D0378832

Holy Ghost Girl

**Center Point
Large Print**

**This Large Print Book carries the
Seal of Approval of N.A.V.H.**

Holy Ghost Girl

DONNA M. JOHNSON

CENTER POINT PUBLISHING
THORNDIKE, MAINE

This Center Point Large Print edition
is published in the year 2011 by arrangement with
Gotham Books, a member of Penguin Group (USA) Inc.

While the author has made every effort to provide accurate
telephone numbers and Internet addresses at the time of
publication, neither the publisher nor the author assumes any
responsibility for errors, or for changes that occur after
publication. Further, the publisher does not have any control
over and does not assume any responsibility for author or
third-party websites or their content.
The text of this Large Print edition is unabridged.
In other aspects, this book may vary
from the original edition.
Printed in the United States of America
on permanent paper.
Set in 16-point Times New Roman type.

ISBN: 978-1-61173-223-8

Library of Congress Cataloging-in-Publication Data

Johnson, Donna M.
Holy Ghost girl / Donna Johnson. — Large print ed.
p. cm.
Originally published: New York : Gotham Books, c2011.
ISBN 978-1-61173-223-8 (library binding : alk. paper)
1. Johnson, Donna M.—Childhood and youth.
  2. Children of clergy—United States—Biography. 3. Terrell, David (David R.)
  4. Evangelists—United States—Biography. 5. Camp meetings—United States.
  6. Large type books. I. Title.
BV3785.T37J64 2011b
269'.2092—dc23
[B]
                                                    2011026089

For Amber and Kirk.

And for my brother and sisters.

There can be no doubt that as a matter of fact a religious life, exclusively pursued, does tend to make individuals exceptional and eccentric.

———————

William James,
The Varieties of Religious Experience

I understood the stillness behind the sky
But never the words of men.

———————

Friedrich Hölderlin,
"In My Boyhood Days"

Prologue

"DONNA, I DON'T KNOW IF YOU'RE COMING TO the funeral, but I heard Daddy's gonna try to raise Randall from the dead. Call me."

My sister left the message as my husband and I stumbled into our darkened kitchen hauling groceries, deli takeout, and briefcases. We had finished another twelve mind-numbing hours at our marketing firm, making deals, finessing budgets, and placating clients, employees, and sometimes each other, racing toward every deadline as though it were life or death. The red light of the answering machine winked at us from the counter. My husband flipped on the overhead light.

"That preacher's going to resurrect his son? We're going, right?"

I shook my head no and said yes. Randall Terrell had been dead twenty-four hours. I was still deciding whether to attend his funeral and everyone else had moved on to resurrection. Even Jesus stayed in the tomb three days, but my family had not followed convention, not in life and apparently not in death.

Randall, his sister Pam, and my brother Gary and I spent our formative years traveling the revival circuit known as the sawdust trail. Our families formed the inner circle of a Holy Roller tribe that preached, prayed, and scared sinners into the fold under giant gospel tents that eventually included the world's largest—a red, white, and blue canvas almost as long as two football fields. I was three and Gary was one when my mother signed on as organist for Randall's daddy. She sold everything and joined the caravan of eighteen-wheelers, faded station wagons, leaky campers, and other gimpy vehicles that limped and lurched from one breakdown to the next. In later years a fleet of Mercedes and a small jet would join the convoy, churning a wake of suspicion that eventually led to the downfall of Brother David Terrell: healer, end-time prophet, and as close to a father figure as I would get.

We descended on towns like a flock of magpies, our public-address system crackling and squawking with cries of "Repent" and "Be Saved," "Jesus Is Coming Soon" and "Be Healed," the phrase that drew multitudes. When Brother Terrell asked those in need of prayer to come forward, most of the congregation rushed toward him. The lines looped around the tent in a human labyrinth of suffering. Strangers pressed against one another, sweat and breath mingling in a collective desire to be touched by that hand. As believers passed under him, they were caught for a moment in a fierce blue gaze just before he squeezed his eyes shut, rolled his head upward, and slapped his right palm on their foreheads. "In the name of Je-sus." They reeled and hit the ground as dead weight. They threw down their crutches. *Praise God.* They didn't walk, they ran. *Hallelujah.* The deaf heard. *Glory be to God.* And the dumb spoke with the tongues of angels. *Amen.*

I had not seen Randall or his father for more than twenty years. It had been longer since I had stepped inside a tent. During the intervening years I had indulged in the posthippie haze of the seventies well into the mideighties before finally graduating from college. Like the woman at the well, I had married and divorced more than one man and lived with several who were not my husband. I had written reams of advertising copy, attended my daughter's graduation from college and graduate school, and married a poet who was also a successful entrepreneur. Somewhere along the line, I had become a semirespectable, doubt-ridden Episcopalian with Buddhist tendencies.

My sister's message on the answering machine brought it all back: blond pine shavings covering the dirt floor of the tent, feathered and piled one upon the other, each singular as a snowflake. My brother and I bedding down with the Terrell kids on that field of sawdust, wrapped in a nest of quilts while the adults paced the tent, praying into the early hours long after the crowd melted away and the last amen was uttered. The warmth of the cannon-shaped kerosene heater roaring beside us on teeth-chattering cold nights, its red tip glowing in the darkness like the all-seeing eye of God.

That November evening as my husband and I stood, mouths agape, in the white-tiled kitchen of our urban home, I felt the past rise up and move toward me like some long-slumbering, pitifully deformed creature. It smelled of pine shavings and kerosene. Its rough, dense texture moved in and out of memory like a tent flap blowing in the breeze. My mother pulsed out a familiar melody on the Hammond organ:

Ain't no grave gonna hold my body down.
Ain't no gra-ave gonna hold my body down.

Somewhere a tambourine kept time.

The Sawdust Trail

1960–1962

THE TWILIGHT SOUND OF CICADA
SINGING OF A DAY
ALREADY GONE BY.

Dōgen

Chapter One

THE TENT WAITED FOR US, HER CANVAS WINGS hovering over a field of stubble that sprouted rusty cans, A&P flyers, bits of glass bottles, and the rolling tatter of trash that migrated through town to settle in an empty lot just beyond the city limits. At dusk, the refuse receded, leaving only the tent, lighted from within, a long golden glow stretched out against a darkening sky. She gathered and sheltered us from a world that told us we were too poor, too white trash, too black, too uneducated, too much of everything that didn't matter and not enough of anything that did. Society, or at least the respectable chunk of it, saw the tent and those of us who traveled with it as a freak show, a rolling asylum that hit town and stirred the local Holy Rollers, along with a few Baptists, Methodists, and even a Presbyterian or two, into a frenzy. Brother Terrell reveled in that characterization.

"I know they's people call me David Nut Terrell. I'm not ashamed of it." He bounced up and down the forty-foot-long platform with the pop and spring of a pogo stick. "I'm crazy for Jesus, crazy for the Lord." The crowd was on its feet, pogoing with him.

The tent went up in all kinds of weather, but in

my memory it's always the hottest day of summer when the canvas rises. A cloud of dust hangs over the grounds, stirred by the coming and going of the twenty to thirty people it took to raise the canvas. Local churches sent out volunteers, but most of the work was done by families who followed Brother Terrell from town to town, happy to do the Lord's work for little more than a blessing and whatever Brother Terrell could afford to pass along to them. When he had extra money, they shared in it. He had a reputation as a generous man who "pinched the buffalo off every nickel" that passed through his hands. He employed only two to four "professional" tent men, a fraction of the number employed by organizations of a similar size. The number of employees remained the same over the years even as the size of the tents grew larger. "World's largest tent. World smallest tent crew," was the joke.

The air smelled of grease and sweat. Men dressed in long pants and long-sleeved shirts (the Lord's dress code) ran back and forth, calling to one another over the gear grind of the eighteen-wheeler as it pulled one of seven thirty-foot center poles into the air. I held my breath as the men wrestled the poles into place, praying that a pole didn't fall and knock a couple of men straight to glory, but making sure I didn't miss it if it did. With a couple of center poles secured, the men broke for lunch, mopping their faces with red or blue bandanas or an already soaked shirtsleeve. Pam and I brought out the trays of bologna sandwiches our mothers had made and walked among them passing out the food. I tried not to wrinkle my nose at the greasy imprints their fingers made in the white bread or the sour hugs that accompanied their thank-yous.

It took three to four days to put the tent up, and the site looked different each time we visited. Some days I picked my way through red and blue poles that lay on the ground in seemingly careless arrangements, imagining them as tall slender ladies who had fainted in the heat or young girls waiting to be asked to dance. Proof that a romantic temperament can take root anywhere, because the only dancers I had seen were believers who jigged in the spirit. The men rolled out sections of canvas over the horizontal poles, attaching the cutout pieces to the base of the now-raised center poles. They laced the sections together and swarmed the flattened tent like a team of tiny tailors stitching a ball gown for a female colossus. With the sewing finished, a man was stationed at the winch attached to each of the seven center poles. Someone shouted, "Go!" and the men cranked in unison. The canvas rose around them, and when it reached waist height, crew members hunched over like gnomes, scrambled underneath, and pushed up the secondary poles. A few more cranks and the peaks billowed thirty feet in the air.

With the tent secured, the crew hung spotlights and secondary lighting from the poles, hammered together the sections of the platform, unloaded the Hammond organ, and positioned the amplifiers and speakers. The expanse of the tent posed a challenge for the sound system, so it was important that the speakers be positioned in just the right places. The tent families unloaded stacks of wooden folding chairs and arranged them in orderly sections that fanned outward from the platform. Twenty-five hundred chairs for the first night, with a thousand more stacked in the truck to be squeezed in as needed throughout the revival. Long one-by-one boards were placed between the chairs' legs to connect them and keep the rows uniform.

By seven o'clock on opening night, a dusty brown canvas and a collection of scuffed-up poles had been transformed into an ad hoc cathedral. People came from near and far. Black and white, old and young, poor and poorer. Women with creased brows and apologetic eyes as faded as their cotton dresses, clutching two and three children who looked almost as worn out as their mothers. Men, taut as fiddle strings, hunch-shouldered in overalls or someone else's discarded Sunday best, someone taller and better fed. They came to find a sense of purpose and a connection to God and one another. They came because the promises of the beatitudes were fulfilled for a few hours under the tent, and the poor were truly blessed. They came for miracles, answers, and salvation. They came to see the show.

It was our first night in Chattanooga. Up on the platform, Mama pulsed out a bass line on the organ and Brother Cotton swung his arm through the air like a metronome as he led the audience through another chorus of "Jesus on the Mainline." He yelled, "Call him up and call him up" into the microphone and the audience screamed back, "Tell him what you want." Brother Cotton's job as song leader and front man was to warm up the audience for Brother Terrell. Sometimes the crowd was cold and unresponsive, and he sweated through his undershirt and dress shirt just trying to get them to say amen. He said the crowd in Chattanooga was so hot, they warmed him up. He and the audience fed off each other, tossing the lines of song back and forth until the words gradually ebbed and music took over.

In the Holy Roller lexicon, "shouting" is another word for dancing in the spirit. Believers clap their hands and sway, stamping one foot and then the other as the organ, trombone, drums, guitars, and tambourines pull them into an ecstatic dance that wipes out the conscious mind and leaves the body with little control over its movements. The crowd was in full shouting mode that night, churning the sawdust and the dirt under it into the air. Floodlights filtered through the dust, casting the scene in an otherworldly haze as Brother Terrell's wife threaded her way through the flailing bodies and herded Pam and Randall and Gary and me under the packed tent. Betty Ann's job was to keep the four of us kids corralled and quiet during a service that lasted from two to five hours, depending on how the spirit moved on a particular night. Given that our ages ranged from one to seven, she may have pulled the toughest tent duty of all. Jostled by the clapping, stomping people, Betty Ann pulled Gary from Randall's arms and shifted him onto her hip. She peered through the crowd to point out a row of chairs, and that's when Randall made his escape. She called after him, then looked around and smiled apologetically at whomever happened to notice. People held the Terrell offspring to a higher standard than other kids, and when they fell short, it was her failing, not Brother Terrell's. She shrugged and steered Pam and me to our seats. We joined the singing just as Brother Terrell walked onto the platform and took the microphone from Brother Cotton. He finished off the chorus with the audience and raised his hands in prayer. Mama slowed the tempo of the music and brought the volume down.

Brother Terrell spoke in a low, quiet voice. "Put your hands up with me and tell Jesus how much you love him. We looooove you, Lord. We magnify your holy name, God. We ask you to look down and bless us tonight, Lord. Open our hearts that we might hear what you have to say. Oooooooooh, God."

In a matter of seconds the mood went from celebratory to somber. Hands were raised across the tent. Hundreds of people, maybe a thousand or more, raised their voices in an orchestration of prayer and unknown tongues that gained in volume and momentum, then drifted to a close. Brother Terrell walked over to the podium and opened his Bible. "I feel like we need to carve deep into the meat of the Word tonight."

Three hours later he was still carving, explicating scripture after scripture. In all that time, he had not once roused the audience to its feet, danced across the platform, or asked a single person to run around the tent for Jesus. His Bible lay open on the pulpit and his finger moved across the page. "Hebrews, chapter eleven, verse one. 'Faith is the substance of things hoped for, the evidence of things not seen.' "

The thin slats of the wooden folding chair cut into the backs of my legs. The crinoline petticoat my mother forced me into sawed at my waist. A three-year-old's version of hell. I yawned and squinted across the curved backs of all those people, leaning over the Bibles flapped opened in their laps. Hungry, hungry, devouring every morsel of spiritual food Brother Terrell handed down.

"Now what does that mean—faith is the substance of things hoped for? Everyone thinks Paul is talking about miracles here, and he is. But that ain't all he's saying. He's saying faith is a real thing in the world. It has substance. It is substance. Amen?" He looked over his shoulder at the preachers lined up behind him on the platform.

"Amen. That's right." Their heads bobbed in unison.

Brother Terrell pulled at his nose, put his hands on both sides of the pulpit, and rocked forward. "Let's go on a little deeper in the Word now. Hebrews, chapter eleven, verse three. 'Through faith we understand that the worlds were framed by the word of God, so that things which are seen were not made of things which do appear.'"

He moved out from behind the pulpit and strolled up and down the platform. He held the microphone so close to his lips, it was almost in his mouth. "Saints, this means the world and everything in it was spoken into existence by the world of faith. What Paul is saying here is that the very earth we walk on, the earth we are made up of, was created by faith. Are y'all with me?"

Amen, they were.

He walked over to the song leader, who sat with the ministers on the platform. "Brother Cotton, what time is it?" The man looked at his watch and mouthed back the answer.

Brother Terrell turned back to the audience. "It's eleven thirty. Time flies, don't it? Y'all ready to go home?"

The crowd yelled, "NO!"

I groaned and dropped my sweaty forehead into my hand. I had faith that if something didn't happen soon, I would die of boredom and go straight to Beelzebub. My legs pumped back and forth, hitting the underside of my chair. Betty Ann reached across Pam, grabbed my knee, and applied pressure.

"What?"

She shook her head from side to side. My brother lay with his head in Betty Ann's lap and his body curled in the chair on the other side of her. My legs slowed. A stream of drool oozed from his sagging mouth onto Betty Ann's skirt. My stomach went queasy.

"You got spit on you."

My words came out in a whisper loud enough that people turned and stared. Pam giggled, and her mother yanked her hair. Pam shot me a look that meant I would get it after church. At five, she was two years older than I was and capable of making me pay for every sin I committed against her. I placed my hands on either side of my seat and pushed my weight away from the wooden slats to relieve the pressure on my bony butt. I leaned forward slightly and the chair tossed me headfirst into one of the metal tentpoles. Two adults jumped up to see if I was okay. One of them helped me up and dusted the sawdust off my dress. The other said too bad there was no ice around. I put my hand to my head and felt a bump rise under the skin. Pam looked at me with suspicion.

"You did that to get attention."

"Did not."

"Did too."

Betty Ann shushed us.

"Donna, sit down. Now. Pamela Eloise, shut up and pay attention."

Pam pointed her finger at me. "She's not paying attention."

Betty Ann pinched her full lips into a hard little knot, raised her eyebrows, and inclined her head toward the platform and my mother. I sighed and sat down. Brother Terrell preached on.

"Faith changes things. When I was a boy doctors diagnosed me with cancer of the bone. They operated nine times and removed all the bone in my leg. I spent so much time in hospitals, I had to drop out of school in third grade."

I sat up and listened. This was the story of the scar. Brother Terrell clipped the microphone around his neck, bent over, and rolled up his right pant leg to just below his knee. He spoke off

24

microphone, and his voice sounded small and distant. "They wanted to amputate, but my mother wouldn't let them. She believed God would heal me." He gripped the white rail of the prayer ramp behind him, balanced on his left leg, and held his right in the air, crooked at the knee. His calf gleamed white under the spotlights, exposed between the dark fabric of his pant leg and sock like some subterranean creature seeing light for the first time. Only it wasn't the first time. Brother Terrell revealed the scar at almost every revival.

"Come on up here, you that wants to see."

People rose across the tent and made their way to the front. Men, women, children, even the scoffers crowded 'round.

"Go ahead, touch it. Jesus told Thomas to put his finger in the nail holes. See for yourself what faith will do."

He lost his balance for a moment and one of the ministers on the platform brought him a chair. He took a seat and stretched out his leg. The scar ran along the inside of his right leg, from knee to ankle. One by one, people laid their fingers in the long trough of purple tissue. It was two fingers wide, two fingers deep, and marbled with yellow and green.

Pam and I threaded our way through the crowd. We never missed a chance to look at the scar. Randall stepped from behind a rear corner of the platform where he hung out with the tent crew and walked with us to the front. Brother Terrell acknowledged each of us with a quick hug and we huddled there beside him as people came forward. Randall was seven years old and not afraid of anything. He laid his fingers in the scar as he always did. Later, I would ask him for the hundredth time what it felt like, and he would tell me that it was as slick and hard as the devil's backbone. As much as I longed to run my fingers down the length of the scar, I could not bring myself to touch it. I stared at it for as long as I could, trying to peer past the outraged skin into the empty cavern of Brother Terrell's calf. There was something there or something not there that I needed to understand, but I did not know and could not have articulated the nature of that something.

Brother Terrell picked up the microphone that hung around his neck and spoke directly into it. "The doctors said I'd never walk without crutches, that I'd be a cripple for the rest of my life.

"Then one day when I was nine years old, Jesus stood in my room. He said, 'David, get up. Walk.' I reached for my crutches. He said, 'Not with those.'"

Brother Terrell leapt from the chair and people scattered like the jacks Pam and I threw between services. "When Jesus heals you, praise God, you don't need no crutches. You don't need no bone. You don't need nothin' but faith to take that first step."

The words flew from his mouth with the ferocity of hornets and we rushed before them to our sections and seats. It wasn't so much what he said, but how he said it. Every word uttered with such urgency that I half expected the world to end before he finished his sentence.

He prowled in front of the audience now, swishing the microphone cord when he turned so that it trailed him like a living thing. His pant cuff fell a bit as he walked, but I could still see the naked glow of that pale patch of skin.

His words slowed and lulled the crowd into believing the storm had passed. "My mama had faith. She believed."

Then he crammed the microphone into his mouth again and the veins on his neck popped up. "You got to have faith. You got to hold on. You can't lie there on your cot and die!"

His voice grew louder with each sentence. "You got to get up. Get uuuuuuup. Get uuuuuuup!"

He went hoarse each time he screamed "get up." The ministers on the platform stood. Mama stood and clapped her hands and amened.

"Yes. That's right. Bless him, Jesus. Tell it, brother."

"When Jesus tells you stand up and walk, you better get on your feet. Get up!"

People all over the tent rose from their seats, hands in the air. Pam and I stood in our chairs, trying to see over or around the grown-ups. My mother began to play "God Don't Never Change," a fast-paced song that turned up the energy.

Brother Terrell stood at the top of the prayer ramp and the crowd moved toward him. The sick, the blind, the deaf, the deformed in body and spirit. By the time the prayer line formed, his right hand was red and hot and jerking like a downed power line.

My mother was deep into the music, a gap-toothed double-wide smile parked across her face. Betty Ann left my brother in the care of a friend and moved to the front to help with the prayer line. Pam and I climbed down from our chairs and made our way to the side of the platform at the end of the prayer ramp. Brother Terrell was someplace else entirely. Randall came and stood beside us, his cowlick standing straight up.

"Look at that."

A woman with a stomach so large she looked two years pregnant labored up the ramp, pulling herself forward by the rails, breathing through her mouth. With each step, her face turned a little redder. Randall put his hand over his mouth.

"Her stomach will be there three days before the rest of her. Daddy'll be lucky if she don't die before she gets to him."

We giggled. Brother Terrell leaned over and whispered something to the woman. She nodded and raised her hands. The people who stood in line behind her on the ramp backed up. Betty Ann and the preachers who waited in front of her on the ramp moved away. If this woman went down in the spirit, no one wanted to go with her. Randall, Pam, and I edged beyond the corner of the platform for a better view. No one was left on the ramp but the woman and Brother Terrell. The music and the clapping stopped. He raised his hand to place it on her forehead, but before he could touch her, the woman's skirt dropped around her ankles. Her big stomach was gone. Randall let out a whoop. Brother Terrell looked over his shoulder at the men on the platform, and they all doubled over laughing. He whirled back toward the audience and jumped up and down, just above the ramp where the woman still stood with her hands raised and her eyes closed.

"She's healed, praise God. The spirit of God has filled this place like a mighty wind, just like in the Bible, hallelujah! The healing power of God destroyed the tumor. It's gone."

Anyone still in their seats rushed to the front. My mother pounded the Hammond and we sang on and on about all that God could do and how he never changed.

The woman stood there in her blouse and slip with her eyes closed, her arms and hands raised, her lips speaking a language that made sense only to her. Betty Ann and the other women recovered their composure and moved toward her. Someone pulled up her skirt and held it in place at her waist. Someone else grasped her elbow and eased her down the ramp. She never opened her eyes or put her hands down. When they reached the bottom, the women talked to her and tried to get her to hold her skirt up. She grasped it for a moment, then let it fall and began to dance in her blouse and slip. Pam, Randall, and I watched in astonishment. The woman didn't seem to know she had lost her skirt, or if she knew, she didn't care. Brother Terrell had that effect on people.

The miraculous and the mundane tap-danced up and down the aisles of the tent together, and it never occurred to me to question if one was more real than the other. I don't think it occurred to the adults either. We experienced the world through the scrim of belief, and that made everything possible. No one followed up to see if the miracles held, but people who said they were healed often returned. The Woman Who Used To Be Big, that's what we called her, came back and gave her testimony several times during the month-long revival.

"I went to the doctor to be checked out like Brother Terrell told me. The doctor said, 'What happened to the tumor?' I said the man of God healed me."

As word of the healing spread, the crowd increased until people stood two and three deep along the outside perimeter of the tent. Ambulances transported people from hospitals. Stretchers and wheelchairs lined the aisles until the fire marshal complained and we moved the sick behind the platform, where they waited until Brother Terrell called a prayer line.

Chapter Two

I'VE ALWAYS THOUGHT OF MY MOTHER'S first meeting with David Terrell as the Holy Roller equivalent of the big bang. It must have seemed as though their twin histories had been spinning toward each other with cataclysmic urgency since birth. They were kindred spirits, each believing he or she had been plucked from the mass of ordinary folks by the long bony fingers of God and set aside for great things. Almost all of the childhood stories told by Brother Terrell and my mother focused on the experience of being chosen. Brother Terrell often said from the platform that growing up he had always had a sense that he was different. No doubt the leg surgeries and hospital stays that were a part of his illness set him apart from other kids. The visit from Jesus at age nine must have sealed the deal. Then there were the visions: He foretold his uncle's and then his grandmother's death; and the voices: when he played alone he often heard God calling his name.

My mother, too, grew up on a first-name basis with God. She was only eight when she heard the voice calling her name in the woods next to the Assemblies of God church where her daddy was pastor. There were no burning bushes, no glowing figures, only an ordinary and somewhat familiar voice calling, *Carolyn*. She wandered through the trees and looked behind the largest trunk. *Carolyn*. No one there. *Carolyn*.

That night as she told her family the story, a feeling of awe swept over her. That voice, the voice that called her name in the trees, the voice that sounded so familiar yet belonged to no one, that voice was the eternal I Am, the same voice that spoke the world into existence. She knew it. When her parents asked how she knew, she shrugged and asked, "Well, who else could it have been?" In her family, no one would have suggested it was her imagination. My Pentecostal grandparents and their children existed in a reality that was an extension of biblical times. They believed the temporal world lay like a fine curtain over the realm of the eternal. At any moment the archangel Michael might reach through the veil and tap them on the shoulder with a heavenly message. Or the devil might slip through and tempt with some cheap bit of finery.

It could be hard to tell one from the other at times, especially given Satan's love of deception, but no one questioned the veracity of the experiences.

Being singled out by God brought the kind of attention that was hard to come by for kids in large, poor families. Born in 1932 to Alabama sharecroppers, Brother Terrell was the youngest of seven kids. The family lived in a shack without running water or electricity. A broken-down horse provided the only transportation. The Great Depression and the death of Brother Terrell's father turned the family's subsistent poverty into a struggle for survival. His mother left him in the care of one of his sisters and went to work in the fields with her other five children. She left at sunrise and came home at sundown. On Sundays, she hitched the horse to a rickety wagon and drove her brood to the nearest holiness church, a backwoods term for a nondenominational Pentecostal offshoot. Her faith was her only source of hope.

Mama's childhood was slightly less desperate. She was one of the middle kids in a family of nine children. Her daddy was the pastor of a string of Assemblies of God churches throughout Alabama and Florida. He farmed to put food on the table. My mother and her siblings picked cotton to pay for their shoes and other necessities. Mama and Brother Terrell were thought to be sensitive children by their mothers and downright peculiar by their siblings. Brother Terrell wrote songs and picked out tunes on a neighbor's guitar early on. For a brief time during adolescence he harbored hopes of making it big on the Grand Ole Opry, but the visions kept coming and he realized that God would not let him go.

Mama was a musical prodigy, further proof of God's favor. Her story is that while picking at the notes on the piano in her daddy's church one day, she was suddenly able to play a hymn straight through. From that moment she could play any song she wanted. When she was fifteen, she saw herself in a night vision playing a big pearly accordion. A night vision is a foretelling of the future, only the seer is asleep. People who have night visions often go on to full-fledged wide-awake visions. When Mama opened her eyes, she could still feel the heft of the instrument against her. She was meant to have an accordion. Her daddy said that might be true, but he didn't have the money to buy one. Another teenage girl might have pleaded or thrown a fit. My mother fasted and prayed. In the early hours of what was to be her fourth day without food, a knock on the door awakened her daddy. He turned on the light and opened the door. There on his front porch stood a man he recognized but didn't know well.

"Preacher, I don't know what's going on, but I've got to give you this."

He thrust a wad of bills at my grandfather and turned to go.

"Wait. What is this? What's it for?" My grandfather tugged at the man's sleeve.

The man shook him off. "Look, I haven't been able to sleep for days. Something keeps telling me to bring you this money. I don't know what it's for. But you have to take it so I can get some sleep."

Later that morning my grandfather went to town and ordered an accordion from Sears, Roebuck. My mother played it in church the day it arrived. She says she never hit a wrong note.

By the time Brother Terrell came along, Mama needed a second chance to fulfill her destiny. She had blown the first one. Her mother had told her, "Honey, any woman can get married and have children. God has something better in mind for you." Mama's plan was to go to Bible school and become a missionary, but she ran away from home, or away from her controlling daddy, instead. My grandfather had the idea that his high-cheeked, leggy daughter was something of a wild girl and he was determined to rein her in. According to Mama, the last straw came when he dragged her out of a boy's car at a local snack shack in "broad daylight" and whipped her with his belt. She was eighteen years old.

She hopped a Greyhound bus to Los Angeles. There she dropped her middle name, Carolyn, in favor of her first name, Betty, and cut her long, stringy hair into a bouncy bob. One broken taboo spawned a host of others: movies, skating rinks, lipstick, slacks, bathing suits, men. The path to perdition is tediously routine for a Holy Roller girl. She went to church, she prayed, but God no longer dropped by. She met my dad in LA, a sinner boy who was everything my grandfather feared. He smoked and drank and indulged a taste for all things fast. Cars. Boats. Women. Mama's religious beliefs and naïveté cast her as something of an exotic in my dad's eyes. Her LA nickname, Betty the Body, tells the rest of the story. My dad wooed her with professions of love, promises of repentance, and declarations that she alone could save him. Six weeks after they met, my parents married. Asked why she married a man she hardly knew and one so different from her, my mother's answer is typical: "I guess I thought I could help him." The cost of bringing a soul into the fold was never too high.

My grandfather's response to the Las Vegas wedding was to the point: "I guess she had to get married."

I was born a year after my parents married. Still, I've always considered their wedding a shotgun marriage of sorts, a trigger-happy God pointing the gun, my mother's guilt egging it all on. She had come close to the fires of hell one night, parked above Los Angeles in my dad's car, the windows steamed with lust. They married soon after. The marriage lasted two years, most of which my dad spent scrambling for the door. He made his final exit when my mother told him a second child was on the way.

Mama discovered he had another woman and her disgrace was complete.

My mother returned to her parents' house pregnant and prodigal with a toddler in tow. She had rebelled against her father. She had eaten of the tree of good and evil. She had known better. She was practically a divorced woman, and in the rural Pentecostal South that put her perilously close to being a hussy. Pentecostals conceded that divorce might be a necessary evil in extreme cases, but remarriage was condemned little more than legally sanctioned adultery. At twenty-three, my mother's vision of herself as God's own girl was lost. She was grateful when her parents allowed her to move into the apartment in the basement of their church. She was grateful when my brother was born healthy, grateful when she found a job, grateful her daddy never said, "I told you so." She woke early Monday through Friday, dressed for work, dropped my infant brother and me at the babysitter's, and headed to Whitman Trailers for another day of typing and shorthand. On Sunday mornings and Wednesday nights she plinked out hymns on the piano at her father's church as she had done for years before her trip out West. She was as grateful as she could be, a grateful corpse of a woman.

And then she heard David Terrell preach. He was a twenty-seven-year-old six-foot looker with black hair, blue eyes, and a smile that flashed Holy Ghost charm to the last soul in the last row of the big tents in which he preached. My grandpa looked out over his congregation from the big throne of a chair that sat between the choir stall and the pulpit and smiled. The pews were full. He was lucky to have caught David Terrell between revivals. Later he would think otherwise.

From her seat at the piano, Mama watched Brother Terrell walk to the pulpit and place his Bible on it. She was close enough to see the light bob off his Brylcreemed hair when he bowed his head and asked Jesus to hide him behind the cross. He opened his eyes, clutched at the sides of the pulpit as if it were a lifeboat, swayed a bit, then let go. He took three steps to the right, turned, and took another three to the left.

"I came here . . . I came here tonight . . . I thought I'd preach on reaching the promised land. But now, now, I don't know."

He didn't sound much like a big-time preacher. His speech was slow and halting, and his shy demeanor stirred Mama's protective instinct. Oh, what a stirring it must have been. Fifty years later and we still feel the ripples.

Brother Terrell cocked his head and stared past

38

the congregation. "I feel like . . . I feel like the Lord is leading me in a different direction. A lot has to happen *before* you reach the promised land, amen?"

No answer. He brought his hand to his brow as if to shade his eyes and surveyed the congregation. "Y'all awake out there? Well? Maybe you will be soon."

He walked back to the pulpit, flipped his Bible open to Exodus, and read aloud the story of Moses. In chapter two, Pharaoh's daughter defies her father and saves baby Moses from drowning in the Nile. He lives in the palace as an Egyptian but cannot forget that he is an Israelite, a member of the slave race. In a fit of pique, he kills an Egyptian. Chapter three opens with Moses on the lam. God appears to him as a burning bush with a gift for gab and tells him to confront Pharaoh and lead the Israelites out of Egypt. When Moses asks who he should say had given him such a charge, the bush says, "I Am who I Am."

Brother Terrell moved away from the podium and walked in measured steps, heel to toe across the small platform, each step, each word a considered choice. His eyes searched the floor as if looking for a path that would take him where the spirit would have him go.

"God chose Moses. That's why he didn't let him drown. God had a plan for him and Moses didn't want any part of it. He was running from God."

Running from God. That was it. That was his way in. "You can't outrun God. When God chooses you, you're chosen for life."

Brother Terrell stepped off the platform into the narrow space between the altar and the pews. "I said you're chosen for life." He moved relentlessly, back and forth, picking up speed and volume as he went.

"You can take a wrong turn!"

Encouragement came from the back of the congregation. "Yes. Amen, you can."

"You can get stuck in Egypt for years." He broke into a run across the front of the church.

The audience couldn't resist. "Uh-huh. Come on now, Brother."

The deacons in the front row raised their eyebrows and chuckled. Maybe this boy really could preach. He stopped and squalled into the face of one of the church's biggest supporters. "You may get stuck on a bench. You may feel like you're wasting your life and your talent."

The deacon was taken aback, but his arms shot into the air when Brother Terrell clapped his hands on the man's head. "Restore his zeal, Lord. Bring him back to that holy ground, that hallowed place where you first made yourself known to him. In the name of Jesus, amen."

Brother Terrell launched back into his sermon with the same volume and fervor as before. He headed down the center aisle of the church. "You may be about to give up. You may think that no one hears your cries, that no one cares. But I'm here to tell you that I AM, the Lord God Almighty, has heard your cry."

He reached the back of the church and started back toward the front. It was as if there were something inside him that would not let him stand still, would not let him shut up. Words and movement and sweat poured from him. His shirt was soaked. The Brylcreem failed and a slick hank of hair fell across his forehead. He ranted like a man possessed.

"I AM has seen your affliction. I AM has felt your sorrow. I AM will deliver you, I said he will take you by the hand and lead you out of the land of bondage." Each time he screamed the words "I am," he threw himself forward at the waist until he was crouched at a ninety-degree angle to the floor, running up and down the aisle. Steady murmurs of "amen," "hallelujah," "thank you, Jesus," and "yes, Lord, yes" ran under and around Brother Terrell's words, a rowdy communion of sounds and syllables that blurred the boundaries between preacher and congregation.

He reached the front of the church and fell to his knees. "Your cry has surely come before the Lord of host and the day of your deliverance is at hand!"

With the service at its emotional peak, Brother Terrell made his pitch for Jesus. He implored

41

every person in the congregation who didn't know the Lord to come to the front and lay down their burden of sin. Usually the invitation was accompanied by music, but there was no music that night. He turned to find out why, and saw an empty piano bench. My mother was on her knees at the altar. She had been seduced by the world. She had lost her way. It poured out of her: guilt, recrimination, resentment, self-loathing, and betrayal after betrayal after betrayal. Her daddy's. Her husband's. Her own. She had come to the end of her ability to make things work. She longed to go back to that time when God was as present as her breath, back to that place where everything had purpose and meaning.

Brother Terrell placed his hand on her forehead, and she felt the weight of her failed marriage and all that had led up to it fall away. She saw her life as it was before, filled with grace and promise and rising on the wind of the spirit. In that moment she was changed.

Brother Terrell preached at Grandpa's church for a week. When the revival ended, he asked Mama to join his evangelistic team and become the organist for his tent revivals. She had never played an organ, but she knew that wasn't a problem. She sold her furniture, the wedding gifts, knickknacks, flatware, all of her slacks, and the more fashionable dresses and skirts in her wardrobe. It all had to go. What she couldn't sell, she gave away. She kept a few of her plainer dresses, a couple of toys, two pots, a set of sheets, a few towels, and her old '49 Ford. She didn't want anything to slow her down.

Chapter Three

BROTHER TERRELL COULD SCAT ON SCRIPTURE like a jazz singer hopped up on speed. He started slow, establishing his theme in a soft melody, circling around and over and through it for three, four, and five hours. He riffed on stories about his childhood, his last meal, or that time he ate a green persimmon, then meandered back to one of his standard themes of holiness, divine healing, the dry bones of institutionalized religion, or a medley of all three—without notes or outlines. I grew up thinking of him as the only one of his kind. He was in fact the last of his kind, or one of them. The sawdust-trail preachers were disappearing even as Brother Terrell joined their ranks. The term "sawdust trail" refers to the circuit traveled by the tent preachers and to the sawdust-covered aisles that a convert walked down to profess his or her new faith. The revivals peaked in the nineteen-forties and early fifties with the healing crusades of A. A. Allen, William Branham, Jack Coe, and Oral Roberts.

Brother Terrell styled himself, consciously or

not, after the preachers he admired most. He emulated the meek persona that was the hallmark of Branham, a mystic who often stared into space and frustrated his backers by walking off the stage when he didn't feel the spirit. As Brother Terrell's ministry grew he exhibited the flamboyance of Coe and Allen. Coe was famous for socking people with stomach ailments in the belly as he pronounced them healed. From Allen came the practice of passing out anointed handkerchiefs.

Brother Terrell pitched his first tent in his late teens or early twenties. It was an old army tent canvas, shot through with so many holes that it let more rain in than it kept out. In the early days he sat at the front of the tent strumming his guitar and singing "I Saw the Light" before an audience that consisted of his wife and infant son and thirty-six borrowed, empty chairs. The odds of him becoming a successful tent preacher were long. Many of the well-known revivalists had died, quit, or succumbed to scandal by the early nineteen-sixties, victims of the backbreaking labor, grueling schedules, and emotional grind that defined their way of life. A few, like Oral Roberts, had enough education and savvy to establish institutions and transform the notoriety of the sawdust trail into a more mainstream, and more bankable, respectability.

By the time my mother joined the team, Brother

Terrell's tents were full most nights and he was considered a comer on the revival circuit. Still, it took a lot of poor people giving their last dollar to support a big tent operation. The crowds he attracted were a fragment compared with the earlier revivalists. Older preachers counseled him to find another way to make a living. The days of the great revivals were over, they said. With radio and movies and now television, the devil could distract people without much effort. Brother Terrell understood what they were saying, but he didn't believe it applied to him. The Lord would make a way. Meanwhile, he stood in front of his audiences, held a white gallon cardboard bucket in each hand, and begged for money for more than an hour at a time.

"I haven't paid my team in weeks. We done everything we can to cut costs. We need five thousand dollars just to make payments on the equipment. I can't do this on my own. I need your help."

People trickled up in ones and twos. Pam, Randall, and I dropped in the quarter or dime we had earned polishing Brother Terrell's shoes and the shoes of the other preachers who traveled with us.

"There's a lost, dying world out there. A world that hasn't heard the gospel. If you don't help us, they'll die and never hear it."

A cry entered his throat. I felt sorry for Brother

Terrell, sorry that he had to cry and plead for money. Late at night when he and the other preachers sat around talking after a long service, I often heard him say he would rather take a beating than beg.

We said we were living by faith, but any reasonable observer would have said we were barely scraping by. Each revival cost thousands of dollars in rent, fees, and ads. Brother Terrell had to make monthly payments on the tent, PA system, organ, and other equipment. My mother and other members of the evangelistic team stayed up all night praying with him that God would meet our needs. And I guess he did, but at the last minute and often with barely enough. Someone donated a house for us to live in during one revival, but it didn't have electricity or running water. Pam and I took baths together outdoors in a galvanized aluminum tub with water that came through a hose connected to a windmill. When we finished, Randall and Gary plopped into the same dingy water and showered off with the hose afterward. We didn't go hungry, but we ate mayonnaise sandwiches and pork and beans for lunch, and bologna sandwiches and pork and beans for dinner. I wondered from time to time why miracles performed under the tent were perfect and complete, while in our daily lives God left things half finished. It was as if something distracted him midway through a job and he wandered off, leaving us with just enough food in our bellies and just enough hope in our souls.

When a windstorm damaged the tent, or one of the trucks that hauled the equipment had engine trouble, or a speaker blew, or a creditor demanded immediate payment, the financial strain increased. The men and women who traveled with Brother Terrell were in their early to midtwenties and completely dedicated to helping him spread the gospel. Mama and the others often signed their paychecks and put them back in the offering, trusting God to meet their needs. Betty Ann found it more difficult. In the eight years she had been married to Brother Terrell, she had watched his reputation grow and his ministry expand, but they still lived like poor people. All of the money that came in went to the ministry. There was no home, no stability, no reliable income. Loud and angry voices sometimes filtered through the walls of the Terrells' bedroom all night long. Brother Terrell emerged the next morning looking beaten. My mother would sit and drink coffee with him and "try to encourage him." Afterward, she counseled Betty Ann on how a minister's wife had to support him, especially in hard times.

One night in Huntsville, Alabama, as Brother Terrell stood in front of the prayer ramp, offering buckets in hand, the Woman Who Used To Be Big walked up and snatched the microphone from him. She had joined the tribes that followed us as we moved in the vicinity of their hometowns. Dockery, the toughest of the tent men, started toward the front to lead her back to her seat, but Brother Terrell waved him off. The woman held a ten-dollar bill by a corner and waved it over her head.

"I'm giving my last ten dollars to Brother Terrell. God healed me of a tumor a few months back. Oh hondalie condalie."

Sufis twirl, Hindus chant, Buddhists sit in silence. Holy Rollers and charismatic Christians babble like fools or speak the language of the angels, depending on who describes the experience. Believers lapsed into speaking in "tongues" or glossolalia when their euphoria stretched beyond the bounds of ordinary language.

The Woman Who Used To Be Big closed her eyes and began to jerk. Brother Terrell ducked a thrown elbow. When the jerking slowed, he thanked her and reached for the microphone. She backed him off with one hand.

"When the doctor checked me out, he said what did the preacher do with the tumor? I said I don't know, and I don't care. I just know I was sick and now I'm well. Hondalie condalie. A mighty wind swept down from the top of the tent, and I was healed."

Brother Terrell reached again for the microphone, but she turned away from him.

"I'm not done yet, Brother. You'll know when I'm done."

He dropped the buckets and started laughing. She waved her ten-dollar bill again.

"This ten dollars is to prove God for my son. He's an alcoholic, but if God can bust a tumor, he can heal a drunk. This man is giving us everything he's got. Y'all help me support him."

As she spoke, the black woman who sat next to Pam and me rose to her feet and waved a bill in the air. The words poured out of her mouth, soft and incessant. "Tell it. Amen. Go on now. Yes. Yes." A soft alto counterpoint to the solo performance of the Woman Who Used To Be Big.

Purses snapped open across the tent and wallets were fished out of pockets. Soon everyone waved bills in the air.

The Woman Who Used To Be Big laid the microphone on the prayer ramp. She gripped Brother Terrell by the shoulder with one hand and with the other she motioned for people to come up to the front. Brother Terrell buried his face in his hands and cried as people walked down the aisles and dropped their money in the buckets that stood at his feet.

We didn't have to worry about money again during that revival. Brother Terrell paid the bills and had some money left over to give to my mother and other members of his team on the payroll, as well as the families who traveled with the tent.

When the people ran out of money to give, they brought bags of clothes and quilts and grocery sacks filled with vegetables from their gardens: tomatoes, peaches, okra, greens, and squash, bushels and bushels of squash. I hated squash. God, I thought, must possess a spiteful sense of humor.

Chapter Four

THE REVIVAL IN HUNTSVILLE, ALABAMA, ended at about midnight. In the hours that followed, Mama, Betty Ann, Pam, Gary, and I exhausted ourselves with waiting for Brother Terrell. He made the rounds among the tent crew, giving last-minute instructions, digging in his pockets, and passing out money. He was close now, just a few feet away, standing next to the eighteen-wheeler, talking to Dockery. The smell of diesel permeated the air, and in the distance I could hear the *thawp thawp* of the wooden folding chairs as they were snapped shut. Closing time.

Randall flitted past Pam and me and taunted in a singsong voice, "I get to ride in the big truck and you don't. Nanny, nanny, nanny."

We pulled at our moms. "Why does Randall get to ride with Dockery and we have to pack into the car like sardines? It's not fair."

Mama shook her head in agreement. "Some things aren't fair. Brother Terrell's about ready. Get in the car, now."

"You, too, Pamela Eloise," Betty Ann echoed. Pam shot her mama a hard look. She hated her middle name.

The next revival was scheduled to start a week later just outside of Atlanta. We had plenty of time, but we would drive all night anyway. Brother Terrell couldn't sleep for hours after a service and saw no reason to wait until the next morning to get on the road.

For reasons mysterious to me, Mama, Gary, and I had been elevated to first-family status during our first year on the road. We loaned our old Ford to one of the tent families and traveled with the Terrells in their old car. And then the Falcon appeared. One minute we were riding in a beat-up rattletrap with bad tires, faded paint, and a wheezing engine, and the next thing you know, we were cruising in the Falcon, intoxicated with the new-car smell and the knowledge that God placed our needs at the top of his to-do list. One of the faithful had slipped the keys to Brother Terrell at the end of a revival. That made it a miracle car.

Gary and I crawled into the backseat with my

mother. He curled up into a fetal position and rested his head in Mama's lap. She pressed her forehead against the window, a gesture of exhaustion or need, maybe both. I gathered my legs onto the seat, fit them around Gary's body, stroked and patted my mother's leg with my feet. She cupped her fingers around my toes. I leaned my head into the corner where the car door and the seat meet. Up front in the passenger's seat, Betty Ann folded her coat into a pillow and placed it on the console for Pam.

"Put your head there, honey."

Pam snuggled into what looked like a comfortable nest, so comfortable it made my own position feel hard and cramped in comparison. I registered my dissatisfaction in my standard way.

"Why can't we go now?"

Mama replied in her flat, end-of-the-night voice, "We'll leave when we're ready. Close your eyes and go to sleep. Now."

"I can't sleep till we're going."

"Then close your mouth and stop talking."

Finally, Brother Terrell opened the driver's-side door and slid behind the wheel and we bumped over the field and onto the road. His long white sleeves glowed in the light of the tube radio. Hank Williams whined "Your Cheatin' Heart." Kitty Wells answered with "It Wasn't God who Made Honky Tonk Angels." We beamed through the night, our headlights reflecting off the molasses-colored two-lane road. On and on we rolled, anywhere and everywhere, across the dotted lines of the map Betty Ann unfolded and folded, across the imaginary boundaries that separated and divided the land into puzzle pieces of here and there.

Betty Ann's head rose like a dark moon above the back of the seat. Dreams merged with reality. A woman moved across the swamps that lined the road, her head rag white, so very white against the night. A long cotton sack hung from her shoulder, but there were no cotton fields here, just water thick as stew and trees that stub and splinter against the night. A hand made its way from the front seat to the back and rested, light and tentative as a mayfly, on my mother's knee. Someone flicked on the overhead light.

Betty Ann's voice rumbled, "Don't think I don't know what you're up to."

Brother Terrell glanced toward her. "What? I didn't do nothing."

No answer. Just the lick of the tires on the road. I looked out the window for the white head rag. Nothing. We traveled deeper and deeper into the darkness until finally the light overtook us and another day began.

The sun hit us like salt on slugs. Every muscle, every dream hardened and cracked under the glare. It hurt to move, breathe, blink. I burrowed into the corner, my hand over my face. The car slowed. I peeked between my fingers as we came to a stop in front of a white wooden restaurant with two big windows. We eased our stiff bodies out of the car and stumbled toward the building.

Brother Terrell called out: "We don't have all day now."

Betty Ann pointed out the restroom to Pam as we walked through the door.

Pam pulled on her mother's arm. "Aren't you coming?"

"I'm staying here with Daddy . . . and Carolyn."

A look I could not decipher passed between the adults. Pam and I took Gary by the hand and headed for the bathroom. When we returned, Mama and Betty Ann were ordering breakfast: two eggs with bacon, grits, and toast for each of them, and the same thing for Pam and me to share. Gary would eat off our mother's plate. The women handed the plastic-coated menus back to the waitress, and it was Brother Terrell's turn. He cleared his throat as if to say something, then didn't. I dreaded what came next. Without looking up from the pad she held in her hand, the waitress asked Brother Terrell if he thought he might order before lunch. She laughed a bit as she said it, but he didn't respond. From the platform, Brother Terrell glided over the most difficult words of scripture with ease. Take him off the platform, replace the Bible with a letter, a contract, or a menu from a roadside restaurant, and he stumbled and stammered and sounded out the words like a kid learning to read. Everyday life rendered him functionally illiterate. My mother said it was God's anointing that enabled him to read during services. She didn't say why God didn't cure him of his illiteracy and spare him the humiliation.

He cleared his throat again and pointed to the menu.

"I'll have this here."

The waitress's pencil hovered over her pad. "And what's that?"

"It's the, the . . ." His face turned red. Pam and I stared at our laps, trying to avoid her dad's terrifying vulnerability. Brother Terrell turned to Betty Ann and dropped his voice. "What's that say?"

"Three eggs, country biscuits, redeye gravy, and ham."

He handed the menu to the waitress and swallowed hard. "That's what I'll have."

She looked up finally from her pad and her eyes went soft. "The writing is so small on these things, it's a wonder any of us can read 'em."

By the time the waitress delivered breakfast, Brother Terrell had recovered. She settled the platter of food in front of him, and the light clicked on in his eyes.

"That looks like my mama's cookin'. I thank you."

She smiled at him like she had never been thanked before and lingered for a moment, hip cocked, before unloading onto the table the other plates that lined her arm.

Betty Ann took it all in with her big, sad eyes. "Aren't chu sumthin'?"

Brother Terrell sawed at his ham without looking up. Pam and I stirred our runny eggs into the grits. Gary crunched into a slice of toast coated with jelly—his mouth a sticky grape outline. Mama picked at her scrambled eggs, then gave up. She mumbled for me to scoot over, all the way over, and slid out of the booth to play a song on the jukebox.

The car felt more crowded than usual that morning when we folded ourselves back into it. The grown-ups spoke only when they had to, and when they did, their words said one thing and their voices another. Pam looked over her shoulder at me from her perch on the console between the bucket seats her parents occupied. Her face was smug. She didn't say anything, but I knew she was thinking, *I get to sit up here and you don't.* I whined that it wasn't fair that only Pam got to sit on the console. Mama told me to be quiet about it. I said it was only right that Gary and I should have a turn too.

Mama cut her eyes at me. "Donna Marie, I'm warning you."

I couldn't stop myself. I reminded Mama and

Betty Ann and Brother Terrell that Pam and Randall had sat on the console during our last trip, that it was in fact my turn, and that I had never gotten to sit on the console even once. Brother Terrell slammed on the brakes and the car skidded to a stop. "Pamela, get off now and let Donna sit up here."

Pam slid into the backseat with Mama and Gary, and I climbed onto the narrow console. I had to sit straight up and my back hurt after about five minutes. I looked over my shoulder at Pam. She nestled against the door and smirked. I shifted from side to side and tried to get comfortable. I couldn't lean forward and I couldn't lean back. I couldn't do anything except sit straight up. After a few miles I offered to trade places with Pam but she said no, she was comfortable, and that I could just ride up there for the rest of the trip.

We uttered a collective sigh of relief as we drove through Atlanta to the community that would be our home for the duration of the revival. The house was located in an area of town that had elements of both city and country life. There were cracked sidewalks, a corner store, and yards that turned into small pastures with an occasional barn or lean-to. Brother Terrell eased the car along the curb, ducking his head slightly and squinting to see the house numbers. Betty Ann looked down at the address she had scratched on an envelope.

"David, this has to be it."

I peered through the car window at the house, white with red shutters. Nice, much nicer than the last place we stayed. Two squares of brown grass lay on each side of the concrete walk that led to the front door. A metal roof extended from the house and covered a porch just wide enough for the glider that occupied one end. A swing. Okay, sort of a swing. A tree hugged the edge of the porch, small, too small for a tree house. We rolled past the house and turned into the dirt driveway that widened into a large rectangle of dirt side yard and extended beyond the house to the ramshackle barn. Brother Terrell jerked the car into park and fished in his pocket for the key his advance man had mailed a week earlier.

We stepped stiff-legged from the car and headed for the side door of the house. Each adult carried two suitcases, all the clothes we owned. The door opened into a large kitchen with a little table pushed against the wall. The five boxes we had packed with pots, pans, plates, towels, sheets, and quilts sat on the table and the floor, delivered earlier that morning by one of the tent families. Betty Ann went to the sink and turned a handle. Rusty orange water poured out of the faucet. After a minute she turned to us and said, "No hauling water from the windmill this time. And if you wait a minute, it turns clear and gets warm."

Mama flicked a light switch on the wall. She

and Betty Ann stared at the ceiling, as if to marvel at the result. It wasn't that we had never experienced modern conveniences; we just never knew when to expect them. We followed Brother Terrell through the kitchen, dining room, little square living room with a couch that folded into a bed, and into the hallway. Three bedrooms opened onto the hall: one for Brother Terrell and Betty Ann; one for Brother Cotton and his wife, Laverne; and one for me, Pam, Randall, and Gary to share. Mama would sleep on the sofa. I pushed through a fourth door. An indoor toilet. I started toward it, but Pam cut in front of me and settled on the seat. She kicked her sturdy tanned legs and beamed a guileless smile, her daddy's smile, dimples denying any wrongdoing.

We unpacked the boxes, placed our plates on the shelves and our flatware into the drawer. We took our clothes from the suitcases, shook out the wrinkles, placed them in the chest of drawers and chifforobes, and smoothed our sheets on the stained yellow mattresses of the beds. Once we settled in, the hours and days turned tedious. It was Saturday and the revival didn't start until the following Friday night. We were people built for the mountaintop experience, not the humdrum routine of everyday life. The mundane grated on us, and we in turn grated on one another.

Everything turned hard. One night as Brother Terrell worked to help lower the tent before a windstorm hit, the winch he turned flew loose and pummeled his arm. Within minutes the arm had puffed up like an inner tube. He prayed for it, and without a call to the doctor, put it in a homemade sling. The tent men dropped one of the big speakers while setting it up under the tent and argued over who was to blame. The house key disappeared and Brother Terrell had to drive across town to pick up another one. And that was just the beginning. The newspaper ads had the wrong dates, and since it was the advance man's fault, we had to pay to run them again. The constable showed up and informed the tent workers that we had filed the wrong permits. My mother went with Brother Terrell to the courthouse to help him read and figure out the permits. They were gone a long time. When they returned, Betty Ann wouldn't speak to either of them.

The four of us kids took refuge in the falling-down barn behind the house and tried to figure out what to do next. We sprawled on the hay and went through our list: Play church? We had exhausted ourselves on that one. Red rover? Not enough of us for two teams. Randall suggested husbands and wives, a variation on doctor that was always his favorite game.

Pam groaned. "We played that yesterday."

He sighed and walked around the barn, hands deep in his pockets. "I got it. We'll play sinners!"

As sinners, Pam and I bunched our dresses into our long white panties to make shorts and stood on street corners holding little sticks between our fingers and blowing imaginary smoke through pursed lips. We thrust our chins out and dared passersby to look at us. When they did, we stared them straight in the eye. Only true Jezebels wore shorts and smoked. We had played sinners all that week, so there wasn't anything new in that idea.

Pam looked hard at Randall, trying to figure out his angle. "We're not playing sinner husbands and wives, Randall."

"I'm not talking 'bout *that,* Pam. I mean we'll be *real* sinners." Randall paused and looked up at the barn eaves. When he spoke again, it was in a hushed voice.

"We won't play sinners. We'll *be* sinners, real sinners. And we'll smoke real cigarettes."

I took matches from the kitchen, Pam stole money from the piles of change her daddy left on the counter every night, and Randall went to the store to buy the cigarettes.

Pam and I traced with our fingers in the air the flight of two flies as they rose through the shafts of light streaming through the holes in the barn roof. We licked each other's arms to see whose were the saltiest and practiced arm wrestling. Gary fell asleep in the corner, sweat trickling down his face, a fly on his lip. Finally, the barn door creaked open and Randall appeared.

"Anybody want an ice-cold cocola?"

"What took you so long?" Pam ran to take the paper bag he carried under his arm. It was wet with the condensation from the bottles of soda, and ripped as she pulled it from him. Four RC Colas, a bottle opener, four slightly melted candy bars, and a pack of Lucky Strikes spilled out onto the hay. Randall ripped open the cigarettes.

"What comes first, cigarettes or candy bars? I vote cigarettes."

Pam held the matchbook in the air. "We vote candy, and I got the matches, so we win."

Randall doled out the chocolate bars and pried off the tops of the sodas with the bottle opener. We took big bites of the chocolate and washed it down with RC. In the rush of sugar I forgot all about the cigarettes, but Randall remembered.

"Time to be sinners. Gimme the matches, Pam."

He put a cigarette between his teeth and struck the match. He puffed and coughed and puffed some more until the tip glowed steadily. He passed the matches to Pam, who lit one and handed it to me, then lit another for herself. We puffed until we grew dizzy and slipped to the ground. Randall tried to stand and stumbled.

My stomach lurched, but I smoked on. Randall threw down his cigarette butt and fired up another. He walked around the barn puffing hard and waving the cigarette in the air. Pam and I put our dresses into our panties and followed him, bony hips swaying. We threw our half-smoked stubs on the ground and pulled out three more. Gary roamed around the barn and stared at us, chocolate smeared across his face.

The fire started in a corner of the barn, just a few sparks at first, nothing to worry about, then a little lick of yellow tinged with blue and another and another. Nothing we couldn't have stamped out, if we had worn shoes, only we saved our shoes to wear to church and went barefoot when we played. Randall grabbed a handful of hay and tried to pat out the flames, but that made the fire hungrier and soon it was dashing here and there like a mad dog with us running behind it, and then in front of it yelling, "Help, help, please help!"

Pam grabbed our jar of drinking water and sloshed it toward the heat. Randall grabbed Gary and headed for the door. Pam and I screamed and pushed behind him. We dashed through the yard screaming, "Fire! Fire! Fire!" Our mothers ran into the yard, long hair flying. One of them grabbed a hose. Neighbors appeared and tossed buckets of water.

The volunteer firemen, mostly farmers, arrived in old pickup trucks, more of an afterthought than a firefighting threat. The barn could not be saved, they declared; too far gone. They stood around in their overalls, talking, spitting, and smoking. So different from pictures of firemen. No boots. No hats. No big red truck that I recall. Just a bunch of old men doing old-men things, there to ensure the fire didn't spread to their properties. Pam, Randall, and I stood behind and to the side of the firemen, watching the flames rush through the small wooden building. The dry wood crackled and popped like a big campfire, only no one roasted hot dogs or toasted marshmallows. On what had been the right-hand side of the barn, a charred skeleton framed the yellow-orange glow of destruction. Long rectangles of corrugated tin dangled from what was left of the beams that just a few minutes earlier had supported the hole-riddled roof. Rivulets of fire lapped the perimeters of the window from the inside, then rushed out in a torrent. Soon the left side, too, would be gone. My mom slumped by the side door of the house with Gary hanging on one hip, a dazed look on her face. Betty Ann stood beside them, arms loose at her sides, her head cocked as if studying the fire for clues. Brother Terrell was still praying in the woods behind the barn. I did not like to think what would happen when he returned. I chewed my fingernails, Pam cracked her knuckles, and Randall hopped from one foot to the other, his neck turning like a periscope as he scanned the distance looking for his daddy. Smoke poured from the barn and formed a tall black column against the Georgia sky. Brother Terrell was bound to see it wherever he was.

Randall spoke for all of us. "Lord, I wished we'd burnt to death in the fire. Or at least been hurt."

Pam nodded. "That way he'd have to feel sorry for us."

Brother Terrell had never whipped me, but I had seen him slap after Randall with a belt. I was more terrified by the redness of his neck and the way he pinched his tongue into a hard little point between his teeth than I was of the belt. When my mother wanted my attention fast, she called out, "Don't make me call Brother Terrell." While none of us, kids or adults, wanted to get caught on the wrong side of Brother Terrell's temper, it was equally true that none of us wanted to disappoint him. There was something about him, something powerful and at the same time fragile, that made us strive to please him. We wanted to be judged worthy, to be close to him, to bask in the blessing of those perfect white teeth, to be chosen by the chosen one. Every man, woman, and child worked hard to gain his approval. When we fell out of favor, it was as if we had been banished from all that we loved most. He was, as we say in the South, tenderhearted, with a soft spot for drunks, losers, animals, women, and kids. But that bucolic place often lay on the other side of treacherous terrain, not unlike the territory in which Pam, Randall, and I now found ourselves.

Randall pointed toward the field that lay

beyond the house and barn. A sliver, no bigger than a speck really, white on top, black on bottom, emerged from the tree line on the other side of the field and moved toward us.

"Get ready. Here he comes."

I blinked and the speck moved faster. When Brother Terrell drew even with the barn, he stopped, looked toward the flames, and then at the house. He was close enough now that I could see the Bible he carried under one arm. Randall considered taking off, but Pam grabbed his shirt.

"Randall, you'll make it worse for all of us."

He tried to twist away, but by that time his daddy had reached our mothers. As they talked to him, he looked over at us, then back at the barn. Two of the farmer-firemen wandered over to where they stood. The five adults turned to look at us. Randall looked over at Pam.

"What on earth are we gonna say?"

"We're telling him the truth, Randall."

"How much?"

Brother Terrell walked toward us slowly, sliding his belt out of his belt loops, his neck growing redder with every step. We scattered across the yard, screaming. Without saying a word, he caught Randall by the arm and began to swing his belt. Pam and I stood by the cottonwood and watched. Randall yelled and danced as the belt hit his jeans. For about the hundredth time, I wished it were not an abomination for girls to wear pants. Brother Terrell let go of Randall's arm.

"Son, you've got to do right. We're supposed to set an example, and here you are burning down barns. And it ain't even our barn."

Randall moved his head up and down, up and down.

Pam and I were next. I looked over at her. Tears rolled down her face and off her chin. She stepped away from the tree.

"I'm over here, Daddy."

She walked over to him. "I'm sorry, Daddy. We shouldn't have done it."

"Pamela, you know I hate to whip you more'n anything. But I got to this time."

"I know, Daddy. I deserve it."

Brother Terrell raised the belt. She didn't move. I noticed the belt always landed on her behind, not on her legs, and determined that I, too, would stand perfectly still. When the belt stopped, Brother Terrell caught Pam up in his arms and held her for long time. By the time he came for me, all the anger had left him. He gave me a few swipes with the belt. It wasn't even as bad as when Mama whipped me.

After the whippings, Brother Terrell went back to the woods to pray. He said he'd lost all his sanctification. When the fire had reduced the barn to a pile of blackened rubble, the firemen said they'd see us at the tent and waved good-bye.

Mama and Betty Ann put us into the bathtub two by two, washed the soot and grime from us, and dressed us in our church clothes. We always bathed and dressed early so that the adults had time to get ready for church. We sat in the living room, quiet and subdued for once. Randall actually looked through one of the books from his homeschool program. Pam showed me how to pop my knuckles. The fire had burned the badness out of us, and Brother Terrell's whipping had chased away any residual demons. We felt relaxed for the first time in days.

We were sitting there being as good as we could be, when Brother Terrell walked back into the house. He stared at us from the dining room and I saw his face go hard. Before we knew what was happening, he had slipped his belt out of his pants and was on us, tongue pinched between his teeth. We did a St. Vitus dance around the living room as the belt popped over our legs. Mama and Betty Ann ran into the room, yelling for him to stop, pleading that he had already whipped us. Brother Cotton and his wife watched from the doorway, mouths open. Then it was over and the three of us kids were scattered across the room, whimpering.

Brother Terrell looked around in a daze, running his hand over his head. "I don't know what come over me. I saw those kids and the thought of paying for that barn . . . we barely have

68

enough money to pay the bills . . . I'm sorry . . . I'm sorry."

He walked out of the room, the belt looped in his hand like a noose.

That night under the tent, he took the microphone from Brother Cotton with his head slightly bowed.

"I know we all like to shout and have a good time in the name of the Lord, but I feel a different spirit here tonight, a grieved spirit. We need to wait and see where it leads us."

"Yes. Amen."

"Brother Cotton, would you bring me my guitar?"

He sat on the edge of the platform and strummed his guitar.

"It's been a hard week. The devil has stirred things up amongst the evangelistic team. Sometimes when you're fight'en the devil, it's easy to start fight'en each other."

"Yes it is."

"The people of God got to pull together. We got to help each other out, not knock each other out."

He chuckled and kept strumming.

"I got a little song I want to sing 'bout how it's s'posed to be."

Brother Terrell's mouth went to the side of his face and he sang about how the rough, hard way was eased when we shared one another's burdens. The audience clapped along but did not join in, even though we knew the words. Brother Terrell with his guitar was a solo performance. He finished the song, unhooked his guitar strap, and stood up to put the instrument back in its case, talking to the audience while he did so.

"The Bible says confession is good for the soul, amen?" He snapped the case shut.

"Amen. Yes it is."

He turned to face the crowd. "Well, sometimes the old natural man gets away from you and you do thangs you wish't you hadn't done. How many done things they was sorry for?"

Hands went up all over the tent.

He tucked the microphone cord through his belt loop and walked down the prayer ramp. "The Bible says don't let the sun go down on your anger. I got mad today, mad at my kids, mad at Sister Johnson's kids. They was just being kids. Y'all know how kids are?"

"Yes, Lord. We do. Uh-huh."

"It's okay to whip your kids when they need it. But I lost my temper. Kids, y'all come on up to the front. I want to make things right."

Betty Ann motioned for Pam, Gary, and me to go to the front. Randall appeared from the other side of the platform. Brother Terrell knelt down and gathered us in his arms. His face was wet with tears.

"I'm sorry. I'm really sorry."

Pam and Randall cried. Gary cried. I cried. He

patted us all and sent us back to our chairs, still crying.

"Now, I want members of the evangelistic team who have grievances against each other to come down here to the altar and pray through." He turned and waved the preachers on the platform forward.

"Dockery, Red, Brother Gunn, if y'all can hear me, come on up here."

The tent men and their wives and kids walked to the front and kneeled. The families who followed the tent joined them. My mother slid off the organ stool and walked to the front of the platform and down the prayer ramp to kneel in front of it. Betty Ann told us to sit right where we were, not to move under any circumstance, and she, too, walked to the front and knelt. Brother Cotton left the platform and joined the others. His wife walked across the tent and stood with him. About twenty adults knelt together. Brother Terrell led the prayer.

"Father, we let the devil turn us against each other. We're supposed to be the light of the world, but we buried our lights under anger and bitterness and jealousy and evil thoughts."

"Have mercy, Lord."

The grown-ups moaned and wailed their repentance, their faces buried in their hands and bowed toward their knees.

"Forgive us, Lord. Have mercy on us. Teach us

to love each other. If we can't love each other, what hope is there for the world?"

All over the tent, people stretched their arms toward the front. "Bless 'em, Lord. Bless every one of 'em. Bless 'em, Jesus. Bless 'em, Lord."

Brother Terrell moved between the adults, laying hands on one, whispering in another's ear. Everyone cried and prayed. The crowd of about three thousand slipped to their knees in front of their chairs or gathered around to pray for the evangelistic team. After about thirty minutes, everyone who traveled with the tent began to stand up. Red hugged Dockery. Mama hugged Brother Cotton. Betty Ann hugged Laverne. Dockery hugged Brother Cotton. Everybody hugged Brother Terrell. Everyone said, "Love yew, love yew," over and over. Mama and Betty Ann patted each other on the shoulder. Neither a hug nor a profession of love passed between them.

Usually a good praying-through made everything better, but something had passed between Mama and Betty Ann and Brother Terrell on the road to Atlanta that could not be undone. It was neither named nor denied, but after that night in the car, it was always with us. I brushed past it when I ran by my mother and Brother Terrell in the hallway, his hand reaching out to steady her when she stumbled. It stood behind Betty Ann in the doorway as she watched my mother and

Brother Terrell sit on the bed, and count the offering, careful not to touch, stacking the ones, fives, tens, and twenties, stuffing the pennies, nickels, dimes, and quarters into the paper rolls from the bank. It elbowed its way to the breakfast table one morning as Brother Terrell related a vision of tanks rolling across the border from Mexico, and my mother stood and told him how the vision ended, because she had seen the same thing. I heard its voice in the muffled and not-so-muffled arguments that drifted from the Terrells' bedroom. And I saw its shadow move across my mother's face when Betty Ann announced her pregnancy.

Chapter Five

AT THE ENTRANCE TO THE TENT GROUNDS hand-painted signs, and later commercially printed banners, proclaimed in large red letters: END-TIME HOLY GHOST REVIVAL! SIGNS AND WONDERS. SALVATION! DIVINE HEALING! EVERYONE WELCOME. The last phrase was code for "segregation ends here." The year was 1961. Our signs went up in Bossier City, Louisiana, as the first busloads of freedom riders made their way from Washington, DC. They were headed for New Orleans, but the rides ended in Alabama, where a succession of mobs organized by men who held dual membership in the local police department and the Ku Klux Klan firebombed the buses and beat the activists.

Brother Terrell stepped down from the tiny trailer he kept parked at the tent grounds and turned to walk toward the tent. Before he reached the tent curtain, three men approached him. The largest man blocked his path and two smaller sidekicks took up positions on either side.

The bigger man jabbed his finger at the preacher. "You David Terrell?"

"Yes, sir, but I cain't talk right now. I got to preach tonight."

"You can damn well talk to us."

"Look, we can talk after service. Right now, I got to go."

The three men tightened the circle around Brother Terrell. One grabbed his broken arm, still wrapped and cradled in a sling. "Preacher, you should'a talked to us *before* you set up this tent."

"We got the permits . . . what do you mean?"

"He means we don't like nigger-lovers in Bossier City."

Inside the tent Brother Cotton made the introduction. "Put your hands together and welcome God's man of the hour, Brother David Terrell."

Brother Cotton turned to hand Brother Terrell the microphone, but there was no Brother Terrell.

The ministers on the platform looked around uncomfortably. Brother Cotton cleared his throat.

"I hope this don't mean there's been a rapture, or we're in trouble."

The audience laughed and craned their necks, trying to catch a glimpse of Brother Terrell. My mother played the opening notes of "I'll Fly Away" and Brother Cotton and the audience started to sing. When Brother Terrell had not appeared by the second verse, Dockery went to look for him. He found him surrounded by the men, one of whom still gripped his bad arm.

"Let him go, mister."

"I don't need no glorified carny tellin' me what to do."

"I'm not tellin' you. I *told* you. Take your hands off him." Dockery had the broad shoulders and ropy muscles of a fighter. He rarely fought since joining the tent team, but sometimes his temper got away from him, and he had to pray through at the next altar call. This would be one of those nights. He grabbed the man who held Brother Terrell's arm.

"Now, Dockery, now hold on . . ."

As the words left Brother Terrell's mouth, one of the men took a step toward Dockery, and another landed a punch on Brother Terrell's jaw. That's when Dockery went wild. Randall came running with the other tent men and gave us an eyewitness account later that night. He said

Dockery punched and kicked and yelled and that it took Brother Gunn, Red, and a couple of others to keep him from killing the man who hit Brother Terrell. Once the tent crew had separated Dockery from the attackers, Brother Gunn, one of the more even-tempered tent men, turned to ask them what they wanted. The largest of the three men shrugged off Red and walked back over to Brother Terrell.

"You better git them niggers out from under that tent. I mean clear 'em out."

Brother Terrell spread his good hand in front them, pleading, "Those people came to worship God. I can't, I won't, ask 'em to leave."

"It's on your head, preacher." The men turned and walked away. One of them lit a cigarette. Dockery started to yell that there was no smoking on the tent grounds, then let it go when Brother Terrell waved him and the others closer.

"Look, I got to take the platform. Someone call the law."

Dockery snorted. "Those men probably are the law."

In a tradition that harkened back to the roots of the modern Pentecostal movement, sawdust-trail revivalists had long welcomed blacks and whites under their tents. It all started when the one-eyed son of former slaves, Reverend William Joseph Seymour, founded a storefront church on Azusa Street in Los Angeles. After praying for months for an outpouring of the spirit, Reverend Seymour and his followers began to speak in tongues one day in 1906. They kept at it for the next three years. What became known as the Azusa Street Revival drew thousands of blacks and whites and was characterized by the *Los Angeles Times* as ". . . a disgraceful co-mingling of the races . . ." Holy Roller churches based on the Azusa Street experience sprang up all over the world, with one notable difference: There was no mingling of the races. Tent evangelists such as Billy Sunday, Aimee Semple McPherson, Jack Coe, and others persevered in interracial worship, but seated blacks and whites in separate sections of their tents when traveling through the South.

Not one for half measures, Brother Terrell said others could compromise with the devil, but bless God, he wasn't afraid to face Satan head-on. "Red, yellow, black, or polka-dotted, we're all God's children, and we all sit together under my tent," he said.

Not that we identified with the civil rights movement. The same whites who hugged the necks of black believers under the tent thought nothing of using the *n*-word in everyday life, and would not abide mixing with blacks under any other circumstance. Brother Terrell told racist jokes in private and most of us, with the exception of my mother, laughed at them. We saw no contradiction in using our "colored" brothers and sisters in Christ as a punch line while risking life, limb, and tent to worship with them.

Brother Terrell's defiance did not go down well in the South. City officials delayed permits, issued noise violation citations for sound checks, and pressured local newspapers and radio stations to deny us advertising. Notes left under the windshield wipers of our cars threatened to cut down the tent and whup our cracker asses. It was clear someone or something was after us, but the adults would not say who or what. When I asked my mother, she hemmed and hawed and said something like, "Oh, honey, the old devil is after us, that's all." That's all? Judging from the fear in her face, I figured the horned one must be close enough to spear our backsides with his pitchfork. When vandals slashed the tent in town after town, I was sure of it. The sheriff or constable or whatever brand of law enforcement that happened to show up walked around the tent saying, "Now, what'd y'all expect?"

The answer revealed itself that night in Bossier City. After the fist fight, Brother Terrell walked under the tent and up the ladder to the platform. Brother Cotton was in the middle of another song. Instead of continuing the song the way he usually did, Brother Terrell signaled my mother to stop the music. He walked to the podium and sat his Bible on it without opening it up.

"Let's move straight to prayer tonight. We ask

you, Father, to hide us behind the cross. Cover us with your blood, Jesus. Deliver us from our enemies. Pray with me, people. There's an evil gathering against us. God is our only defense."

Brother Terrell walked away from the pulpit and fell to his knees in the middle of the platform, rocking back and forth. "Oh God. Oh . . . oh God. . . . Throw up a hedge, Lord. Protect us from the powers of the enemy."

The ministers on the platform knelt at their seats. My mother knelt beside the organ stool. Across the audience, people slipped from their chairs onto their knees and began to plead with God for protection. Betty Ann told Pam and me to bow our heads and pray, and she, too, began to keen.

"Ooooooooooooh God . . . Have mercy, Lord. Have mercy. Ooooooooooooh God . . ."

Brother Terrell paced the platform and exhorted us to call out. People all around us entered into what we called travail, a weeping and mourning that came when the worst had happened or was about to happen. In travail we experienced the emotion of the situation, wrestled with it in prayer, and believed we could change it. It was as if we could sense the onset of some evil, could hear its heartbeat as it approached, but could not see or name it. The woman kneeling next to me prayed aloud and with her eyes open wide. Her lips exposed her teeth in a weird half grin, half grimace. She made a strange high-pitched sound.

"Neh, neh, neh, neh, neh, neh, neh."

A collective wail rose from the congregation. We didn't know what we needed protection from at that point, but when Brother Terrell told us the enemy threatened us, we believed him. The wailing went on for about forty-five minutes, reached a crescendo, softened, and died away. By the time we took our seats again, it was dark outside.

Brother Terrell flipped open his Bible just as a long line of cars began to turn from the highway onto the tent grounds. Usually when people arrived late, they switched their lights off to avoid creating a distraction, but these cars kept their lights on, and instead of parking, they circled the tent. Betty Ann's mouth opened and closed like a fish as she watched them. People turned and stared over their shoulders. A black woman sitting close to us murmured, "Lord, Lord, Lord."

Brother Terrell glanced up, and then looked down at his Bible as if nothing were amiss.

"Turn with me to Second Corinthians, chapter four, verse eight: 'We are troubled on every side, yet not distressed; we are perplexed, but not in despair; Persecuted, but not forsaken; cast down, but not destroyed . . .' "

Around and around the cars drove, maybe twenty, maybe more, high beams glaring. When they finally came to a stop, they left their lights on, pointing toward us. After a minute or two, people turned toward the front in their chairs and opened their Bibles. They tried to focus on Brother Terrell, tried to take in the encouragement he plucked from the scripture, but the car lights beamed a steady stream of anxiety our way.

"We need to keep our minds on God tonight, people, no matter what the devil throws at us."

Pam and I asked Betty Ann what was going on. She put her finger to her lips and told us to pay attention as she always did. Her hands worked the handkerchief she held beneath her swollen pregnant belly, twisting it back and forth until it was the shape of a dog bone. She asked Pam if she knew where Randall might be. Pam raised her eyebrows and arranged her face in the self-righteous expression we wore when we referred to the morally and spiritually inferior. "Mama, there's just no telling."

As she scanned the audience for her brother, the prim look on her face turned to shock. I followed the line of her raised arm and pointed finger. Twenty, fifty, a hundred figures in long white robes materialized along the perimeter of the tent. Black eyeholes gaped out of tall, pointed heads. Backlit by the headlights, the apparitions billowed and glowed like angels of destruction, or one of the hybrid creatures that roamed the end of time in the Book of Revelation. The hair on my legs and arms stood up. The end of time. The moon would turn to blood. Stars would fall, trumpets would sound, and the veil between heaven and Earth would be rent. I wanted my mother. She sat behind the organ, hand over her mouth. All around us, people turned and whispered. Pam worked herself into the crevice between her mother's arm and body. Betty Ann bounced Gary on her lap until he started to cry, but she didn't seem to notice.

She whispered, "Where's Randall? Where's Randall?" Her eyes rolled across the tent looking for a blue checked shirt.

Brother Terrell called to us from the platform. "Please, let's keep our minds on worshipping God here tonight. Don't let the devil scare you. That's what he wants to do, scare you."

The devil. That explained why the adults were so scared. I shut my eyes tight and pled the blood of Jesus in silence, the way the adults did when Brother Terrell cast out demons.

"The blood of Jesus, the blood of Jesus, the blood of Jesus. I plead the blood of Jesus."

I opened my eyes. Lines of black people shuffled down the sawdust aisles. The woman who sat in front of us pulled three kids, two little boys and a girl of about ten, off the pallet she had spread for them. She shook out the quilt and folded it in half, bringing one end under her chin and holding the other in her long outstretched arm; the edges matched just so, her movements slow and meticulous. She repeated the process and handed the quilt to the girl. *Her daughter, that's her daughter.* She pulled a creased paper bag from her purse, placed the jar of water and the saltines the boys had snacked on earlier into the sack and handed it to her daughter. Her right arm settled on the girl's shoulders as her left hand snapped shut around the wrists of the boys. They joined the exodus. Some said angels led the people safely through the white robes. Others said the Klan never intended to hurt us; they only meant to scare us. If that were so, they only partially succeeded. The woman and her children did not seem frightened, and neither did the others who left the tent that night. Bone-weary, but not afraid.

Those of us who remained were scared to death. A smattering of whites sat twisted in their seats, staring out at the robed figures. The crowd in Bossier City had been about half that of other towns, and now with a third of the audience leaving, the tent was almost empty. Quiet, too, except for the sigh of bodies in motion and the shuffling of feet on the ground. A woman a few rows ahead of us licked her lips constantly. A few men and women caught one another's eyes and raised their brows, as if to ask, "What now?" Everyone looked ready to leave, if only they didn't have to pass through those white robes. Several of the devils stood behind and to the side of where we sat. I cut my eyes toward them, and noticed for the first time the pant legs and shoes, regular men's shoes, beneath the hems of their robes.

Up on the platform, Brother Terrell tried again to regain his audience. "Let's focus our attention on the Lord. A time is coming in this country when God's people will worship without fear. Amen?"

A dry cough and the whimper of a child were his only answers.

He tried again. "I said there is coming a time when the powers of this world will fade away and God's kingdom will last forever. The lion and the lamb *will* lay down together. Amen?"

Not a single amen floated up.

"Don't lay down and die on me tonight. I said there is coming a time when the devil will be defeated once and for all! Now, can I get a real amen?"

A lone voice called out of the silence. "CERTAINLY!"

The shout came from the other side of the tent. Brother Terrell put his hand to his eyes and peered through the spotlights.

"Well, that's not an amen, but bless God, I'll take it. When the devil wins one battle you got to believe there will be another battle, one you can win with God's help. Amen?"

"CERTAINLY!"

Brother Terrell paced the platform and his words picked up speed as he moved. "You got to fast and pray until you've put on the whole armor of God. Then you got to go back out and win the next battle. Because there will be a next one and a next one until righteousness triumphs over evil, hallelujah."

He took out his handkerchief and mopped the sweat off his brow.

"Ain't that right?"

"CERTAINLY!"

Brother Terrell started to laugh.

"Well, Certainly, whoever you are, come on up here. I want to get a good look at a man who ain't afraid to speak up when the devil is looking him in the face."

A small man stood up on the left side of the tent and walked toward Brother Terrell. He wore a plaid sports jacket, dark pants, and a white shirt, all of which were at least two sizes too big. His short gray hair stuck up like pinfeathers. Brother Terrell left the platform and met him in front of the prayer ramp with his hand outstretched. He grabbed the little man around the shoulders and began to drag him back and forth in front of the audience. Certainly's jacket flapped around him as they walked. People began to turn from the white robes and back toward Brother Terrell.

"Bless God, they's some people will stand with

you no matter who or what is standing against you . . . ain't that right?"

The man blanched when Brother Terrell stuck the microphone in his face.

"Yes, sir, I . . . I . . . guess that's right."

"They's some people won't back down when the devil takes a pitchfork after 'em. Ain't that right too?"

"Yes, sir, Brother Terrell." Certainly seemed to grow more confident with each step.

"Some people when you ask 'em to say amen, they don't just say amen. They say . . ." Brother Terrell turned toward the man beside him. "What was it you said?"

The man hesitated, then took the microphone, leaned back as far as he could, and whipped his body forward as the word shot out of his mouth. "CERTAINLY!"

"Look, saints. Look, Brother Certainly. I b'lieve you scared the devils. I b'lieve they've turned tail and run."

We turned in our chairs. The white robes were stomping back to their cars and the cars were backing up and pulling away, the glare of their headlights finally receding. Brother Terrell ran up and down the aisles, dragging Certainly by the hand.

"We may not have won the battle tonight, but we didn't lose it either. God protected us with his shield."

Brother Terrell urged us to have courage, to have faith, to hold on. He told us that our brothers and sisters would be back, that we would raise our hands and pray together again. That God was still in his heaven, still in charge, and that in the end, we would be the victors. People wanted to believe him. They clapped their hands because they knew that's what they were supposed to do. They said amen and hallelujah, but their voices fell flat. Brother Terrell took his white handkerchief out of his breast pocket and mopped his face.

"You know what we need tonight? We need a victory march. Sister Johnson, play us a victory march."

My mother played the opening notes of "When the Saints Go Marching In" and Brother Terrell pounded out the rhythm with his fist and sang.

Oh when the saints go marching in
Oh when the saints go marching in,
Oh, Lord, we want to be in that number . . .

The ministers on the platform marched down the prayer ramp and queued up behind Brother Terrell. They shot one another quick, nervous looks as if they were on their way to a firing squad. Brother Terrell seemed determined not to notice how sick at heart everyone felt. As they proceeded down the aisle and around the tent, he pumped his arms and legs and grinned like a maniac. He marched with his hand in the air. He beat the tambourine double-time. He danced with his hand on his hip, stepping back, then shuffling forward. He spoke in tongues: "Lama bahia ma so may oh me la bahandala." He acted as if the hosts of heaven had paid us a visit instead of a bunch of men wrapped in bedsheets. When he passed our section, Betty Ann, Pam, Gary, and I joined him. My mother left the organ and marched with us. Oh, Lord, we wanted to be in that number, but mostly we didn't want Brother Terrell to march alone.

The crowd did not respond. Whether from fear of the Klan returning to the tent or of waking later that night to the sound of breaking glass and a cross burning, they remained in their seats. Brother Terrell would not give up.

When the Klan is dead and gone
When the Ku Klux Klan is gone
Oh, Lord, we want to be in that number . . .

Maybe people began to feel sorry for Brother Terrell or maybe they realized there was something to dancing like a madman in the face of fear and adversity. On about the second or third turn around the tent, a few folks from each section joined us. We were fifty, then one hundred, five hundred, a thousand, maybe more. Sometimes we tripped over a tentpole or a rope, but we picked ourselves up and marched on. Betty Ann spotted Randall leaning against a curtain pole and grabbed him by the ear. She pulled him into line and pushed him along in front of her round, swaying stomach. We marched until our legs grew heavy. We smiled until our faces hurt. We sang until our voices overwhelmed the dread inside us. Finally, Brother Terrell, my mother, and other members of the team made their way back to the platform and the rest of us drifted back to our seats. Mama took her seat at the Hammond and began to play a slow, soft hymn. From the platform, Brother Terrell urged people not to let fear keep them away.

"Don't be afraid to come back. We'll be here three times a day tomorrow and every day for the next few weeks. Now hug your neighbor around the neck and tell 'em you'll see 'em here tomorrow."

Once the crowd cleared, Brother Terrell gathered the evangelistic team together behind the platform and asked everyone to stay and pray for a few hours. "We haven't seen the end of this. I feel like they'll be back, and we need to make sure we have what it takes to stand firm."

The four of us kids fell asleep on a pallet of quilts in front of the altar and were awakened by yelling. Randall jumped up. Pam and I moved slower. Unsure for a moment whether I was dreaming or awake, I watched a group of adults across the tent pull into a tight little circle, scatter apart, then collide one against the other, hard, harder, in a fierce, weird dance. Randall called, "Daddy. Look out!" Brother Terrell turned and threw up his bad arm to shield his face just as a wooden folding chair wielded by a short bald man crashed over him. He howled like a cat with his tail on fire. Mama came up behind the man attacking Brother Terrell and brought another chair down over his head, then turned and ran. *Go, Mama. Go. Go.* The man tried to catch her but was brought down by two tent men. The women screamed and screamed. A police car drove up, lights flashing, and two lawmen got out and waded into the fray, threatening to take everyone to jail. The voices grew quiet and the bodies drifted together again, softly this time. I spotted Mama, chin thrust out, hands moving like birds as she talked to the policemen. Brother Terrell and the tent men told us later they recognized the faces of the three men who had shown up earlier that night among the attackers.

The black people stayed away from the next day's services. Brother Terrell asked everyone to remain in prayer for the safety of those who had been driven out by hatred. I thought of the three kids I had watched pack up and leave the night before.

Please let them be okay. Please let them be okay. Please.

That evening as the sun flamed out in the windows of the old Fords, Chevys, and Buicks that rimmed the field, the black portion of our congregation gathered in little groups just outside the tent and stood throughout the service. Their numbers increased throughout the week, even as the white audience dwindled.

The Klan did not come back in uniform, but we found several anonymous letters on our porch. The writer of one threatened to cut the unborn baby from Betty Ann's body if we didn't leave town. Brother Terrell ended the revival early. He told what was left of the congregation that he wasn't tucking his tail between his legs and running from the devil. He cast our retreat as a victory of sorts. "It may *look* like we've lost the battle, but we haven't. We stood up to the devil. We showed him we're not afraid. There is coming a time when those who hide behind the sheets will be spat upon as the scourge of the earth. There's coming a time when people of all colors will worship together in spirit and in truth, and that's thus saith the Lord."

Until the dawn of that Edenic age, there would be a new seating arrangement: blacks on one side of the tent, whites on the other, with a sawdust aisle in between. It was for the safety of the congregation, the evangelistic team, and his family. He began every revival with an announcement of the segregated sections.

"They threatened to cut the baby out of Sister Terrell's stomach. They'd do it too. Y'all know who I'm talkin' about." Blacks and whites nodded. "Now before we move on in the service, I want those of you who are white to cross the aisle and hug the necks of your brothers and sisters. Tell 'em Jesus loves them and you do too." That, at least, we could do.

Chapter Six

THE END WAS ALWAYS UPON US AND THE situation always dire. The revival in Bossier City just upped the ante. Unable to recoup the thousands he had spent on the revival, Brother Terrell left Bossier City owing everyone in town, plus the monthly equipment payments and staff salaries. It all added up to what Brother Terrell called his financial burden, and it got worse with each revival. If we didn't raise a certain amount of money, we would lose the tent or the eighteen-wheeler or the sound system. Millions would die and go to hell. Their blood would be on our hands. Meanwhile, we had our own blood to worry about. As tensions increased in the South, the three-foot-wide aisle that divided black from white did not satisfy the more violent racists. Brother Terrell was beaten a few more times. One story has cops looking on as one thug holds

Brother Terrell and another slugs away. Harassment by local officials increased. Our speakers were always too loud, the aisles in the tent too narrow, and the electrical system not quite up to code. Everything about us disturbed the peace. Authorities threatened to charge Brother Terrell with practicing medicine without a license, a tool that had been used before against faith-healing evangelists. One set of cops dropped all pretense and said they were taking him to jail for preaching to a mixed-race crowd. Brother Terrell grinned and held out his wrists to be handcuffed. "Last I heard that wasn't illegal, but at least you boys are honest," he said.

Our lives were a mess, and when the baby was born everything became even messier. There was less sleep, less space, less money, and more arguments, especially when Brother Terrell insisted on naming his new daughter after my mother. Betty Ann agreed, reluctantly I assume, and then called the child by the nickname Tina instead. The adults all seemed on the verge of a nervous breakdown. They displayed tremors in their hands with solemnity and pride.

"Look at that," they said, holding their hands out at right angles to their bodies. "My nerves are shot." Nervousness was a badge of honor; why, I never figured out, but it carried over to us kids. When Pam and I argued with Randall or resisted his schemes in any way, he held his hand out and told us we were turning him into a nervous wreck. He played up the tremble to win our sympathy, but when he held a pencil or spread peanut butter on bread, I could see that his hands really did shake. I faked a quiver in my fingers on occasion, but Randall outed me. My insides were another matter. I felt as though we lived our lives on a tightrope and that at any moment the baby would cry unexpectedly or Gary would wet his pants or Pam or I would argue too loudly and everything, everyone, would fall to the ground. It didn't take a divine revelation to figure out something had to change.

We were in revival in some nameless town that was like every other town we passed through. The evening service was long over, and I lay half-asleep under the tent, stretched out across two or three folding chairs, head to toe with Pam. My mother and Betty Ann sat in the row in front of us, talking with a group of believers under the floodlights that hung from one of the center poles. Gary slept on a pallet with Baby Tina beside him. Randall had disappeared as usual, but no one worried about him; he always showed up before it was time to go home. The adults talked endlessly, and I was lulled by the rise and fall of familiar voices discussing topics that should have been harrowing but had become comforting in their familiarity.

"You know Brother Terrell says communism is about to spread all over Central America and into Mexico."

"He had those visions of tanks rolling into the US from Mexico."

"If we're gonna do something for God, we got to do it quick."

A hum of voices agreed. "Uh-huh. Yes, we do." Several different conversations split off from the main one: talk of Brother Terrell's fast, money, faith, the lack of faith. I sought out Mama's low, reassuring voice. "We're planning to go to Central America next year." I was wide-awake.

"Sister Johnson, my heart goes out to those people."

"Brother Terrell says he wants to start a Bible school down there."

"I heard an orphanage too."

"He cried the whole time he was in Guatemala last time, seein' those babies wandering the streets hungry, half-naked with no one to take care of them."

The voices took on an urgent tone with everyone talking at once, excited about the prospect of starting a school and an orphanage where those poor kids who didn't have anyone, not a soul, could live and be taken care of.

I kept my eyes closed and listened again for my mother. "I wouldn't mind spending my whole life there. I've always dreamed of living in a foreign country and doing missionary work."

"What about your kids?"

I waited.

"They could live . . . at the orphanage . . . while we traveled and preached . . . and helped the people." Mama spoke slowly as if awed at how perfectly everything would work out. I sat up and looked around. I wanted to ask, "But wouldn't that make us orphans too?"

Someone said, "The Lord always makes a way, doesn't he?" One of the women who sat close to me reached over and smoothed my hair out of my eyes. Mama smiled. Everyone *looked* sane.

I didn't tell Pam or Randall what I had overheard. Somewhere in the corner of my mind was the half-formed belief that if I never repeated what I had heard, it would never happen.

Some people said Randall brought the situation on himself by giving his daddy one more problem to worry about. He was only eight, but most of the time he did as he pleased. While his daddy railed from the platform against the evils of sin, Randall hung around the tent with boys as old as twelve and thirteen. You could see them leaning against the parked cars. Some people said they smelled cigarette smoke as they passed by, but Randall denied it. From time to time he went missing from the tent grounds and Dockery or some other hand would find him in a nearby pool hall. He was always in trouble, but unless his parents wanted to whip him all the time, there wasn't much anyone could do about it.

As much as Brother Terrell disliked and worried about Randall's behavior at the tent, I think it was the trouble he gave my mother over his schoolwork that sealed his fate. Mama was one of the few in the evangelistic team with a high-school diploma, so the job of home-schooling Randall fell to her. When it was time to study, she dragged him kicking and screaming from clothes hampers, closets, the tops of trees, and on one occasion, the trunk of his daddy's car. She said it would take an act of God to teach that boy anything. They only had a few hours between the afternoon and evening services to study, and by the time she found Randall and they sat bent over one of the thin homeschool booklets, it was almost time to go back to church. Mama tried to hurry him through his reading lesson, but Randall couldn't be rushed. It took him what seemed an eternity to sound out the one-syllable words.

"G-g-g-ga-o-o, go-oh . . . go." He pulled and twisted a short hank of hair toward his forehead and studied the ceiling before he returned to the page.

". . . T-t-tah—o-oh—mmm. Tah-om?" He dug in his nose and rolled the pickings between his fingers.

"Tom, Randall. It's Tom."

"Oh." He slid his finger to the third word and chewed his lip.

Mama sighed and rolled her eyes toward heaven. "It's the same as the first word."

"Ga-oh?"

"So what does the whole sentence say?"

"G-g-oh, go, Tah-ah-om . . . g-g . . . hmm . . ."

Mama's leg jiggled up and down. "The last word is the same as the first word. What is the first word?"

"Well, um . . . um . . ."

"Oh, for heaven's sake." She grabbed the book off Randall's lap and sailed it across the room.

"Go, Tom, go. Go, Tom, go."

Randall looked up, earnest and perplexed. "I was just about to say that."

Brother Terrell and Betty Ann thought second grade would be easier for everyone if Randall went to school in Villa Rica, Georgia, and lived with his aunt Marie and uncle Raymond. Randall didn't want it to be easy.

"I won't try your patience no more. I'll be good. Please don't leave me," he begged.

Brother Terrell reasoned with him. "Son, the law says you got to go to school."

"But Jesus will come soon, and I won't need no education."

"Son, it's outta my hands."

"But Carolyn can teach me." He rolled his big, baleful eyes toward my mother.

"Son, you done wore Sister Johnson plumb out. Now stop arguing, before I wear you out."

I experienced my family, the Terrells, and the other members of our nomadic tribe as a single unit, a holistic entity incapable of functioning without each individual. The earlier mention of the orphanage and Randall's impending exile made it clear that some members could be left behind: the kids. Mama could leave Gary and me, and the life we had lived with her would go on without us. The hot, dusty morning services where time stood still, the blur of the afternoon services, the wild singing and shouting at night, the long drives between revivals. Everything would be the same, but we wouldn't be there.

The drive to Villa Rica was miserable. Randall rode in the backseat with Mama, Gary, and me, and his unhappiness took up so much room we couldn't breathe without brushing up against it. Mama tapped her foot and Randall moaned. I cracked my knuckles and he wailed. Gary tried to make him feel better by offering my Etch A Sketch.

"Git that thang away. I'm too miserable to play."

Betty Ann's standard warning of, "Randall Terrell, you better straighten up," started a new round of begging and pleading.

"Please, Daddy. Don't leave me. I want to go with you. Mama, make him take me with you. Please, y'all. Please take me with you." He choked on his words. Pam began to weep softly. Brother Terrell glanced up from the road and looked over at Betty Ann, who looked over her shoulder at Randall, then back at her husband. Randall ratcheted up the crying. That was a mistake.

The longer and louder he cried, the less we felt sorry for him. His daddy warned him. "Son, I need you to stop crying right now. And I mean right now." Randall had nothing to lose and he had never minded whippings, so on he wailed. The atmosphere in the car went from sad to mad in a couple of miles, but Randall didn't notice.

"I just want to goooooooooo with you. Please. Please. Don't leave meeeeeeeeee."

Mama sighed and rolled her eyes. Brother Terrell doubled his tongue between his lips and hunkered over the steering wheel. Gary and I worked on making ourselves smaller. *Any minute now,* I thought, *any minute.* Brother Terrell glared at Randall over his shoulder. "Randall, son, I warn you, I've had enough."

My mother yelled, "David!" and Brother Terrell turned around in time to jerk the Falcon back into the right lane and miss an oncoming car. Mama threw her arm over Gary and me and kept it there until we bumped to a stop by a weedy water-filled ditch that ran along the side of the road. We sat there at an angle, breathing hard, the car leaning toward the ditch and all of us leaning with it. Mama put her arm down, sighed, and said, "If you're not careful, you'll kill us all."

Brother Terrell gripped the wheel and stared out the windshield. He seemed calm. Close calls on the highway affected him that way. He accelerated and tried to straighten the car a bit before slipping the gearshift into park and turning off the engine. "Son, why do you leave me no alternative but to whip you?" Randall didn't have an answer.

Father and son opened the doors and walked to the back of the car. Randall stretched out his arms and put his hands on the trunk as his daddy unthreaded his belt. Pam mumbled, "He's gonna get it now." Mama put her hand on my head and turned my face to the front. My shoulders and neck tensed in anticipation of the first whop of the belt. Brother Terrell pleaded with Randall that he didn't want to whip him, not today, especially not today. His words receded under the blast of a horn from a passing car. As the horn grew fainter, we heard laughter. No one laughed during a whipping. I whirled around and stared through the rear window. Brother Terrell stood pulling his pants up over his boxers while Randall looked over his shoulder at him, one hand still on the back of the car, the other hand slapping at his thigh over and over. Brother Terrell gripped his pants at the waist and tried to swat Randall with the belt, but he couldn't stop laughing long enough to take aim. The two of them were laughing as hard as I had ever seen.

I tugged at my mother's sleeve. "What's going on, Mama?"

She arched her eyebrow. "I'd say God just answered Randall's prayer."

In a moment Brother Terrell and Randall collapsed back into the car, bodies shaking, faces crinkled, wiping tears from their eyes with the backs of their hands. Brother Terrell beat the steering wheel and wheezed. Randall rolled from side to side in the backseat, holding his stomach, gasping for air.

"Oh, Daddy . . . oh, Lordy . . . Daddy done fasted so much, when he, when he . . . took his belt off, his pants . . . his pants just slipped down on the road."

Brother Terrell turned to Betty Ann and took up the story. "You should'a seen that carload of people passed by. Five mouths flew open at once."

My mother said, "Next thing you know, they'll have the law on you for exposure."

Brother Terrell started the car. "Randall, I don't want to hear another word about school. Not another word, or I'll have your uncle beat the tar out of you with *his* belt when we get there. He ain't been fasting."

102

Randall sat quiet for the rest of the trip. When he started to tap his foot too hard, Mama or Betty Ann said, "I feel a whipping coming on, better grab your pants," and we all laughed a little.

When Brother Terrell finally turned off the Falcon and announced, "We're here," Randall opened the car door, shook his uncle Raymond's hand, and hugged his aunt Marie. Betty Ann joked that someone had stolen her boy and left this well-behaved child in his place.

Aunt Marie invited us in, but Brother Terrell said we had to get back on the road and couldn't stay. Randall asked his daddy for the keys and opened the Falcon trunk. He hoisted a little brown suitcase from the trunk with both hands, then dropped it on the ground and buried his face in Brother Terrell's concave belly.

"Son, I'm sorry 'bout this, but I got to preach and you got to go to school."

"I know, Daddy. I know."

We piled in the car with Randall watching, biting his nails. Brother Terrell turned the key and the engine cleared its throat. I waited for Randall to grab the door handle and run screaming behind us, but he stood there, hands in his pockets, and watched us back the car onto the highway and drive away.

I thought for a long time that some essential part of Randall had broken when we left him behind, and that it was from that damaged place inside him that the blood issued, the blood that would spurt and seep from his body for the rest of his life. It was an explanation that made sense to a four-year-old, and it continued to feel true long after I was old enough to know better. People said all the time that Sister So-and-So had worried herself sick, that Brother What's-His-Name had died of a broken heart. Separated from his mother and father, forced to go to school, to become just another kid in a town where no one knew or cared who he was or whose he was, Randall fretted and grieved himself sick. Under the tent, he was David Terrell's son. Away from the tent, he was nobody, and if there was one thing Randall couldn't stand, it was being a nobody. Pam and I knew this about him. We knew it in the way kids sniff out the tender areas of one another's psyches, little gardens of feeling to be skirted or trampled upon, depending on the day and the situation.

Randall lived in Villa Rica only a few months before the bleeding started. There was no warning that first time, none of the symptoms that later signaled the onset of a hemorrhage. One minute he sat at the kitchen table arguing with Aunt Marie about baths or chores and the next minute he was covered with blood. Not the soul-cleansing blood of the Lamb. Not the bloody handprint posted on the doors of the Israelites in the Exodus story, a plea for God to spare the firstborn son inside. The thick dark liquid that erupted from Randall's lips was death itself. It splattered across the table where he had sat with Aunt Marie and Uncle Raymond every day and thanked God for all his blessings. It hit the wall below the window that looked out on another pristine day and ran in rivers toward the pine slats of the floor. Blood. His blood. Everywhere he looked. *Please, God*. He pushed up from the table as he did every morning and evening, but he didn't get far. His foot slipped in one of the dark pools, and down he went. He listed there on his side, a pale little ship in a sea that darkened and widened around him, fed by the stream that burbled from his lips. Outside, a cloud the size of a man's hand drifted past the window.

We were in a revival in West Virginia when the news came. Brother Terrell said he knew something was wrong when he opened his eyes that morning, that he felt a weight pressing against him. He ended the morning service early and shook the hands of all the preachers as fast as he could. He asked Brother Cotton to preach the afternoon service, and turned to make his way through the next line of people as he moved toward the camper trailer he kept parked behind the tent.

"Good to see you. Thank y'all for coming. Later, we'll talk later."

Once the door of the trailer clicked shut behind

him, he began to move up and down the tiny corridor. He felt as though something inside him had slipped out of place. There was nothing to do but pray, and as he prayed, his son's face came before him. Randall was giving Raymond and Marie fits. Several times a week Brother Terrell fed a bag of change into a pay phone and called the neighbor who lived nearest to his sister and brother-in-law. She ran across the pasture to get Randall and Marie or Raymond, and he called back fifteen or twenty minutes later. His sister and brother-in-law kept him up-to-date on all Randall's shenanigans. He skipped school and picked fights and no one could do anything with him. He had called that morning to check on Randall, but the neighbor had not answered her phone.

He prayed all afternoon. Usually after a day of prayer, he felt relieved, purged, but not this time. He tried to read scripture to prepare for the evening service. It was of no use. Reading was hard for him. In fact, the only thing he could read was the Bible, but on this day the letters on the page seemed particularly stubborn and refused to arrange themselves into words. He didn't know what to do about Randall. He opened the door, stepped out of the trailer, and headed into the tent to preach.

He had taken the first step up the ladder to the platform when he felt the hand on his arm. He turned and looked into a face filled with concern.

"Brother Terrell? It's Randall. He's real sick. He's in the hospital in Atlanta."

At the edge of the tent, Betty Ann clutched the baby and leaned against one of the poles. Her face crumpled with pain. "Oh, my boy, my boy, my boy."

Brother Terrell took her arm. "Let's get in the car. We got to go to Atlanta." For the first time in a long time they were in agreement.

It seems logical that my mother would have stayed in West Virginia to provide the music for the services, and that Gary and I would have stayed with her, but I can't recall anything after the Terrells left. What I remember are the stories of the trip as told by Brother Terrell and later Randall and repeated so many times that they took up residence in me and began to function as memory. Only it is not my memory. It can't be, because I am not in the stories. The only characters are Brother Terrell, Betty Ann, Randall, and the bit players who recite their lines on cue.

The Terrells drove a couple of hours before stopping for coffee and calling the hospital in Atlanta for an update. The nurse told Brother Terrell that the doctors had no idea why Randall was hemorrhaging. They had given him transfusions, but he continued to throw up blood. They wanted to do an exploratory surgery; it was the only way to find out what was wrong. Brother Terrell said he would think about it. He didn't trust anything he couldn't understand, and that included banks, government, lawyers, and doctors— especially doctors. He always said if his mama had let the doctors have their way and amputate his leg, he'd have ended up a one-legged faith healer or worse, dead. He couldn't figure out what to do, so he prayed, silently and aloud, throughout the trip. He didn't beg, plead, or bargain with God to save his son's life; he demanded.

You said all things are possible to those that believe. I'm holding you to your promises. You can't let my son die. I command you to heal my son.

When he finished haranguing God, he started in on the devil. *I rebuke you, you foul spirit of death. You can't have my son. I won't give him to you. You have no authority over me or my family. Git away!* When words failed, he spoke in tongues.

Somewhere on the road, God began to talk back. The voice of God always came to him first as an impression, something he felt rather than heard. *If you let those doctors operate on Randall, he will surely die.*

Lord, he's dying now.

I'm telling you those men don't know what's wrong with Randall. They want to use him as an experiment.

What am I supposed to do?

Trust me.

My son is bleeding to death.

Trust me.

He's my son. My only son.

Trust me.

What do you want me to do?

Prove me.

What do you mean?

There's a tent revival in Atlanta. You know the preacher. I want you to give him a hundred dollars.

That man's a flat-out crook.

You're not giving to him, you're giving to me.

But I don't have an extra hundred dollars.

Trust me.

Brother Terrell rolled down the window and let the cool, damp fall air hit him in the face. Beside him, Betty Ann sat stiff and silent, a wall of grief. It was always Brother Terrell's stories, Brother Terrell's struggles, Brother Terrell's pain that mattered. His suffering dwarfed her own and that of everyone around him. We were there to bear witness and offer support. The closer you were to him, the more this was true. When his voice fell silent Betty Ann would have prayed that most common of prayers: *Oh, God. Not my son. Please. Not my son.* Her petition would have beat against the wall of her mind like a trapped fly. She would not have dared remind God of all she had sacrificed: a steady paycheck, a home, security for her children, the occasional new dress, the casual comforts. In a world of mythic struggles and divine visitations, Betty Ann was the most ordinary of women. Sure, she grumbled from time to time. Lamented all she and her children had done without.

I'll stop complaining. Please. Not my son.

She might have wondered why, after all Brother Terrell's fasting and praying, after all the miracles and the sacrifice, Randall lay dying.

Please, forgive me. Forgive my lack of dedication. Please. Don't take my son.

The car slowed, surged forward, slowed, and surged again, rocking back and forth down the highway. Brother Terrell always drove with one foot on the accelerator and one on the brake. In the distance, tiny points of light pierced the darkness. They were almost in Atlanta.

They parked the car and entered the colorless glare that was Grady Hospital. Each step down the narrow corridor diminished Brother Terrell. Away from his milieu, he lost his status as celebrity preacher and became again the son of sharecroppers, a cripple boy whose family depended on charity to get by, an uneducated man to whom the workings of the greater world remained a mystery. By the time a nurse approached and asked what it was he needed, his gaze was fixed on the toes of his spit-shined wingtips.

"Yes, well, ah, we come here to, to see Randall. Randall Terrell."

The woman looked down from beneath her big white hat. "It's five thirty. In the morning, sir. Come back later, during visiting hours."

He plunged his hands into his pockets and jingled the keys and coins. "Well, uh, look, we, uh, we drove straight through and all. To, you know, to get here."

"Sir. He's asleep. Everyone's asleep."

Betty Ann whimpered.

"My wife here, she's real worried. She needs to see her boy."

The nurse raised her voice as if he were hard of hearing. "Surely you want him to get his rest."

Another nurse stepped from behind the desk. "What's going on here?"

"These people want to see their son. I told them to come back later."

"Who's your son?"

Brother Terrell shifted his weight from one foot to the other. "Randall. David Randall Terrell. We drove all night."

"Oh, the Terrell boy. He's been asking for his daddy and mama. Go on in, let him see you're here, but don't stay long."

They opened the door to the sound of moaning. Long white curtains hung from the ceiling, dividing the room into three small rectangles. Each area held a bed and hospital machinery that

111

whirred and churned and cast a gray watery light, enough to see that the first two tiny, ancient faces in the beds did not belong to their son. Randall occupied the third bed, the one next to the wall, the one from which the moaning came. They stood over him together, quiet and still, watching his body move and twitch. His arms sprouted tube after tube. Betty Ann's hand flew to cover her mouth. Brother Terrell whispered in her ear: "Trust God, Betty Ann. We have to trust him."

The next morning Brother Terrell sat under the crooked preacher's tent and watched him take the offering. People stood in line and waited to give him money. The man didn't have to plead or beg. He was glad he didn't have the hundred dollars God had told him to give the preacher. As the service drew to a close, he stood to leave and a man who sat in front of him turned around.

"Brother Terrell, is that you?"

"Yes, sir, it is."

"We came to see you last year in Chattanooga. You healed my wife's rheumatism. I been wantin' to thank you." The man shook his hand and palmed a twenty-dollar bill.

"Brother Bob," he yelled to a man three rows over. "This here is David Terrell. That tent evangelist that healed Marie."

Within a few minutes Brother Terrell found himself in the center of a crowd. People reached toward him, grabbed his hands, hugged his neck, and put money in his hands and coat pockets. When they finally let him go, he had a thousand dollars. He counted out five twenty-dollar bills and went to find the preacher.

Later that afternoon, Brother Terrell went to the hospital alone. He stood over Randall's bed and looked down at his sleeping boy. "Son, son, I need to talk to you." Randall opened his eyes. "God told me he is going to give you a miracle, but you have to believe. Do you believe?"

"Yes, Daddy. I believe."

"That's what I wanted to hear, son. I'm taking you outta here."

He pulled the needles and tubes from Randall's arms, scooped him up, and walked out of the hospital room. A nurse called to him in the hallway. "What are you doing?"

"I'm taking my son."

"Sir, please. Wait. Let me get a doctor."

"We don't have time to wait." He walked past her and continued down the hall into the waiting room, carrying Randall wrapped in a blanket the same way he had carried him as a newborn home from the hospital. A flock of nurses and a couple of doctors trailed behind them.

One of the doctors grabbed his arm. "I can't let you take that boy out of here. He'll die."

"He'll die if he stays."

"Mr. Terrell, we'll get a court order."

"You better get it fast, 'cause we're leaving now."

He walked out of the hospital and laid Randall in the backseat of his car. The boy looked scared and pale. He had not noticed earlier how pale. If he had, he might not have had the nerve to do what he was doing. "Son, you're not going to die. God is going to give you a miracle."

"I know, Daddy."

Brother Terrell and Randall drove a hundred miles an hour, never stopping or slowing down until they crossed the state line. They made it back to West Virginia in time for Brother Terrell to preach the morning service the next day. He sent one of the tent men back for Betty Ann and the baby. By the time they arrived, Randall was raking leaves to make money to put in his daddy's offering.

Randall hemorrhaged off and on for the rest of his life. Years later we learned that he suffered from a rare birth defect. A vein intended to route blood to his heart dead-ended in his stomach. His body produced a network of tiny capillaries to ferry the blood supply. It was an ingenious work-around, but from time to time the network ruptured. At first the blood showed up as dark patches in his stool, subtle and easy to miss. Then the blood began to engorge his belly and there was nothing to do but wait and pray for a miracle. Once the hemorrhage reached critical mass, blood spewed from his lips. I remember the splattered chaos of that blood and the fear that came with it, long urgent journeys through the night with the car windows open and the heavy, honeysuckled air of the South pressing down upon us like the left hand of God.

The events I witnessed and the stories about these events have intertwined to form a single thread of memory. Sifted and shaped over time by the adults around me, my recollections have distilled into a mythology of faith, hard to believe, harder still to deny. Here is what I think I know: Randall was sick most of his life, he came close to death again and again, and his father refused to let him go. It was his father's voice, his father's faith that tethered him to life. That's what Randall believed. That's what we all believed.

Chapter Seven

TENSIONS BETWEEN MAMA AND BETTY ANN eased a bit after Randall rejoined us on the road. My mother's story is, she decided Brother Terrell should stay with his family for the sake of his ministry. There was no such thing as a divorced holiness preacher. Mama said she avoided Brother Terrell as best she could, a difficult feat considering we all occupied the same house during revivals. She and Gary and I went back to traveling in our own car for a time, and I remember her yanking me and other bystanders into any room or space in which she found herself alone with Brother Terrell. She said Brother Terrell pursued her constantly and that she resisted, reminding him he had a wife. That wife would soon give birth to two more daughters. My mother managed to take responsibility for their births, saying, "If I hadn't talked him into staying with her, they wouldn't have had all those kids and things might have been different."

Randall remained healthy for nearly a year, and we did what we always did: moved every three to six weeks, stayed up after the evening service until two or three in the morning, got up early for the morning service, raced back home for lunch, then back to the tent for the afternoon service. If pictures existed from those days, and in my family they do not, they would reveal a pasty-skinned, pinwormy lot with baggy clothes and dark hollows under our eyes. Maybe it was too much "light" bread or not enough pork and beans. We began to physically resemble our metaphoric conception of ourselves—a battlefield on which God and the devil duked it out. The cosmic implications of our hardships and the fact that we expected Jesus to touch down at any moment made the normal touchstones of childhood an afterthought. My mother homeschooled Randall and then Pam as time and energy permitted, enough to keep the authorities off the Terrells' backs. We lived in fear of "the government." Whatever it was, there were whispers it might take us kids away. I don't know if the threat was real or simply an extension of the adults' increasing mistrust of the larger world, but the rumors added to everyone's nervous condition. Sometimes Mama or Betty Ann would notice how tired and unkempt we kids looked. "Poor little things," they said. "This is no life for kids." Their eyes watered but never quite spilled over into tears.

On the calendars it was mid-October, but in Dallas it was still summer. The tent collected and radiated heat like a cast-iron frying pan. Daytime services were the worst. About three hundred people sat scattered among the seventeen hundred or so wooden folding chairs. The employers of the elect insisted that they show up for work, revival or no revival, and that kept the morning and afternoon services small, quiet, and dull as dirt. The only movement was the occasional flick of a fan fashioned from the "Repent and Be Saved" flyers we printed and handed out as advertisements. Beyond the rows of empty chairs, beyond the rolled-up canvas curtain, beyond the hot white light reflected off the dusty automobiles parked in neat lines across the gray clumpy field, beyond the field and the sticky tar of the highway lay the world with its oscillating fans, water-cooling units, and *air conditioners*. I eyed the glare beating through the tent above me and wondered why it never stormed during the morning services.

Brother Terrell perched on a chair in the middle of the platform. He was early into his latest fast and already everything about him seemed sharper, more focused. He had declared fasts before, for a week, two weeks, thirty days. This time it was different. This time he wouldn't eat until he heard from God. Fasting mortified the flesh and honed the spirit, and that made it easier to get to God. He was dark as a crow with his black hair and black suit. The Bible lay open on his lap and his finger traced Jesus's red-letter words. "Verily, verily I say unto you . . ." The visiting ministers sat behind him in rows, all dressed in the same dark suits. My mother had moved away from the organ bench and arranged herself at the end of a row, legs crossed, face eager, her body pointed toward the true north of Brother Terrell. Under the dark heavy fabric of her ankle-length skirt, her leg pumped back and forth. Mama had taken to wearing long skirts and dresses as a consecration, a sort of secret pact between her and God. Despite her high-necked, long-sleeved blouse and heavy skirts, she looked unfazed by the heat. I picked up my paper fan and moved it across my face. Hot air. My mother, the preachers, and Brother Terrell seemed so removed up there on the platform. Their zeal for God turned the ordinary comforts of life into something as unnecessary as a dime-store whatnot.

Down here in the valley things were different. Pasted to the back of my chair with nothing to distract me, I counted seven new beads of sweat rolling down my body. I slumped in my seat, head lolling on my shoulder. My dress, petticoat, panties, and socks were soggy. I was indeed a poor little thing. My eyes rolled up to Laverne, Brother Cotton's wife, searching for pity. She bent over her Bible, following Brother Terrell as he marched through scripture, hup, two, three, four, verily, verily.

Gary and I sat through the services with Laverne now instead of Betty Ann. When Betty Ann became pregnant, Mama said it was too much of a burden on her to watch us. And then the baby came and it really was too much of a burden. Pam still sat with her mama and the baby, and her absence made the tedium of the daytime services almost more than I could bear. I watched my foot swing round and round, then switched directions. A horsefly landed on my wrist and crawled up my arm, feathery-legged and red-eyed. I gave him a limp swat and slumped lower in my chair. Just when I thought I couldn't take another minute, Randall slid into the seat next to me and whispered, "If it's this hot in hell, they may as well not send me 'cause I won't stay."

I rolled my eyes at him. "At least you don't have to sweat to death on Earth."

He grinned.

"What is it?"

"That new tent man, John, the young one, said he would take us swimming."

"Swimming?"

Laverne cut her eyes at us.

"I'll talk to your mama. I'm gonna get Pam. You and Gary meet us round back."

In less than a couple of minutes, Randall was on the platform, whispering in Mama's ear. She nodded and they left the stage together. *How did he do that?* Pam and the new tent guy appeared at the side of the tent, and Mama and Randall joined them. My mother waved Gary and me outside. *Yes.* We walked up just as John told Mama he wanted to take us and a couple of other kids who traveled with the tent to a big swimming hole outside of town. He would have us back before church that night. Mama didn't look convinced.

"My kids don't know how to swim."

Pam and Randall stood on either side of her and tugged at her hands. "Please, Carolyn, let 'em go. Please."

John reassured us. "Don't worry, Sister Johnson, I'll keep 'em in the shallow water."

Pam and Randall piled into the cab of the pickup with John, and Gary and I climbed into the bed of the truck with two boys from one of the families who followed the tent. We held on to the sides of the truck as we bounced across the field toward the highway. I made Gary sit between my legs; that way I could keep him safe and he could hold my dress down. As we turned onto the highway and the tent grew smaller, the thrill of what we were doing rushed through me. Swimming was one of those things Holy Roller kids didn't do. When our parents felt sorry for us they might let us stick our feet in one of the slimy pools of whatever motor court we happened to spend the night in. And if my mother or Betty Ann felt especially guilty, we might do a drive-by vacation, as in we drove by the Gulf of Mexico or the Atlantic Ocean en route to the next revival. "Looky there, kids," they said, and we would jump up and down and clap our hands at the sight of the waves rolling up on a Mississippi or Florida beach. It never occurred to them to stop, and it never occurred to us to ask them to do so. And now, here *we* were, here *I* was, about to do the impossible. *Yes, Lord.* My legs and arms wanted to pound the bed of the truck. My voice wanted to whoop. I looked at the two skinny tent boys who sat beside Gary and me. They were about my age with blond crew cuts that shimmered in the sun. Their faces wore the serious, self-conscious expression of the true believer. One of them smoothed his long-sleeved white shirt deeper into the waist of his dark, baggy dress pants and tightened his belt. Neither would meet my eye. I clamped my jaw shut. The wind whipped my hair into my face and stung my eyes. I didn't care.

The pool parking lot was a field, not unlike the field on which the tent sat, only with large pecan trees that cast a generous shade over the parked cars. Kids and grown-ups lazed against the cars or strolled casually between them, arms and legs long, brown, and naked, chests and bellies forested with thick black hair or smooth as stones. Swimsuits stretched tight over curves that dipped and swelled, a mound of breast here, a crescent of white buttock over there. So much skin. The tent boys dropped their jaws. I knew how they felt. My mother screamed and crossed her arms over her chest if I caught a glimpse of her in a full slip. Gary stared and pointed up into the trees. "Look. Look."

"It's a bird," I said, but my eyes never left the bodies around us.

Doors slammed and Randall, Pam, and John were at the back of the pickup, letting down the tailgate. The seven of us stood there for a moment, feeling exposed and unsure what to do or where to go. The two tent boys shoved their hands as far into their pockets as they would go, hunched their shoulders, and pulled their heads in like turtles. Randall slapped one on his back. "Come on outta there, Lynn. Let's have some fun."

"This way, kids." John led us toward a clump of buildings in the distance.

Uneasiness mounted as we approached the line of kids waiting to enter the pool. Most wore swimsuits, but some were still clothed, in shorts and sleeveless shirts mostly. They turned to look as we joined the line, all of us dressed in what appeared to be our Sunday best.

"Why don't they mind their own beeswax," Pam muttered. I shrugged and focused my attention on the ant that crawled into a crack between the light-green cinder-block walls. The girl in front of me leaned one tanned arm against the wall. She threw the other one around her friend. Someone yelled. Someone else laughed. Another ant moved into the crack. Pam pushed me forward until we stood on wet cement looking out at the long pool. Grass and boulders lined the sides. Little boys cannonballed into the water. Teenage girls in two-piece suits rode atop the shoulders of boys and wrestled other girls on other shoulders. Kids walked through the water with their eyes closed and their arms extended in front calling out, "Marco! Polo!" Everyone smiling. Water flying. Bodies glistening. "Marco! Polo!"

John nudged Pam and me toward a small room. "Go get ready in there. Then come on out." The dressing room was a revelation. I didn't know where to put my eyes. Naked women sat on benches pulling on or peeling off swimsuits, talking to one another or to their kids.

"And then I told him if he wanted someone to do that, he'd better find a new wife."

"Wait, Jimmy. Over there. Shelly, come here."

One of the women smiled at me. I looked down. Pam pulled me into a small stall with a curtain. We unbuttoned each other's dresses, took off our slips, and put our dresses back on. I took my shoes and socks off. My toes spread in all directions on the damp concrete. With crinolines and shoes in hand we tiptoed out of the dressing room toward the pool. Randall, John, Gary, and the tent boys stood there in their black pants and long-sleeved white shirts holding their shoes, socks, and belts. Randall's grin took up his entire face. He bounced up and down on his naked feet.

"Come on. Let's go. Let's go."

We placed our shoes and other things on a dry patch of ground and walked over to the white concrete steps. John put Gary on his shoulders and he and Randall ran down the steps into the water, leading with their bellies. They began splashing each other as soon as they hit the pool. Pam told the tent boys to go ahead, and they descended into the water with slow, measured steps, hands white-knuckling the rail.

Randall splashed at them. "Come on, y'all. This ain't no baptism." The tent boys assumed a martyred air as the locals retreated toward the sides and the deep end of the pool.

Pam pulled at my hand. "Our turn." I kept my eyes fastened to her back as we walked down the steps. My ears thrummed. We moved oh so slowly. The water tugged at my legs like quicksand, only cold. I had not expected it to be so cold. Little waves lapped at my knees and thighs. Chill bumps popped up on my arms and legs. Our dresses floated open like flowers around the white stems of our legs as we stepped down into the pool. I didn't know what to do, so I began to move slowly from right to left, watching my dress trail behind. I looked anywhere, everywhere, except at the kids staring at us.

Randall pointed at me and Pam. "I see your panties, both of you."

John shushed him. We walked back to the steps, tied the hems of our dresses around our thighs, then waded back in the water. Randall splashed us and we splashed back. The splashing helped us pretend that we didn't care if people stared at us, didn't care that we were in a public pool fully clothed, and after a while we really didn't care. John took Gary off his shoulders and began to swing him through the water, holding him under his arms. Gary laughed so hard he started to cough. The two tent boys hoisted themselves out of the water and sat on the side of the pool, determined to remain apart or unable to overcome their sense of separateness. The rest of us played sharks, pirates, mermaids, even Marco Polo. Pam figured out how to swim underwater and we had contests to see who could hold her breath for the longest time. She won. Groups of local kids gradually made their way back to the shallows and resumed their games. If they ventured too close, we glared and they backed off. Riding in the back of the truck on the way home, I thought about how happy everyone at the pool seemed. They either didn't know or didn't care that they were practically naked and on their way to hell.

Chapter Eight

IN HOT SPRINGS, BROTHER TERRELL OPENED the little half door at the back of the platform and walked to the center of the stage with his head slightly down, chin tucked in. After weeks of fasting, his shoulders were coat-hanger thin and his shirt billowed about when he moved, almost as if there were no one inside. Every week his black belt snaked a little farther around his waist. Soon it would touch his back. He took the microphone from Brother Cotton and began to speak in the middle of the chorus.

"Y'all ever been tempted? It's a lonely place to be."

The singing died away and the crowd sat silent.

"Bathsheba tempted David and he murdered a man. Delilah seduced Samson and destroyed him. Jezebel caused a king and an entire nation to stray with her painted lips and idols."

Jezebel. The pagan princess who painted her face and seduced the king of Israel into marrying her. Jezebel. Thrown from the castle window and devoured by dogs who left only her skull, hands, and feet. I saw her severed hands lying there in the street, rings stacked on slender fingers that ended in long red nails. The sun reflecting off gold sandals crisscrossing her tiny, unbloodied feet. Her skull rolling to a stop against the curb. She never should have worn all that makeup. I tore the Kleenex Laverne had given me in half and wrapped one piece around each of two small sticks I had fished from the sawdust, glad Pam couldn't see me making ladies out of sticks and Kleenex.

"Seems like every time a man of God falls, there's a woman in the picture."

"That's right, there is."

"Uh-huh. Preach it, brother."

He stumbled and one of the preachers brought him a chair. He sat, reconsidered, and stood again.

127

"You women who set your cap for a preacher better be careful not to end up like Jezebel."

Brother Terrell moved the folding chair aside and began to walk up and down the platform. His steps grew steadier and his voice stronger as he paced.

"You women like to fix yourselves up to look good. Even you holiness women." He dropped the microphone and let it hang from the cord around his neck. With one hand on his hip and the other crooked at the arm so that his hand flapped in the air, he pranced forward on his toes, hips swaying. He pitched his voice to falsetto. "Why, I just want to look nice. Nothing wrong with that." His voice fell back to its normal timbre. "And you smear on a little more of that *tinted* chapstick." Again he mimicked a female voice. "It's flesh-colored. Nothing wrong with that."

The women who sat around me fidgeted and shifted in their seats. Brother Terrell didn't mince words. He preached the Word and he preached it like it was a double-edged sword. It hurt sometimes, but they came to hear the truth and that's what he gave them. Besides, he was really talking about women like Sister Corinne two rows back. She had been looking a little like the world lately, hadn't she? Brother Terrell dropped the falsetto and laughed. They laughed with him, relieved, a bit more at ease. They met one another's eyes and shook their heads. That

Brother Terrell. He was something, wasn't he?

An electronic screech shot through the speakers as Brother Terrell grabbed the microphone again and began to yell directly into it. "Pretty soon there's nothing wrong with anything and the flesh has got you. It's the *flesh* you gotta watch out for."

His body trembled and the tremble grew stronger until he shook all over. He was gripped by a power that would not let him go. It arched his back and propelled him across the platform. Its voice tore through him and came out as a loud rasp. "It's the flesh you got to deny, mortify, crucify. If you don't, you're worth nothing. I said you're worth nothing to God. Did you hear me? You may as well be fed to the dogs."

He reached the edge of the platform and teetered there as if about to tumble into a ravine. Before Brother Cotton could reach him, he jumped onto the prayer ramp and ran up and down, screaming, "Harlots! Hussies! Jezebels!" His face turned red and the veins on his neck popped out. "You women who wear your pants so tight a man can see your crack."

He stopped suddenly and faced the audience straight-on. "You women who tempt the men of God to lust, and cause them to forget their calling. The wrath of the Almighty will fall upon your heads and there won't be enough of you left for the dogs to eat."

He pulled a folded white handkerchief from his breast pocket, wiped his brow again, and threw it onto the sawdust. A man and a woman dived for it, scrambling to grab hold of its miracle-working powers. The man came up with the cloth, holding it stretched out above his head like a prize, one end in each hand. The woman shrugged and turned to go back to her seat.

"Wait a minute, ma'am. Here you go. Here's another one." Brother Terrell took a second handkerchief from his pocket, wiped his brow, and threw it to her. She caught it and walked back to her chair bucking at the waist, waving the cloth in front of her.

The evangelistic team huddled around Brother Terrell after the service that night, congratulating him on a powerful sermon. He leaned against the outside railing of the prayer ramp. He always left the platform exhausted, but lately he could barely stand at the end of a service. He fingered his keys in his pockets and stared past us. "I can feel the powers of the enemy. He's trying, he's gathering against us. I feel it . . . in my soul. The devil, he's, uh, he's getting ready to test us." He paused and fidgeted. "Something big . . . I don't know what. Remember what Jesus said about the demons, that some, uh, some respond only to prayer and fasting. We got to . . . you know, we need to be ready." Everyone waited for him to say more, something about how to get ready, maybe, but he was finished.

Mama spoke first. "Brother Terrell, we want to stand with you."

"Thank you, Sister Johnson. Those of you who are able, it would be good if you stay and pray with me."

The praying lasted a long time that night. Voices lowed, "Oooooooooh God. Oooooooh God." In the dim after-hours lighting, shadowy figures glided up and down the sawdust aisles and around the periphery of the darkened tent. I watched the thin smudge of my mother move across the tent. She threaded her way through rows of chairs and disappeared in the twilight that lay beyond the reach of the light and just this side of the night.

I woke to Mama's hands under my shoulders, pulling me up. My body felt thick and heavy as a tree stump. "Is it the middle of the night?" I always wanted to wake up in the middle of the night. No answer.

"I'm worried he's gonna fast hisself to death." My mother's voice sounded strained, higher than usual.

Brother Cotton nodded. "I don't know how he's standing up under the stress. The churches are pulling back on their support, the Klan threatening him night and day. The crowds aren't what they should be. He's carrying the burden for a lost and dying world by himself."

Dockery sat up suddenly. "Has anyone *seen* Brother Terrell in the last hour or so?" After the altercation with the Klan and the threats and beatings, Dockery made sure someone stayed with Brother Terrell at all times when he was at the tent.

Brother Cotton cleared his throat. "He left a little while ago."

"Where'd he go?"

"He said he needed to take Sarah back to her room. Said he wouldn't be gone long."

My mother's lips pursed, then relaxed. She exhaled through her nostrils and they flared, the way they did when she was mad. Betty Ann sat stiff-backed, ankles crossed, hands folded in her lap. She placed her gaze someplace beyond us. Sarah, tall and thin with long soft hair that flipped on the ends. She worked in Brother Terrell's office in Greenville, South Carolina, scheduling crusades, opening mail, and taking out checks and money orders to put them in the bank. She smiled at Pam and me like we were her special friends. When we played grown-ups, Pam always got to be Sarah. I picked up one of the stick ladies I had dropped when I fell asleep and twirled her between my fingers. Her Kleenex dress floated through the air. Pretty.

"Mama, what is lust?" She whirled around from the kitchen sink. Soapsuds drooled from her hands onto the floor, but she didn't seem to notice.

"Where did you hear that word?"

"I heard it in church. Brother Terrell talked about it the other night. You know, the night he took Sarah home."

She looked down at the puddle of suds on the floor. "I might have known you'd be paying attention at that moment." She tossed a dish towel to me and turned back to the sink.

"Wipe that up."

I wiped up the suds and handed the towel back to her. "Do men lust after you?"

Her back stiffened. "Donna Marie, did anyone ever tell you that children are to be seen and not heard?"

"But . . ." I dropped the subject. "Do you think I'm pretty?"

"Of course."

"Pam's prettier."

"Pretty is as pretty does."

"What does that mean?"

Mama dried her hands, turned around, and put her hands on my shoulders. "It means how you treat people matters more than how you look." She cupped my chin, tried to run her fingers through my hair, and ran into a nest of tangles. I gritted my teeth.

"You're supposed to brush your hair occasionally."

"I do brush it, occasionally."

"When's the last time you washed it?"

I didn't want to get caught lying. "A few days ago."

"Come on, let's pretty you up a little."

"But . . . you said . . ." My arms and legs went heavy with dread.

"This will be fun."

It was not fun. First Mama put me in the tub and tried to scrub the skin off my arms, legs, neck, and even my ears. "Why do you rub so hard?"

"Because you don't use soap when you bathe yourself. Now close your eyes and let's wash your hair."

I looked up at the ceiling and shut my eyes tight. Mama laid her hand on my forehead to keep the shampoo from running into my eyes. It didn't work. "It's burning. It's burning." I jerked my head up and thrashed my legs. More shampoo ran into my eyes.

"No, no. Please, no."

With one hand under my head and the other pushing down on my chest, she held me under the faucet.

"Don't. Don't." The water ran over my forehead and into my nose. I gasped for breath and swallowed a mouthful of water. "I'm drowning. Let me up. Please."

By the time she helped me out of the tub, we were exhausted. We still had to comb the tangles out of my hair, roll the slippery strands onto the pink sponge rollers, and sit around and wait for the curls to dry. I had to be careful how I played (no chase, no bungled cartwheel attempts), careful how I turned my head (not too fast), and careful how I sat (no rolling my head from side to side on the back of the couch). By the end of the afternoon, I was exhausted.

"Donna Marie, hold still." Mama sat on the side of the bed and I stood in front of her. She emphasized each word with a little jerk on the pink sponge curlers she pulled from my hair.

"It hurts."

Mama wrapped each curl around her finger and shellacked it with hair spray. My hair felt hard and prickly against my neck.

"Now hold your arms up and let's get your petticoat on."

"But it itches."

"Hold your arms up."

I thrust my lip out and my hands into the air. The petticoat pricked my skin as it fell over my shoulders and around my waist.

"Now, step into your dress."

I stomped into the dress she held open at my feet. She pulled it up, fastened the buttons on the back, and tied the sash.

"Put these on." She handed me a pair of white ruffled socks and my church shoes, black patent-leather Mary Janes.

"Try not to scuff your shoes tonight. Now, let me see you."

I locked my knees and held my arms away from me. She cupped my chin and studied my face. "You are just as pretty as Pam Terrell. In fact, you're pretty as Marilyn Monroe."

"Who?"

"Marilyn Monroe. Go ask the ministers if you aren't just as pretty as Marilyn Monroe."

I skipped into the living room, ready to show myself off. Brother Terrell and Brother Cotton sat on the edge of the couch, deep in conversation. Children did not interrupt adults, especially preachers. My face burned and my heart pounded. I stood in front of the men and without explanation pitched myself up on my toes and began to whirl.

I heard the soft tapping of my patent leather shoes on the floor. One more twirl. Faster. My dress and petticoat flew up; a show of lacy panties. I came to a stop in front of Brother Cotton and looked him in the eye.

"Do you think I'm pretty?"

He pursed his lips and whistled. "Very pretty."

I lowered my eyes and smoothed the skirt of my dress. "Pretty as Marilyn Monroe?"

His big hands encircled my waist. He looked me up and down and turned me around. "Honey, you are prettier, much prettier than Marilyn Monroe. Don't forget it."

"Thank you, Brother Cotton. I won't forget. But who *is* Marilyn Monroe?"

"Nobody you need to know. Now, go play."

"Tell me, please."

Brother Terrell cut me off. "We got business to discuss. Now go on back to your mama."

Brother Cotton slapped my bottom, end of discussion. I flounced from the room. Maybe I did look pretty. I ran to the bathroom, climbed on the side of the tub, balanced on the sink, and stretched to see my reflection in the mirror. Bangs lay pasted on my forehead in thin, sweaty strands. The rest of my hair was separated into ugly little dishwater-blond sausages. All that primping and I looked worse. I walked outside and kicked at a tree.

Chapter Nine

EVERY DAY THERE WAS A LITTLE LESS OF Brother Terrell. Cheekbones rose like canyon rims from the planes of his face. His Adam's apple bobbed exposed and lurid above the pit at the base of his throat. A glimpse of him ambling to the bathroom in his T-shirt and pajama bottoms featured a clavicle that ran like a rail over the sinkhole of his chest. A boneyard of a man. What once were muscles had thinned to curtains of skin that hung from the sticks of his arms. I passed him in the hallway and shifted my eyes as he slunk by, his shoulder pressed against the paneled wall for support. I could not bear to look at him directly. His frailty encompassed a growing desperation that embarrassed me. He was naked in his need, and it was terrible to witness. He said he was fasting to hear from God, but it was the world after which he seemed to hunger. His eyes, round and swollen, slipped over every person, every object in the room, searching, searching, searching. It was as if he found himself locked outside life and looked for a way back in. On occasion he gathered the four of us kids close, Pam and Randall nestled under each arm, Gary crowding in. I pulled away, unable to laugh and snuggle and hold my hand out for the silver dollar he offered, terrified by his vulnerability.

The house we had rented in Birmingham, Alabama, was still and quiet. Without the perpetual hum of Brother Terrell in motion, everything slowed down. The adults talked in worried, hushed voices, always about Brother Terrell. Had he eaten? Had he tried? Oh my God, what if he dies? The women made soups: vegetable, chicken noodle, beef stew.

Betty Ann nagged. "You've got to eat something. You're gonna kill yourself. It's hard on the kids. Please. Eat. Just try."

At the beginning of the fast he joked and told

her to get thee behind me, Satan, but three months later the pleas for him to eat came from every direction, and he gave in and took a few spoonfuls of soup. His stomach rejected it. He drank broth, but that, too, came back up. He drank water and Sprite through a straw to keep from drinking too much at once and throwing it back up. His eyes bounced like pinballs. He was afraid. He wanted to eat, but couldn't, and the more he wanted to eat, the more he tried to eat, the harder it became for the rest of us to put food in our mouths.

Late one afternoon, Pam, Randall, Gary, and I sat in the white painted kitchen around a square table covered in pink, blue, and red flowered oilcloth, about to dig in to plates of hamburger meat and tomato sauce ladled over piles of macaroni. Goulash, we called it, and it was my favorite. I loaded the first bite into my mouth just as Brother Terrell shuffled around the corner into the kitchen, his twenty-eight-year-old body frail and stooped as an old man's. The meat frying and the sweet tang of the tomato sauce had lured him from the back bedroom where he lay resting before the evening service.

He leaned into the counter and gripped its edge. "Hey. Y'all eating?" His voice was soft and whispery, and he sniffed the air as he spoke. He parted his lips and pulled them away from his teeth, an attempt at a smile that made his face appear more skeletal. Pam yelped and ran from the room.

"Pam. Honey, what is it? Come back." He turned to follow her but lost his footing and slipped. My mother leapt toward him and kept him from hitting the floor. He clutched her arm and rested his head on her shoulder. She looked down at him for what seemed a long time, fear and tenderness passing like clouds across her face. He searched her eyes. "I'm dying."

"You are not dying." She called for help. "Brother Cotton! Come here!"

Brother Cotton's dark curls and big red face appeared above Mama and Brother Terrell. Betty Ann and Laverne trailed behind.

"I'll take him, Carolyn." Brother Cotton slid one arm around Brother Terrell's waist and the other arm under his knees, and carried him like a small child back into the bedroom. Laverne followed, but Betty Ann lingered in the kitchen, circling Mama.

"You're always there, aren't you, Carolyn?"

"I'm trying to help."

"Keep your help to yourself."

Mama thrust her face close to Betty Ann's. But instead of saying anything she just shook her head, threw the dish towel, and walked out of the kitchen, through the living room, and out the front door. Betty Ann stared after her, as if the air my mother moved through held a clue about what to do next. She glanced at Randall, Gary, and me as she left the room. "Y'all eat. Before it gets cold."

The grease had separated and congealed around the edges of my plate, and the bite of goulash I took before Brother Terrell came into the kitchen lay in my mouth like a dead thing. I gagged and ran to the trash can to spit it out, wiped my mouth with the back of my hand, and walked back to the table. Randall dropped his head into his hands. The nurses in the hospital had warned that Randall shouldn't get upset, that it could aggravate his bleeding condition. Gary took his thumb out of his mouth and patted his arm. "It's okay. It's okay." Randall jerked his arm away, pushed back from the table, and walked out the back door. Through the window I watched him pick up an old baseball bat and beat it against the skinny trunk of a tree. His belly swayed with each swing. It seemed to get bigger every day, a sure sign that the blood was backing up in his stomach again. We had not taken him to the hospital because Brother Terrell said we had to hold on to the promise that God had healed Randall and not let the devil steal our faith. The Bible was filled with stories of people who, as Brother Terrell often reminded us, paid the price for their faith. How much would we have to pay? I slid my fork tines through hollow tubes of macaroni. The bare scraggly branches of the tree trembled each time Randall cracked the bat against its trunk.

Everything seemed harder in winter. Bark flew off, exposing the soft white flesh beneath.

"I wish he'd stop."

Gary looked up at me. "What?"

"Nothing. Just eat."

Brother Terrell eased himself down on the edge of the platform, resting his feet on the prayer ramp below. "Somebody bring me my guitar." He slipped out of his suit coat and held it up. Brother Cotton exchanged the guitar for the coat. "Can I have a little water too?" Three men jumped up to get the water.

"Fasting leaves a funny taste in your mouth. Y'all ever notice that?"

Yes, amen, they had noticed.

He strummed the opening chords of "They That Wait Upon the Lord." "It's hard to wait on God, but if you're a man of God, there ain't nothin' else to do."

He closed his eyes, strummed his guitar, and began to sing.

> They that wait upon the Lord
> Shall renew their strength
> They shall mount up with wings of an
>   eagle . . .

The lyrics are an affirmation of faith, but the tune is slow and melancholy. That night Brother

Terrell's bare-bones guitar playing and his ragged voice turned the song into a lament. Mothers stopped shushing their children. Teenage girls held on to the notes they were supposed to pass. The tattooed young men who were dragged to the revival or bribed by their mothers to come stopped elbowing one another and listened.

Brother Terrell had started over again on the first verse when a high, reedy laugh made its way up from the audience. Goose bumps popped up on my arms. The spirit sometimes moved people to wail when Brother Terrell sang a sad song, but never to laugh. Up on the platform, my mother half-stood at the organ bench looking for the source of the laughter. She gave Brother Cotton a look that meant someone ought to do something. He nodded and left the platform. The laughter stopped as suddenly as it had started and was replaced by a low burble of words and sounds. I scrambled up in my chair and scanned the back of the tent for a better look. Laverne pulled at my hand, but I ignored her. The women in front of us inched to the edge of their seats and craned their necks to see. Others turned in their seats and looked around. Brother Terrell continued to sing and sway, eyes closed.

They shall walk, but not be weary
They shall stumble
But not fail . . .

143

Brother Cotton hurried toward a group of people, mostly men, who stood in a little clutch in the middle section of the crowd. Someone, a girl, broke free of the group and ran up the aisle toward the platform. She passed so close to where we sat I could have reached out and touched her pale, puffy arms or felt the strands of her long blond hair whip against my fingers. She was barefoot and wore a sleeveless flowered shift that rode up her thighs as she ran. She flung herself against the sides of the prayer ramp below where Brother Terrell sat. She reached up and grabbed the railing that ran along the outside edge of the ramp and shook it. She whinnied, "David Ter-rell, David Ter-rell," in the same high, eerie voice that had laughed aloud. Perched on the edge of the stage above her, Brother Terrell sang on, his black shoe tapping out the time.

Brother Cotton, Dockery, and Red converged on the girl, pulling at her from behind. Dockery pried one of her hands off the ramp and pinned her arm behind her. She twisted away from him and ran back toward the congregation. Brother Cotton and Red grabbed her around the waist, but she flipped like a fish from their hands. The congregation stood and prayed aloud, "Blood of Jesus, blood of Jesus, blood of Jesus."

Men and women left their seats and walked toward the girl with their arms outstretched in her direction. Someone ululated, "Lelelelelelele-lelelele."

Voices layered one over the other as people began to speak in tongues. "Ma ma so mako. Shondiddy-i. Shondiddy-i. Nenen la ma hi."

The girl turned, holding her arms out and away from her as if for balance. The two tent men and Brother Cotton circled her like a gyre. The audience threw a wall, two to three people deep, around the four of them. "Blood of Jesus. Blood of Jesus. Blood of Jesus." I looked up at Mama. She had stepped away from the organ bench and had both hands outstretched toward the girl, her lips moving.

An older woman pushed through the crowd, calling, "Doreen, Doreen." The girl turned her head and when she did, Brother Cotton tackled her and took her down. Sawdust flew, and the crowd that gathered around them fell back a bit. He straddled her waist, his hands catching and pulling her arms back. She flailed her legs until Dockery caught and held her ankles. Red knelt down and tried to talk to her as she banged her head against the ground. Finally, he gave up and held her head still.

After a few minutes, the praying, ululation, and tongue-talking died away. Calls for the blood of Jesus grew less frequent and the crowd shuffled and looked at one another as if to say, "What now?" Brother Cotton looked over his shoulder at

Dockery and shrugged. The ministers on the platform stood and whispered at one another. My mother stood. No one knew what to do.

"I came here for you, David Terrell." The voice, now low and full as a promise, came from the ground.

Brother Terrell kept singing. One of the preachers on the platform started toward him as if to alert him to the situation, but someone caught his shoulder and pulled him back. The Lord and Brother Terrell had their own way of handling things.

The voice rose from the sawdust in a singsong pattern. "Da-vid Ter-rell . . . Da-vid Ter-rell . . . Oh, Da-vid Ter-rell . . ."

Brother Terrell finished the song and opened his eyes. He looked down at the girl, the tent men, and the crowd that stood around them. Without saying anything, he unhooked his guitar strap, pushed himself up, walked across the stage, and slipped the guitar, body first, then neck, back into its case. He walked down the prayer ramp and leaned on the rail for support. "Y'all can return to your seats now. Everything's okay."

The crowd fell back but continued to stand.

"The Bible says some demons come out only with much prayer and fasting, amen?"

"Amen, yes it does."

"The Lord has been readying us for this. Is someone here with this girl?"

The short, square-shaped woman who had called Doreen by name stepped forward. Her gray hair was slicked back in a bun, and she wore a brown sack of a dress, its plainness broken by a thin black belt. She looked like hundreds of women who came to the revivals, the ones who seemed rooted wherever they happened to be standing, feet planted apart, hands hanging in fists at their sides. They may not have been able to control what came at them, and plenty did, but bless God they were not going to let the devil or anything else mow them down. Brother Terrell put his arm around the woman's shoulders and inclined his head toward her as she spoke into his ear.

He nodded and picked up the microphone that hung around his neck. "She says this girl's been this way since she was sixteen."

He turned back to the woman. "How old is she now?"

He unclipped the microphone from his neck and held it in front of the woman.

"Doreen's nineteen years old, Brother Terrell."

"You her mama?"

She nodded yes.

Doreen howled and tried to roll on the ground. Her shift rode up and an expanse of thigh came into view. Dockery took one hand off the girl's ankles to tug at her shift and was rewarded with a foot to his chin.

Brother Terrell addressed the audience. "Can someone help cover this girl up?" A woman ran up and draped a sweater across the girl's thighs.

Brother Terrell turned back to Doreen's mother. "Go ahead, sister."

"She was sneaking off with older boys at night, hanging out at pool halls. I took her to a revival in Chickasaw, but she sat in the back and made fun. That night on the way home, she grabbed the wheel of the truck and tried to kill us all. She been that way ever since. She tried to set the house on fire with us in it. She came at her daddy with an ax, liked to kilt him. She tries to eat raw meat."

"Blood of Jesus. Blood of Jesus. Blood of Jesus."

"What do the doctors say?"

"We can't afford no doctor. I took her to every preacher I could, but not one done anything for her. Her daddy and me pretty much give up. Then two days ago she asked me could she come see you."

"Oh, Bro-ther Ter-rell." Doreen called his name in that soft voice. "Brother David Ter-rell."

Her mother moved toward her. "Hush, Doreen."

"It's okay, sister." Brother Terrell steadied himself against the railing of the prayer ramp. "That's not your daughter talking, that's the demon inside her."

The word "demon" ran through the crowd.

People picked it up and whispered it back and forth to one another, nodding. Demon possession wasn't exactly common, even in our circles. Two or three times a year some poor soul interrupted the service spewing obscenities or a relative brought them through the prayer line bucking and frothing at the mouth. Exorcism, or the casting out of devils as we called it, was a terrifying and thrilling experience. The possessed were preternaturally strong and on occasion had broken free from the men who restrained them and had to be pulled off of some audience member. Worse was our belief that demons could fly out of one person and into another. I didn't want to end up like these people with their wild eyes, strange habits, and damned souls.

Brother Terrell told the men to let the girl up. They looked at him as if he were nuts. "Really, Dockery. Y'all go on and let her up." The men tried to pull her to her feet but she buckled at the knees. Red grabbed her under one arm and Dockery held the other. Brother Terrell put his hand on her forehead. Her body stiffened.

"Neeee neee naaaah lo si me lay lo. We speak in tongues, too, Brother Terrell." As the girl spoke, small red marks appeared on her face and arms, a field of ripe strawberries.

"Blood of Jesus. Blood of Jesus. Blood of Jesus."

Brother Terrell dropped his hand from Doreen's

149

head and faced the congregation. "I need every one of you to keep your eyes closed and your hearts and minds on the Lord. Don't let fear get a hold of you and don't open your eyes, or next thing you know, the demon will be in you."

Laverne closed her eyes and covered Gary's eyes with her hand. I squeezed my eyes shut, but they wouldn't stay closed. Brother Terrell put his hands on the girl's head. His face turned red and purple, just like when he was mad at one of us kids.

"You foul spirit of death! Come out of this girl. In the name of Je-sus. Depart! I command you. Go!" His voice sounded stronger than it had in weeks.

"Hallelujah. Stay with me, people. Keep your eyes closed. Doreen, can you hear me?"

"I hear you. I hear you, Brother Terrell." Doreen sounded like a normal girl and she smiled, a soft, pretty girl smile. Brother Terrell's shoulders relaxed. Dockery and Red let go of her arms. She reached out to Brother Terrell as if to hug him, then spat in his face. A murmur of protest came from the crowd. Several men stepped toward Doreen, but Brother Terrell waved them away. He took his white handkerchief out of his pocket and wiped his face. Dockery backed the girl away from Brother Terrell, but she sidestepped him and charged the preacher headfirst. Brother Cotton stepped between them and took a blow in the stomach. He doubled over, hands clutching his sides.

Doreen laughed. "What will you give me if I leave this girl, preacher?"

"That's enough!" Brother Terrell walked toward Doreen with his right hand outstretched. "I'll not bargain with you, Satan."

"You will, Brother Terrell. You will."

"Keep your heads bowed and your eyes closed. Stretch your hands in this direction and believe with me, pray with me. I need every ounce of faith I can get tonight."

I was so frightened my teeth chattered, but my eyes would not stay closed. Arms and hands all over the auditorium beamed all the belief that could be summoned toward Brother Terrell and Doreen. Lips moved in incessant prayer, voices layered and formed a dense chorus.

The voice that was not the voice of the girl rose above it all: "What will you give me if I leave Doreen?"

The din quieted. We waited for Brother Terrell to answer, but all we heard was silence, a sure sign that something strange was going on. The crowd pressed against Doreen and Brother Terrell. I hopped off my chair and moved into the aisle for a better look. There he was, kneeling in front of Doreen, drawing or writing with his finger in the sawdust, just as Jesus had in the Bible with the adulteress. All around me eyes were closed, faces tensed, bodies rocking to and fro. Doreen kicked at Brother Terrell, but he continued to write. When he stopped, he placed his hands on Doreen's feet and looked up at her. His expression was tender.

"Lord, have pity on this girl. Have pity on her family. The Bible says, for God so loved the world, he gave his only begotten son. For the sake of your son Jesus, drive these tormenting spirits from this girl's mind and body."

He stood up and walked in a circle around Doreen, then stopped and clapped his hands on her head and shook it from side to side. "Satan, I refuse to let you have this girl. In the name of Jesus, I command you be gone. Be gone!"

Doreen trembled, then crumpled to the floor. She looked like a baby lying there with her legs crooked at the knees, her arm slung carelessly in front. Her mother fell beside her and wept.

Brother Terrell stood over the pair and urged the congregation to praise God. "The Lord has just delivered this girl. Raise your hands and praise him. We've witnessed a miracle here. A child of God has been restored tonight." He knelt beside Doreen's mother. "Sister, when your daughter wakes up, she'll be whole. God has made her whole."

A cacophony of praise rose throughout the tent. People flooded the altar and in a moment, the throng swallowed Doreen and her mother.

My mother played "I'm so glad Jesus lifted me, glory, hallelujah, Jesus lifted me."

Brother Terrell walked up the prayer ramp, ignoring the arm Brother Cotton offered him, and stepped up onto the platform. He reared back, then bent forward at the waist, his chest parallel with his knees. "Glory! I said glory!"

He laughed and with his eyes closed put one hand on his hip and moved his feet in the quick shuffle step that was his trademark. He danced from one end of the platform to the other with Brother Cotton running beside him, worried he might stumble and fall. When he started across the platform for the second time, Brother Cotton gave up, put one hand on Brother Terrell's shoulder, and fell in step behind him. As they danced across the stage, other preachers joined them until they formed a chorus line of men in white shirts and black pants, hands resting on the shoulder of the man in front, everyone dancing like Brother Terrell. My mother bounced up and down as she played, her eyes fixed on Brother Terrell and the line of dancing men.

Laverne took Gary out of her lap, placed him in the seat beside her, stood up, and began to jig. I climbed back onto my chair to see what had happened to Doreen, but I couldn't see her in the crush of bodies. I hopped down and pushed through the crowd to the altar. A tall, skinny woman with big curls on her head moved her feet in dainty steps, two forward, one back, her hands crossing in front of her, then behind her with each step. A young woman with red hair that fell to her waist held a child's hand and skipped in place. Stout black women in faded blue or gray cotton dresses wobbled here and there on black sturdy shoes, arms flailing to no particular rhythm.

"Thank you, Jesus. Yes, Lord. Yes, Lord."

An old man in overalls marched in place. Children about my age danced with their eyes closed. Some peeked from under half-closed eyelids to see if anyone noticed, but there were others whose faces wore that vacant, rapturous expression that separated the real from the faker.

In between the arms and legs and torsos and backsides I saw Doreen sit up and look around. Her mother helped her up and they stood with their arms clasped around each other, the daughter's head resting on her mother's shoulder, the mother's hands smoothing her daughter's blond hair, whispering in her ear while several thousand sang, "Glory, hallelujah, Jesus set me free." Brother Terrell made his way back down the prayer ramp and waved at my mother to bring down the volume of the organ.

"I want everyone who needs a miracle, I mean a real miracle, to come on up here tonight. This isn't the night for nervous conditions and alcoholism. God is going to heal the lame here tonight. Glory hallelujah. He's going to open blind eyes and deaf ears. Lama la bahia. Everyone else, please go on back to your seats."

As the crowd drifted back, an old black man with a cane felt his way along the aisle, one arm in front. He wore a brown suit and a dark fedora. He overshot the altar and Brother Cotton brought him back. Brother Terrell walked down the prayer ramp and met them at the altar. He took the man's arm from Brother Cotton and they stood on level with the congregation in front of the prayer ramp.

"Sir, how long you been blind?"

"Ever since I can remember."

"You were born blind?"

"No. There was an accident when I was little. At my grandmama's."

"Do you believe Jesus can heal you?"

"I promised him I'd stay away from the juke joints if he would."

Brother Terrell laughed. "You won't be going back after tonight. Let me see your cane." The man drew back and held the cane close to his chest.

"You ain't gonna need that piece of wood no more." He took the cane and handed it to Brother Cotton. The man grabbed in the air after it. Brother Terrell took his hands. "Sir, I want you to bow your head and pray with me. Believe with me."

"In the name of Jesus. In the name of Jesus. Y'all believe with me here tonight."

He placed his hands over the man's eyes. "Lord, look down in your infinite mercy. Take pity on this man, blind since he was a boy. Restore his sight."

He removed his hands from the man's eyes. "Close your eyes, sir. I feel led to do one more thing." Brother Terrell bent over and scooped dirt, then he spit into the palm of his hand and swirled the dust and spit into a paste. He dabbed the paste onto the man's eyes, just as Jesus had done in scripture.

He took his handkerchief and wiped the mud off the man. "Open your eyes now." The man blinked several times. "Sir, can you tell us what you see?"

"I see long, big things . . . with spots on top." He tottered over to one of the center poles, keeping his hands in front. He placed his hands on the pole and moved them up and down.

"This here, it's a pole, ain't it?" He looked at Brother Terrell and beamed. The congregation erupted in applause and thank you Jesus glory be to his name praise God hallelujah.

Brother Terrell took the man's arm and raised it in the air. "You're healed, brother. Now give God the glory." The man raised both hands and the crowd turned up the volume. When the noise died back a bit, Brother Terrell took the man's cane from Brother Cotton and broke it over his knee.

"You won't need that anymore."

The man nodded and stumbled back into the crowd as the music and shouting started up again. Brother Terrell handed the microphone to Brother Cotton and walked up the ramp to the platform. He looked strong as he headed toward the half wall that ran along the back of the platform and pushed through the gate. Laverne shepherded Gary and me to the area behind the platform. She didn't say anything, but I thought I knew what she was thinking, what we were all thinking: that maybe this was the turning point. That maybe now, after casting out a demon and healing a blind man, Brother Terrell would be able to eat. She pulled back the canvas curtain that separated the backstage area from the view of the audience on one side just as Pam pulled back the curtain on the other side to let her mother and the baby pass through. Brother Terrell climbed down the four or five steps that led to the platform. His face was white and strained and he was shaking.

The backstage area was reserved for the very sick and those who knew someone who could get them a one-on-one audience with Brother Terrell. Ten or fifteen people waited there for him, waited to tell him their troubles and hear him say, "I believe it'll be all right. Let's pray." Lanky young men in ill-fitting suits sidled up next to the steps, longing to hear him prophesy, "Thus saith the Lord, God has surely chosen you for a great work." Women, old and young, yearned toward him; surely it was the Holy Ghost that pulled them toward him. He often said he couldn't sleep at night, that he felt the needs of the people pulling at him like quicksand.

At the bottom step he reached out to shake someone's hand and collapsed. Someone screamed. Exorcisms took a lot out of Brother Terrell, but this was the first time he had fainted. My mom looked over the half wall at the back of the platform and continued to play the organ. Men in suits poured through the gate, down the ladder.

"Step back, please. Give us some room here."

They closed over him. "We need to get him outta here. Move back, now, y'all hear? Please."

The knot of people loosened and as it did, two men rose with Brother Terrell hoisted between them, their arms wrapped around his waist, his arms propped up on their shoulders, hands dangling from his wrist. They carried him out from under the tent. Betty Ann, Pam, Laverne, Gary, and I followed the men and Brother Terrell into the night to the tiny trailer parked behind the auditorium. Randall was already at the door, his hand on the long silver handle. One of the preachers spoke to him and he moved aside. In they went, pulling the door closed behind them. The latch clicked into place. We stood there staring at the handle.

Randall looked at his mother. "We got a right to

know." He pushed the handle down and tugged on the door. Nothing. He knocked and a preacher, a stranger, appeared in the darkened crack.

"He needs to rest, son. Y'all go on home. Someone will be there in a little bit to let you know how he's doing."

"I need to see my daddy. Mama needs to see him."

"He needs rest."

"We ain't leaving till we see him."

"Who is it?" It was Brother Terrell's voice. Betty Ann breathed a sigh of relief.

The preacher mumbled something about Randall over his shoulder.

"Let 'em in."

Two preachers walked out and Betty Ann, Pam, and Randall stepped up into the Airstream. I felt conspicuous waiting around in the dark outside the trailer. The Terrells always said members of the evangelistic team were like family. I realized at that moment that being *like* family was a long way from actually being family. Mama, Gary, and I were insiders, but the Terrells were the inner circle itself and we hovered just outside their circumference. Members of the congregation approached us and asked about Brother Terrell. Laverne's eyebrows came together and she dropped her head and shook it slowly from side to side. After a few minutes the door opened and Randall's belly came through the opening. His mother and Pam followed. They were crying. Randall mumbled something about how God was going to let his daddy die. Someone drove Betty Ann and her kids home.

Laverne, Gary, and I picked our way through the dark, stepping across electrical cords and around tent stakes until we were back under the tent. Brother Cotton had called for an all-night prayer meeting for Brother Terrell and almost the entire congregation remained. Several hundred people knelt at their seats or walked around and around the building, praying. Kids curled up on makeshift beds of pushed-together chairs. I didn't see my mom, but I knew she was there somewhere, calling on God over and over again, asking him not to let Brother Terrell die. Laverne put Gary and me to bed on the chairs and walked to the altar to pray. I told her I was going to stay awake and pray, but a few hours later my mother dredged us from sleep. She settled Gary onto her shoulder and walked me outside the tent to the Cottons' car. She settled us in the backseat, then climbed into the passenger's seat as Laverne started the car.

"Where's Brother Cotton?"

Mama turned and looked over her shoulder at me. "Shh. You'll wake Gary. Brother Cotton's staying in the trailer with Brother Terrell."

"Why are they staying here?" No one answered.

Laverne steered the car through the parking lot

and turned onto the highway. She threw a quick glance at my mother. "You think he'll make it, Carolyn?"

Mama stared into her own face in the glass of the passenger window. A soft rain had started to fall and the water ran in rivulets through her reflection. "The devil has done everything in his power to stop Brother Terrell. Money problems. Randall. The Klan. Family problems . . . I don't know.

"He's fighting for his life tonight, Laverne." Her voice broke.

I stared out the window and let myself drift through the night. The sound of the tires on the road, the way the night softened the edges of the world, these things soothed me. I patted my mother's shoulder. Her hand closed over mine. I wished that we could drive like that forever.

Chapter Ten

MAMA FUMBLED THE KEY INTO THE LOCK while moths beat against the porch light overhead. Tomorrow, thin, dry wings would litter the stoop. Sometimes I cupped my hand and swept them out of the flow of traffic, but most days I ground their flimsy bodies under the heel of my shoe without a thought. I hopped from one foot to the other and hugged myself to stay warm.

Mama pushed the door open, flicked on a lamp, and put her finger to her lips. "Go get in bed and don't turn the bedroom light on, you'll wake up Pam and Randall."

"But how will we know if Brother Terrell is okay?"

"Lower your voice. Brother Cotton will let us know."

"But how will I see to undress?"

"I don't have the energy to explain everything to you. Put your gown on. Don't turn on the light. And don't wake up the other kids."

"But I'm scared of the dark."

"If you've been good, there's no reason to be scared." She popped me lightly on the bottom. "Now, go on!"

She turned to pull out the couch and click it into a bed for her and Gary. I walked down the hall wondering how good I had been lately. Laverne startled me as she brushed past. *Not good enough.* I turned the handle on the bedroom door and stepped into the darkened bedroom I shared with Pam and Randall. My eyes found the window, then darted away from it. I didn't want to see a demon peering in at me. *Blood of Jesus. Blood of Jesus. Forgive me for peeking tonight.* I felt my way over to the end of the bed, peeled off my church clothes, and left them in a pile on the floor. With my hands held out in front, I fumbled over the chest of drawers and counted down one, two, three to the third drawer, found what felt like my nightgown, and pulled it over my head and shoulders. Something in the corner caught my eye. *What is that?* I backed up until I hit the end of the bed and scrambled up between the Terrell kids. Randall sprawled along the outside edge of the bed. I threw his arm across his chest. He didn't stir. Pam was hunched into a tight little ball with her face toward the wall, her arms wrapped tight around her abdomen, knees drawn in close, a cocoon of grief. I lay on my back and shut my eyes. Whatever I had seen a moment before, I did not want to see again.

My thoughts shifted to Brother Terrell. It wasn't until that night that I considered the possibility that he might really die. I imagined the tent packed with thousands of people, the platform empty. I waited for a wave of sadness to roll over me, and was shocked to find relief instead. No more feeling guilty each time I ate a Hershey's bar. *I didn't mean it. I didn't mean it.* If he died, what would happen to all those souls who had not heard the gospel? Would they burn in hell? Babies too? I thought how much it hurt when I burned my finger. I made myself imagine my body burning like that forever.

I thought about how Brother Terrell always had a gift for me and Gary each time he gave Pam and Randall a present. He didn't have to do that. He wasn't our daddy. I thought how good it felt when

163

he patted my head and asked how I was doing, how I always wanted to say something funny to make him laugh, but never could. Everyone seemed more alive when he was around. *Please, God. Let everything go back to normal, please.* A selfish prayer when so many souls were at stake. Why was it so hard to be good? I felt myself drifting into that lake of eternal hellfire when the front door creaked open and startled me fully awake. A man's voice. Brother Cotton's. Then my mother's and Betty Ann's. No one screamed or cried. The door closed again. *Thank you.* I curled around Pam and pressed my knees into the bend of hers. Sleep blanketed my thoughts and everything that could go wrong in the world slipped away.

I woke the next morning to a warm, doughy smell. Biscuits. No one had baked biscuits since Brother Terrell started his fast. He could stand the smell of beans bubbling, cornbread baking, and chicken frying, but the smell of biscuits brought him to tears. I inhaled deeply and opened my eyes. A rheumy water spot stared down from the ceiling. On one side of me Randall snored, mouth wide open. On the other side, where Pam should have been, was an empty space. Voices rose and fell in some other part of the house. I pulled myself above the quilt, scooched to the foot of the bed, and lowered my feet to the wooden floor, smooth and cold. I slipped over to the door and pulled it open. Laughter. I walked down the hall to the living room, past the couch, cleaved in two with Gary sleeping in the middle. I wanted to rub my hand over the dark wool of his curly hair but thought better of it. There would be more biscuits if Gary and Randall stayed asleep.

Bright light washed across every surface of the kitchen. Shiny enameled stove and round-shouldered fridge, pale no-color countertops, cabinets with peeling white paint, faded linoleum traced with indecipherable patterns. My mother stood on one side of the stove, hand on her hip, stirring a cast-iron fryer full of tomato gravy. The light blurred and softened the strong features of her face and brought out the red and gold in her hair. On the other side of the stove stood Laverne. She flipped one strip of bacon, then another, jumping as the grease popped and splattered, laughing at the brief, sharp pain, so ordinary and expected. Betty Ann faced the counter, cutting into biscuits with a wooden handled knife and spreading butter, then fig preserves into the warm, flaky centers.

She let go that deep, throaty laugh, then whipped around to Mama and Laverne. "The steak!"

Mama dropped the long-handled spoon into the gravy and knelt in front of the oven broiler. "Laverne, hand me that hot pad." She pulled out the pan with smoking meat and placed it on the counter in front of Betty Ann. "A burnt offering."

They laughed, voices mingling in a loose, rough harmony.

"Hey, can we get some of that food? We got a hungry man over here." Brother Cotton's voice drew my attention to the table where Brother Terrell sat, elbows propped on the round white table, a fork in one fist, knife in the other, a shiny white platter in front him. The haggard quality his face had assumed during the fast was softened by an eager, boyish grin. He turned that smile on the women and they giggled and bumped around, placing platters loaded with bacon and sausage, biscuits, eggs, and toast onto the table. Bowls of tomato gravy, cream gravy, and grits oozing with butter followed. The sun streamed through windows and across the table, catching on mason jars filled with honey in the comb, strawberry preserves, and fig preserves, turning them into jewels of light. Pam sat beside her daddy, beaming her big snaggletoothed smile at him. Something bubbled over on the stove and Mama scolded herself. I stood in the doorway, taking it all in: Brother Terrell, the light, all that food.

"Well, Miss Priss, are you going to stand there all day or do you think you might eat?" Mama held up a plate. I walked over and sat across from Pam.

Brother Terrell waved the women over. "Let's bow our heads and pray together."

Laverne stood behind Brother Cotton's chair

while Mama and Betty Ann flanked Brother Terrell. Mama bit at her lips and Betty Ann twisted a dish towel. Laverne placed her hands on her husband's shoulders.

Brother Terrell dropped his head and prayed. "Father, we thank thee for this food. Bless it to the nourishment of our bodies, and bless the hands that prepared it. Oh Lord, we ask that you would be with us. We ask that you would enable our bodies to accept and use this food, so that we might be strengthened, Lord, to do the work that thou hast given us to do . . ." His voice grew softer as the prayer progressed until I couldn't hear him at all.

The clock ticked. The coffee perked. Brother Cotton cleared his throat. No one wanted to disturb Brother Terrell's prayer, even when he wasn't saying a word. I opened one eye to see what was going on. Mama's, Betty Ann's, and Laverne's heads were bowed. Pam's eyes were squeezed shut. Brother Cotton's head was tucked so low his chin almost rested on his chest. Brother Terrell's eyes were open and he was chewing a biscuit and licking his lips. My mouth fell open and I looked right at him.

He winked at me, put the biscuit on his plate, and spoke. "Brother Cotton, when you're done praying, could you pass the bacon?"

It was his old joke. Somehow we had forgotten it, or maybe we were glad to play along again.

Betty Ann popped him with the dish towel. "David, you're a mess."

He spooned a lake of grits onto his platter, flipped three over-easy eggs on top, and stirred it all together. He shoveled a tablespoon into his mouth and didn't put the spoon down until he scraped the platter.

Mama's brow furrowed. "Maybe you should slow down a bit."

"Jesus released me from the fast and told me to eat. Bless God, I'm eating."

Mama exhaled a long-suffering sigh. "Maybe Jesus expects you to use wisdom."

Betty Ann put one hand on Brother Terrell's shoulder. "Honey, you ready for this steak?" In her other hand she held a platter on which rested a piece of meat bigger than her face.

Pam chimed in. "Yeah, Daddy, you want that steak?"

Betty Ann forked the meat onto his platter and he added bacon, a sausage patty, and two more biscuits covered with Mama's tomato gravy. He chewed through it all, mouth open, slowing down only to sop the leftover grease, butter, and egg yolk with two more biscuits.

A whoop came from the doorway. "Daddy, you're eating!" Randall jogged to the table, belly swaying. "We thought God was gonna take you." He stood by his dad and draped an arm about his shoulders.

"I thought he was, too, son. Guess he ain't done with me yet." He let go a long, satisfied belch.

"Y'all got some cream to go in that coffee I smell? I ain't had coffee in months."

"I'll get it, Daddy." Pam jumped up and dragged her chair to the counter. She climbed onto the chair, lifted the percolator with both hands, filled the cup, and with slow, measured steps, walked it to her father. Brother Terrell flashed her a smile and took the cup. He scooped spoonful after spoonful of sugar into the coffee and poured in the cream. He lifted the cup to his nose and breathed in the aroma, took a long slurp, and set the mostly empty cup back down.

His eyes rolled back in his head and he drew a deep breath of satisfaction. "I feel like I've died and gone to heaven."

The next instant, Brother Terrell opened his eyes wide and pointed toward the living room. "My God, my God. It's an angel of the Lord, right here in this house." His voice was a whisper.

A small figure stood in a shaft of light that poured through the living-room window.

It was Gary. Mama and Laverne groaned.

Brother Terrell slapped his knees and laughed. "I had y'all that time."

Gary moved toward us, rubbing his eyes. "What? What?"

Mama stretched out her arms. "It's nothing. Come here, honey."

He toddled over to her. I cupped my hand over my mouth and leaned toward Randall. "He don't look like no angel to me."

Unsettled by the attention, Gary asked again, "What?"

Mama glared at me and reached down to pick him up. "It's okay, honey. Brother Terrell said you were an angel."

A big grin spread across my three-year-old brother's face. "An angel."

Mama picked the sleep from Gary's eyes. "Let's go wash your face."

Mama stepped into the living room with Gary on her hip as Brother Terrell cleared his throat. It was what he always did when he had something important to say. "Listen, I need to tell y'all something. Carolyn, can you come on back in here? In the trailer last night, I had a vision."

Mama let Gary slide down her body until his feet touched the floor. Three quick steps and she was back in the kitchen. Betty Ann turned off the water at the sink, dried her hands, and drifted back to the table, pushing her hair out of her eyes. Laverne set the dirty dishes she had gathered on the counter.

Brother Terrell looked at me, Pam, and Randall. "You kids go on and play now. We need to talk."

"But Daddy . . ."

Betty Ann cut Randall off. "You heard your

170

daddy, Randall. Now get dressed and go outside. All of you."

As the four of us left the kitchen, I heard Brother Terrell say, "Jesus stood in my room last night."

We shivered in a miserable little huddle on the tiny patch of a front porch. The gray mud of our yard oozed into the lighter brown mud of the dirt road that ran past our house and four other unpainted houses, and dead-ended at a dark, soupy field. Pam looked around. "What in the world are we gonna do?" It was cold and everything was still wet from last night's rain. There was no dry place to sit or play.

Randall sighed, and his swollen belly strained at the fabric of his thin plaid cotton shirt. "Well, if there's nothing else to do, I guess we could play husbands and wives again." His tone was regretful, as if he had exhausted all other possibilities.

Pam allowed herself one comment. "You are a nasty boy." She pointed across the street to the last house on the road. "I saw some kids there the other day. We could ask them to play."

Randall shook his head no. "Them's worldly kids."

There were many reasons to avoid the unsaved. First of all, they were dangerous. Their picture-show-watching, ball-playing, honky-tonking ways might tempt us from the straight and narrow.

171

Second of all, they made us uncomfortable. Everything about outsiders—their clothes, speech, habits—seemed to belittle us, and that put us on the defensive. Mama mimicked the speech of the store clerks and bank tellers we encountered: "Oh mah. What dahling children. So smaht." There was only one way to be in the world, one right way anyhow, and that was the way we were. Even local churchgoers with their smooth ways were suspect. They might be saved, but they were lukewarm at best, unwilling to make the required sacrifices. It was just a matter of time before God spewed them out of his mouth. These prejudices, spoken and unspoken, gave me, Pam, Randall, and Gary license to treat outsiders however we wanted, though I'm not sure the grown-ups would have seen it that way. If some local kid raised an eyebrow at the goings-on under the tent, we stalked and harassed them for the rest of the revival. Their brains would be splattered on the highway for making fun of God's anointing. The devil would deep-fry them in a vat of boiling oil. Sores would cover their bodies and they would burn forever. We pronounced their doom in solemn oracular tones, and if they tried to defend themselves, we invited them to step out from under the tent to settle things. I was too scrawny and way too chicken to fight, and Gary was too young. That left the Terrell kids to wage our battles, and they usually won.

Pam walked to the side of the house and came back with an empty bucket. She scooped mud into the bucket with her hand and stirred it with a stick. She wiped her hands on her dress and looked at me thoughtfully. "Let's play soda shop. We need some glasses."

The back door opened and out came Brother Cotton. "You kids having fun?"

A chorus of "uh-huh"s affirmed our fun. Randall walked toward him. "Y'all done praying?"

"No, son. I'm just going over to the tent to cancel the morning and afternoon services, so we can spend the day in prayer with your daddy."

Pam looked up at Brother Cotton and smiled. "Would you get some glasses for us?"

"How many do you want, honey?"

"Just four."

He stepped inside and brought out four of our best glasses, no questions asked. I realized for the umpteenth time how different life would be if I had dimples.

Pam picked up the bucket. "Come on, Donna. Let's play like we're making chocolate milkshakes."

We mixed the mud in the pail until it had the right consistency and the right color and poured it into a glass. Pam wiped the sides with the hem of her dress and held it up. "Just like the chocolate malts from the A&W."

Randall took the glass. "That gives me an idea.

Those kids at the end of the street? Let's tell 'em these are real milkshakes and see if they'll drink 'em."

Randall dispatched Gary and me to bring the kids to our soda shop. "They'll trust y'all 'cause you're about their age."

We found them, a boy and girl, sitting on the edge of their porch, hands propped on their knees as if waiting for something to do to come up and grab them by the hand. Gary called hi, but neither of them answered. We walked to the bottom of the steps and looked up at them. I made a megaphone of my hands and called, "My brother said hey. Can't y'all hear?"

The girl nodded yes.

"We got chocolate milkshakes. Wanna come over?"

They nodded. Neither of them said anything on the walk to our house. I asked the girl if they were idiots and she shook her head no.

"Well, is your brother a deaf-mute?" Again she shook her head no.

"If he is, you could bring him to the revival and get him healed. You know about the revival?"

She nodded yes, but I didn't believe her. "Do you know you'll go to hell for lying?" She didn't have time to answer because by then we were approaching our front stoop. Gary ran and took a seat on the bottom step as Pam stood and held up a glass of chocolate mud.

"Y'all want a milkshake?"

The girl didn't move but her brother nodded eagerly and took the glass. He brought the glass to his face, hesitated, then took a big, greedy drink. Gary and I fell in the mud laughing. Randall laughed so hard he had to lean against the house. The boy began to retch.

Pam jumped from the porch and bent over him. "I think he's really sick, y'all."

The boy's sister didn't flinch. Pam glared at her. "Girl, I said your brother's sick. Get over here and help him."

Randall grabbed a glass and headed for the faucet at the back of the house. He brought back a glass of clear water and held it up to the boy. Pam took the glass and put it to the boy's lips. He wouldn't look at her.

"Rinse your mouth out. It's not a trick this time. Really." He sipped just enough water to wash his mouth out. Pam rubbed his back with her free hand. The girl wedged herself between Pam and her brother. She pulled him up by the hand and they walked across the yard. Randall scurried after them. "Hey. We're sorry. We didn't mean nothing. Can't we be friends? Come on, now."

They walked down the middle of road and turned into their yard. Pam figured if they were going to tell on us, they would head straight into the house. We were relieved when they sank back down on the porch instead. Randall sloshed water from the pail across the steps and washed the mud away.

"There's no telling what some people will do," he said. "Just no telling."

The Brother Terrell who took the platform that night was a scythe, a blade beveled and honed so that all that remained was the thin quick edge of purpose. He was the will of God personified. He took the microphone from Brother Cotton, clipped it around his neck, and the audience went still. He moved to the pulpit and we moved with him. He inhaled and expectation rose in our chests. He exhaled and we hung there, waiting.

The preachers' heads turned in unison as he paced. They had arrived early to stake out seats on the stage, eager for their congregants to know they were associated with Brother Terrell. Privately, some said his popularity wouldn't, couldn't last long. His lack of education caused him to make wild, improbable claims about the nature of God, the Bible, and the world in general. Besides, rumors of marital infidelities had surfaced. It was only a matter of time. Midway across the platform, Brother Terrell stopped and stared at the preachers, without speaking. After a couple of minutes, they began to cross and uncross their legs. A nervous chuckle passed among them.

He rubbed his forehead as if trying to banish a

particularly troubling thought, then turned to face the audience. "I broke my fast this morning." The audience and the preachers applauded.

Brother Terrell did not smile. "Some of you may not be clapping when I finish here tonight. Some of you may be running for cover.

"I broke my fast because Jesus appeared in my trailer last night. He touched me here, in the palms of my hands."

He held up both hands. "Jesus said, 'If I be lifted up, I'll draw all men to me.' He said he was bringing a great revival to the earth, a revival that would not be corrupted . . ."

He dropped his hands, picked up the microphone around his neck, and turned back to the preachers. ". . . A revival that would not be corrupted by the churches. The Pentecostal revival that began on Azusa Street back in the twenties has lost its fire. People ain't getting healed like they use to. They ain't getting delivered like they use to."

He kept an even, rhythmic pace, the delivery of his words timed to his steps, his right hand striking the air for emphasis. "Why? Because you preachers are more interested in buildings and comfort and glory than you are in preaching the truth."

He stood in front of them. "Don't you wag your heads at me. Don't you cross your arms like it ain't true." He walked up to one of the ministers and threw open the man's crossed arms. "You know it's true!" He gestured back at the audience. "They know it's true! And I'm telling you God knows it, too, and he's tired of it!" The audience rose in sections as he spoke until every person was standing and clapping.

The preachers sat slack-jawed, arms at their side, legs open at the knees. Some of these men were from the local churches, some from farther afield. They clearly didn't like what they were hearing. Evangelists often employed a shake-'em-up, wake-'em-up strategy in dealing with organized religion. It was part of their role and everyone expected it. But this unrestrained animosity was something else. Brother Terrell had no mercy and showed no signs of relenting.

"Jesus told me he's sending a revival the likes of which the earth has never seen. He showed me a vision of a revival where people speak the Word and missing arms and legs grow back."

He stepped off the platform, walked down the prayer ramp, and stood level with the audience. He raised both hands and looked up. Light bathed his face and hands.

"I saw men of God healing waterhead babies. Bless God, I saw a dead-raisin' revival! That's right. I saw the people of God walking into funeral homes and raising those who had died in the faith."

He began to run in front of the crowd and

scream. "The Bible says death shall have no dominion over them! This is the revival Jesus was talking about when he said in the scripture, 'These things ye shall do and greater.'

"Jesus showed me a vision of this revival spreading like wildfire across the whole earth. Then before the devil and the churches could get into it and destroy it, it was over. And then a time of great tribulation came upon us." He buried his face in his hands and his shoulders shook. His voice wheezed out a cry.

"I saw Christians persecuted in this country for refusing to renounce Christ, just like I saw in my vision back in fifty-nine.

"Then it was over and I saw the Son of Man, Jesus, coming in the clouds. We don't have much time, people. We got to lift up Jesus. We're entering into a new dispensation. It's got to be Jesus, Jesus, Jesus from now on out. I don't understand everything that this means, but I believe as we seek the Lord, he'll tell us."

He stretched out his hand toward the congregation. "And one more thing. Jesus told me if I would obey him, he'd supply all my needs. He said, 'You'll never have to beg for an offering again.' That's thus saith the Lord, people."

Brother Cotton brought the four offering buckets and handed them to Brother Terrell. My mother began to play softly on the organ. Brother

Terrell set the buckets up on the ground in front of him. "Whatever y'all give tonight will be given back to you multiplied. The Lord will bless those that bless this ministry. That's what he said."

The audience filled the buckets, then began to press money into Brother Terrell's hands and pockets, telling him it was for his personal use. He shook hands and thanked people for their support. He inclined his head to listen to prayer requests. He hugged the older men and women and blessed the children of the younger ones. When people grabbed him and refused to let go, he waved Brother Cotton aside and patted their hands and nodded while they told him how much he meant to them. In him they saw a more powerful, dazzling image of themselves. He came from the same grim poverty that had shaped them, but it did not cling to him. His smile held out a promise; what it was they couldn't have told you, but the memory of it lingered for days after they saw him. He was one of them, but his face lacked the hopeless, haunted expression they glimpsed as they walked past streaky storefront windows. When he spoke he sounded like them, and people *listened*. He stood on that platform in those fine store-bought suits and told stories of huntin' coons and eatin' stewed squirrel, and when the newspaper men came to take his picture and write about him, he laughed and didn't try to talk in a prettified way. He was them without the shame. He was them without the hopelessness. And oh how they loved him for it.

Just as Jesus promised, Brother Terrell never had to beg or plead for money again. Crowds went up and down, and sometimes we had to cut corners, but the bills were paid on time and the old desperation about money was gone. So were the ministers who sat on the platform that night. Others took their places, but over time they, too, left as Brother Terrell's "revelations" led him further away from traditional church doctrine. After Brother Terrell's one-on-one with Jesus, my mother immersed herself in the Bible, looking for scriptural backing for what she and Brother Terrell called the Revelation of Jesus Christ. What she found took on heightened significance in light of the Visitation.

Scripture referred to Jesus as the firstborn of many brethren; that meant God was raising up a people who would be just like Jesus. Brother Terrell taught it was Jesus's choices rather than his birthright that made him a son of God. The churches responded with charges of blasphemy and preachers issued not-so-veiled warnings about him in front of their congregants. And then Brother Terrell piled on the soggy straw that broke the camel's back: He began to baptize in the name of Jesus, instead of the Trinity. Mainline Protestant preachers, always tepid supporters at best, stayed away. The Assemblies of God hierarchy officially withdrew its support, and he was banned from preaching in their pulpits. People said publicly the split was based on doctrine. Privately they said it was about Brother Terrell's dalliances with women. All of that was true, but the real deal-breaker was money. When Brother Terrell came to town, church coffers dwindled. He responded to their disapproval by forming the New Testament Holiness Church, a tax-free nonprofit under which followers began to organize congregations based on his teachings. The men and sometimes women who headed those churches were subject only to Brother Terrell.

Chapter Eleven

BELIEVERS SAW THE COURT CASE OF DAVID Terrell vs. Richland County as a mythic battle. It was Moses vs. Pharaoh, David vs. Goliath, and Jesus vs. the Antichrist all rolled into one. Newspapers cast the struggle in less grandiose terms: EVANGELIST TOLD TO CURB NOISE; HEARING SLATED. The story was written up by the Associated Press in three-to-five-inch installments and carried on the inside pages of newspapers throughout the South and as far west as California. The two realities never came together, and the faithful still talk about the revival in Columbia, South Carolina, as, "That time Brother Terrell fought the devil and made front-page headlines across the world."

It began on opening night with Brother Terrell exhorting a smaller-than-average crowd to make up in volume what it lacked in size. "If the people of Columbia won't come out to praise the Lord, the same God that turned a valley of dry bones into a living army in the Old Testament will command these old wooden chairs to stand up and praise him!"

He ran back and forth across the stage, his mouth stretched wide over the microphone. "Will somebody, oh somebody please stand up and say hal-le-lu-jah with me?"

His question and the response it generated reverberated through the living rooms and bedrooms of people who lived up to a mile away from the state fairgrounds. Not prone to late-night religious ecstasy, the neighbors picked up the phone and gave the sheriff an earful. By the time the patrol car crawled through the parking lot, the crowd was so caught up chanting "Hallelujah!" that no one noticed. The sheriff parked behind the tent and waited inside the car with his deputy, windows down, cigarette tips glowing in the night. Brother Wilson, the new tent manager, walked over to talk to the officers. He assured them that neither he nor Brother Terrell wanted any trouble and that he would personally turn down the sound system.

After the service that night, the tent manager relayed to Brother Terrell and the rest of the team what the sheriff had said: too many complaints, turn down the speakers.

Mama snorted. "They don't tell those worldly entertainers to turn down anything. This is the state fairgrounds! They must be used to noise around here."

Everyone agreed we were being persecuted, but the speaker volume was lowered before service began the next morning. Brother Terrell asked the sparse daytime audience to move closer to the large speakers at the front of the platform so they could hear. The lower volume worked with the smaller, more compact seating arrangement, but posed a problem at night, when the crowd, though small for us, was still too large to be contained in one or two small sections. The volume crept back up and the sheriff began to make regular appearances. The sound system had posed problems before, but the tent team and authorities had usually reached an agreement. Before we reached that point in Columbia, someone called the press. We didn't make the front page as folks would later remember, but the newspaper coverage did stir up interest. Our crowd size increased, and so did the noise and the pressure for a showdown.

Brother Terrell began to point out the sheriff's car from the platform. "That viper out there that's supposed to protect us is out here trying to shut down the revival. They're trying to stop God. You can't stop God."

Mama played "I Shall Not Be Moved," and the crowd joined hands and sang, swaying to the music. Inspired by the civil rights movement, two hundred of the faithful descended on the Richland County courthouse demanding freedom of religion. The sheriff scratched his head and told Brother Terrell's followers and the reporters who accompanied them he wasn't out to restrict anyone's religion. The people who lived in the area just wanted a little peace and quiet, that was all. He wasn't aiming to run the tent revival out of town, just to get the speakers turned down. Cameras clicked and reporters scribbled away and we made the next day's papers.

One night as Brother Terrell paced and preached below the prayer ramp, two men in suits approached him from the middle aisle of the tent. One of them said something in his ear. Brother Terrell pointed the microphone at him, but he brushed it aside. Brother Terrell spoke for him.

"He wants to know if I'm the Reverend David Terrell." He looked at the man. "Yes, sir, I am."

The other man took Brother Terrell's hand and placed an envelope in it, then both men turned and walked back down the aisle in no particular hurry. A couple of guys with beefy arms started toward them, but Brother Terrell waved them away.

"Please, y'all, stay seated. We'll not respond with violence of any kind here tonight."

He opened the envelope, pulled out the document inside, and stared at it for a moment. "I don't read so good, so I don't know what all this says, but I believe it's from those devils that want to shut us down."

He held up the paper and ripped it down the middle, then shredded each half. "Whoever signed this, whoever has aligned himself with the powers of the enemy, will be dead within the month."

He tore the strips of paper into small pieces and tossed them into the air. They fluttered in the light around his shoulders and drifted to the ground. "That's thus saith the Lord."

Reporters wrote that Brother Terrell had torn up a court order in the middle of a church service. People who had never been to a tent revival showed up to see what would happen next. The crowd was so large we couldn't seat everyone, and the speaker volume crept up again. When the sheriff didn't appear, people congratulated Brother Terrell on showing the devil who was boss. He said he wasn't convinced it was all over, that he still felt uneasy in his spirit. Brother Terrell's spirit was the divining rod in all things.

If a tent man decided to marry a particular woman and Brother Terrell told him he didn't feel settled in his spirit about it, there was no marriage. Increasingly, believers sought his input on changing jobs, taking trips, making major business decisions, and other life decisions. There was always talk among the inner circle about how he had saved someone from making not just a mistake, but a tragic mistake. His intuition held sway in his own business as well. If plans had been made to hold a revival in a certain place and Brother Terrell began to feel uneasy about it, plans were changed.

His uneasiness didn't necessarily lead to a clear view of what was wrong. He and the evangelistic team speculated on whether the Klan might be driving the problems with law enforcement. Mama said under her breath several times that it sure would be good if they knew what was on that paper he had torn up. We found out about a week later when two more men approached Brother Terrell just before he walked onto the platform. One of them touched his shoulder and reached out as if to shake his hand.

"Reverend Terrell?"

"Yes, sir." Brother Terrell stuck out his hand and when he did, the other man handed him an envelope.

"If I were you, Reverend, I'd read that before I tore it up. Could save you more trouble."

After church that night, my mother and a couple of ministers puzzled over the paper and figured out that Brother Terrell had to appear in court the next week. Looking back, it's clear no one understood what was going on. Dreams, visions, prophecy, and scripture, our primary tools for making sense of the world, offered no insight on how to deal with legal issues. Late one night while my mother was praying, she had a vision in which she saw the finger of God pointing toward an angel, a youngish man with dark, curly hair.

"It means God is sending an angel to help us. We just have to hold on and believe."

Members of the congregation approached Brother Terrell a couple of nights later and told him an angel had been present while he preached. They described him as having dark, curly hair and a presence that glowed. Mama said it was her angel, it had to be; he had the same hair.

The adults gathered in the middle of the tent after church on most nights and talked about the Persecution of the Saints into the early morning hours. It was upon us, they said. This was it. While Pam and I sat in our chairs and played here's-the-church, here's-the-steeple and bit our fingernails to the quick, they spoke of the government pressuring them to deny Christ, of having 666 carved into their foreheads, of being thrown into jails and insane asylums for refusing to give up their faith. They spoke of Christian women strung up naked in public. Of children turning their parents in to the authorities. No one mentioned turning the speaker volume down. What began as a misdemeanor charge had escalated into the apocalypse. But then, that's what we expected.

Our lives became the twenty-four-hour prayer channel. When the grown-ups were not pacing and praying all night and in between services for the courage to stand up for Jesus, they were laying hands on Randall. His stomach had been swelling for months and now it was so large, he had to wear a man's shirt to keep it covered. During the evening services, Brother Terrell called him to the front and had the congregation put their hands up and pray for him.

After these prayers, Randall examined the profile of his body in the dresser mirror. "Hey, y'all, I b'lieve it's gone down a little. Look."

Everyone said yeah, maybe he did look smaller, at least a little, when it was plain he looked the same or larger.

About a hundred of the faithful accompanied Brother Terrell to court. My mother and Betty Ann and key members of the evangelistic party like Brother Cotton stayed behind to organize an all-day prayer meeting under the tent. I was relieved. If they put Brother Terrell in jail, if they yanked his fingernails out with pliers and tortured him for his faith, someone would still be around to drive to the store and buy groceries. As it turned out, the four of us kids were on our own that day. We started a couple of halfhearted fights with local children that didn't go anywhere, wrote cusswords in the dust on believers' cars, and played a lot of chase. Randall ran backward on his heels, his belly bouncing slow like a beach ball. As Pam, Gary, and I closed in on him, he turned around to run in earnest and slammed face-first into the ocean of humanity that was Sister Waters.

The Waters, as Pam called her, was five feet tall and weighed at least two hundred pounds. She lived in Andalusia, Alabama, but she followed the revivals from town to town and had decided that she was called by God to keep an eye on us children. Her calling compelled her to grab Randall by the shirt and me and Pam by our ponytails at every opportunity, hissing under her breath, "You better sit your tails down before the devil gets a holt of you."

She was so worried about Brother Terrell that day that she swatted Randall aside and continued in prayer. "Help him, Lord. Help him, Jesus."

We watched in relief as she rolled by, her hands stretched open against her sides, fingers wide. Each time she took a step, she pointed a short, squat foot and the opposite hand moved forward in tandem. The effect was a dainty, mincing walk that set her body vibrating against the thin, strained cotton of her dress. Once she was out of earshot, Randall made a wavy motion with his hand and said, "God moved on The Waters."

Late that afternoon, a man named Sam, a longtime follower of Brother Terrell, delivered the news. The evangelistic team, the tent crew, and the families who followed the tent gathered in the backstage area to hear the news. Sam was a short, wiry man with a t-shaped nose and a brown, well-creased neck. When he spoke, his eyes hopped about like a bird and his face turned red.

"Judge said he should'a not torn up that paper. They took him to jail."

Mama spoke up. "For tearing up a paper?"

"I don't know what for. They just took him. He didn't say anything, didn't speak a word against 'em."

Brother Cotton started up the steps to the platform. "I better tell the people. Don't turn the sound system on, Dockery. I don't want to make things worse."

I slipped to the side of the platform and watched him walk to the middle of the stage. He beckoned people to move in closer. "Those of you who can hear me, come on up to the front. I can't use the microphone. Everyone, move on in here."

Brother Cotton didn't sugarcoat it. "They've taken Brother Terrell to jail."

Silence.

"I know how y'all feel. But I'm not in despair. And don't you be either. We're gonna go right on holding services. We'll let you know when we hear news of Brother Terrell. We're going to rest a bit now, but we'll be back in a couple of hours to carry on the night service, and we'll be here tomorrow morning, tomorrow afternoon, and tomorrow night. The devil may have pulled the plug on our PA system, but he can't shut us up. Amen? Can y'all hear me out there?"

Someone yelled no and Brother Cotton laughed. "Well, come on back tonight, and I'll say a lot more you can't hear."

Brother Cotton stayed at the little trailer behind the tent to prepare for the evening service and the rest of us—Laverne, Betty Ann, the baby, Mama, and the four of us kids—went home for a couple of hours. The house was quieter than a three-bedroom house with eight people in it should be. Betty Ann took the baby and retreated behind the door of her bedroom. Pam and Randall and Gary and I scrubbed the day's dirt off, dressed for the evening service, and made peanut-butter sandwiches for dinner. There were no fights and no play either. Three weeks of waiting for the worst had finally worn us out.

Brother Cotton walked up and down the aisles, yelling at the top of his lungs without a microphone that night. When his voice played out, he grabbed the four offering buckets from a back corner of the platform and held them, two in each hand, in front of the prayer ramp. People began to sing, "What you give to the Lord, give it in Jesus's name, and he will give you some more." They waited in line to give money and they filled the buckets twice.

Two days later Richland County set Brother Terrell free. A newspaper photograph shows him smiling for the cameras, riding on the shoulders of followers as they carry him away from the jail. He told reporters he harbored no hard feelings, that the whole thing was a misunderstanding. He said the revival had been such a success he was going to enlarge his tent to seat another twenty-five hundred people. The judge survived, though some believers still contend he died within the month. "Touch not my anointing, touch not my anointing," they mumbled, underscoring the biblical warning with meaningful looks only they could decipher.

Chapter Twelve

SAWDUST-TRAIL PREACHERS LOVED TO BRAG about their tent size. During the nineteen-forties, Oral Roberts claimed his tent was the world's largest. The faith healer Jack Coe covertly measured Roberts's tent and had his own extended by three feet, just enough to transfer bragging rights to his operation. A few years after Coe's death, Brother Terrell was able to make the same claim. The new tent was big, but no one can remember just how big. It accommodated anywhere from five to ten thousand people, depending on who is giving the estimate. My mother remembers it as stretching the length of two football fields. Others put the length at a football field and a half. Brother Terrell made the proud claim that the tent was bigger than the Ringling Brothers and Barnum & Bailey circus tent.

It was hard to feel persecuted under the world's largest tent. Every night was one long hallelujah party. In the midst of all the celebrating, Randall's stomach rose like a harvest moon. His long, mournful face bobbed above his thirty-six-inch belly, giving him the appearance of a sideshow freak: nine years old and eight months pregnant. His energy diminished until the tent men carried him into the services on a cot. Brother Terrell prayed for Randall night and day, but he didn't get any better. Everyone agreed the Lord was putting Brother Terrell's faith to the test. And Randall, was he being tested too?

I asked my mother once if God hated kids. She looked shocked and said no, of course not. The story of Abraham offering his son as a human sacrifice at God's bidding had convinced me otherwise. The adults interpreted the story as a test of Abe's faith. I remember thinking, *He has a knife at his son's throat, and it's only a test?* Small wonder that when the grownups spoke of the necessity of trusting God, I always heard an unspoken "or else." I banished these thoughts as soon as I had them. I didn't want him coming after me.

As Randall lay on his cot growing weaker and God tested his daddy and his daddy pursued my mother and my mother prayed for the strength not to acquiesce and acquiesced anyway, people began to get healed right and left under the tent. During one service, a man stood a few rows from where Randall lay and began to yell, "Je-sus, Je-sus, Je-sus" in the flat throaty monotone of a deaf-mute. Brother Terrell ran over and interviewed his sister, who said the man had been deaf since birth but had been healed spontaneously while listening to Brother Terrell preach. Brother Terrell brought the man to the front and put him through his standard tests. He stepped behind him and clapped his hands, and the man jumped. Still standing behind the guy, he spoke simple words to see if the man could repeat those words; he could. While this was going on, a young man on crutches stubbed to the front. He said he had broken his leg a couple of weeks before, and . . . before he reached the end of his story, Brother Terrell slapped his hand on the man's head, shouting, "In the name of Jesus! Be made whole!"

He hit the guy so hard, the man fell to the ground.

"Now, get up and walk. Don't be afraid. Come on."

He pulled the man up and together they walked across the front of the tent. When they reached the altar area, the man grabbed his crutches and beat them into splinters on the ground. The spirit, and some would say frenzy, could not be contained. A woman who sat close to us and who had been too shy to make eye contact earlier was suddenly running around the tent at full speed, hair and skirts flying. Another woman close by thrust her baby into the arms of a nearby stranger and took off after her. I figured they would be walking by the time they made it all the way around, but they didn't even look winded when they returned. Men all over the tent climbed the new tent poles for Jesus. Brother Terrell made his way to Randall's cot and knelt beside him. We expected him to rise with Randall on his arm, but he stood up alone.

Brother Terrell preached on divine healing every night. "I feel the presence of the Most High God tonight. Someone, oh, someone is reaching out to God tonight. Some-oooooooooone is touching the hem of his garment."

He paused and looked over his shoulder at the

men on the platform. "Would some of y'all go bring Randall up here? I want him to be right in the middle of this divine power."

Just as the men settled Randall and his cot at the very front of the tent, the blood came. It covered the sheet that draped Randall and turned the sawdust around him red. The crowd issued a collective *ooh*.

Brother Terrell never missed a beat. "Clean him up."

A couple of women scurried to the front and washed Randall's face with a damp towel. Someone exchanged the bloody top sheet for a clean one from a nearby camper, and Brother Terrell preached on.

"By the spi-rit of the Most High God, I was sent here tonight to set the captives free. By his stripes we are made whole, not just better, but whole. I proclaim victory over death, victory over disease, victory over the devil, victory over everything that would destroy God's people."

He stood over Randall and began to sing "Victory in Jesus" a cappella and the crowd joined in. He broke down by the end of the chorus and someone led him away. Dockery and the other tent men carried Randall behind the platform and the crowd sang on.

Randall went to the hospital for a transfusion. Brother Terrell didn't want him to go, but the evangelistic team talked him into it; just so the boy could get some blood in him, they said. Two days after the transfusion, Randall was back at the front of the tent on the cot. A couple of weeks later, he was off the cot, and by the last night of the revival, he was well again.

The last service of the revival was over and we were packing up to move on. Pam shimmied up one of the thin six-foot poles that held up the outside curtain of the tent. She hung there for a second and looked down at me, dangling a long chain of spit from her lips, and then sucked it back up before it escaped. I grunted and strained on the pole next to her. She dropped to the ground, sprang up like a coil, and hauled herself up again, hand over hand. My spaghetti arms gave out before I was halfway up, and I plopped down hard, dress flying up, panties exposed. No way to pretend I meant this to happen. I stood up and looked around. On one side of us the night: layers of black broken by blasts of artificial light blaring from tall, dark poles and spilling from the mouths of squat machines rolled from place to place, thick cords snaking behind like tails. Adults strolled in and out of the electric glare, animated with the business of breaking down the tent and moving on. Generators, giant cicadas of sound, whirred an incessant drone, while three eighteen-wheelers grunted and wheezed and the tent men pitched their voices.

"Back it up, Red."

"Tell me when."

"Come on. Come on. Stop. *Whoa,* I said."

I pushed my back against the pole, spread my legs into a wide *v,* and stretched my arms level with my shoulders as far as they would reach. Half of me in the dark, the other half in the bright light of the empty tent. Folding chairs slapped shut one by one. Randall, Brother Terrell, Brother Cotton, and assorted other brothers walked down the long uniform rows, plucking each chair off its legs, picking the rows clean, stacking the chairs end to end, section by section. Someone threw a quilt over the big Hammond organ. Soon they would pull apart the platform, dismantle the prayer ramp, and lower the tent to half-mast. Most of the men worked until two or three in the morning, slept a few hours, and returned at first light. They would remove the poles and the augers that anchored the tent deep in the ground, and as the sun came up, they would pull the tent apart and load her into the back of the eighteen-wheeler.

Usually we were long down the highway by the time the tent was loaded. But on this night, there were no adults hurrying us into cars. They sat together under the floodlights that hung from the center poles and talked and talked. Sister Waters was there. Randall said she was like the measles, hard to get rid of. The baby cried and Sister

Waters took her from Betty Ann and thumped her on the back like a watermelon. The harder Tina cried, the harder she thumped. It was late at night or early in the morning and Pam, Randall, Gary, and I fought to stay awake.

"Afraid they'll miss something," the adults murmured, and they were right. We threaded a circle of twine through our fingers and snapped it. We arm-wrestled and popped our knuckles and kicked our feet until our bodies began to wind down and we moved slower and slower and then hardly at all. Gary went down first, then Randall. Pam and I hung on, despite knowing looks from the adults. I tried to figure out what those looks might mean, but couldn't follow a thought.

My head grew heavier until it leaned against Mama's shoulder and my eyes shut for a minute, only a minute. They opened again as someone, a man, carried me from the tent into the cold, damp night air. He held me high on his shoulder, his arm wrapped tight around my legs. I breathed in familiar aftershave: Dockery or Brother Cotton, someone I knew. My head bounced and I saw my mother close behind with Gary in her arms. Low, serious voices moved around us. Smoke shot from a tailpipe, gray and blue against the blackness. Odd, how the mind records the most random detail and leaves the larger picture a blur. A car door opened and hands reached out and pulled me in and down, onto a scratchy weave of upholstery. My head settled on a broad thigh. A woman's sob broke through the static of voices. *What?* A question, soft and unformed, rose from the bottom of my consciousness. I tried to push myself up and was pulled back down by hands, warm and soothing, on my shoulders, my forehead. The door closed. Car wheels crunched through gravel. We were moving. I let myself sink back into sleep. Everything was okay as long as we were moving.

The Road Through Hell

1962–1966

NOTHING IS SO MUTE AS A GOD'S MOUTH.

Rainer Maria Rilke,
"Straining So Hard Against the
Strength of Night"

Chapter Thirteen

I WOKE THE NEXT MORNING WITH RANDALL'S feet in my face and Pam curled beside me. A familiar arrangement. We were used to rolling out of bed after a long night of travel, and tiptoeing around the new house or trailer while our parents slept. Their sprawled bodies and slack faces communicated everything we needed to feel secure. We must have lived in the cheapest and shabbiest of places, but I didn't experience them that way. My mother's presence, and her determination to scrub every corner of every place we lived in, made these temporary dwellings feel like home.

Pam stirred and we sat up together and looked around. The dingy little room in which we found ourselves felt utterly forsaken. There was no window with morning light streaming through, no heater, no sad-sack Jesus staring down from the colorless wall, no boxes of sheets and bedspreads and whatnots waiting to be unpacked. I could feel my mother's absence. She was gone; worse, she had never been here. I looked to Pam for reassurance. She put her fingers to her lips, took my hand, and we crawled to the other end of the bed, where our brothers slept. She shook Randall's shoulder. He pushed her away and sat up, wiping the sleep from his eyes with his fist. Gary startled awake. I put my arm around him and rocked him against me. The four of us said nothing, hoping, I think, to keep the forlornness of this place from hardening into a more solid reality.

Sister Waters rolled into the doorway. "Y'all going to sleep all day?"

When people said Sister Waters was half-Hi-waiian, I always imagined a little line drawn down the center of her. This split somehow explained her dual personality. The Waters was two women: the one who smiled and told our mamas how much she loved us, and the one who grabbed and twisted and pulled at us till it hurt when they were not looking. It was the mean Waters with whom we now found ourselves living. The mean Waters who explained that we were so much trouble our parents had sent us to live with her, *without saying good-bye,* so they could preach the gospel without having to stop and tend to us every five minutes. The mean Waters who huffed down the hallway of her shotgun house every night, grabbed Gary from the bed, and kicked him to the john, saying it was time he learned to pee in the pot, while Pam, Randall, and I wound ourselves around her legs and begged her to stop.

I spent most days waiting for Pam and Randall to come home from school. The Waters often locked me out of the house when they left in the morning and didn't open the door again until they returned. If it rained, I sat in a corner of the porch and watched the water pour from the sky. When the rain stopped, I set my naked one-armed baby-doll adrift in a mud puddle and played out the Moses story. I sat on the front porch steps and turned the knobs of the Etch A Sketch until I became the darkened endpoint that moved across the light-gray slate, creating a world of lines and boxes and losing myself in that world. I tried not to think about food because most days there was nothing between breakfast and dinner. Sometimes I dug turnips from an abandoned vegetable plot to eat, and when I was thirsty I put my mouth over the water hydrant at the side of the house. If I needed "to go," I went to the old outhouse in the field. Having no idea I was a poverty-stricken kid, I pretended to be poor. I didn't feel mistreated. I felt fortunate. Gary was too little to play outside all day and had to stay inside with Sister Waters. I wasn't sure why I had to stay outside and didn't want to risk asking. It was clear who had the better end of the deal.

At some point in the day, my thoughts went into hibernation. I sat on the porch, elbows to knees, and watched the clouds move across the sky, careful not to think, not to want, not to anticipate. Longing rooted me in time and deepened the chasm between where I was and where I wanted to be: with my mother, or at the very least playing freeze tag with Pam and Randall. I spent my time looking instead of thinking. I studied birds, ants, trees, bushes. If I looked at something long enough, the veil that separated me from it fell away. There was no I. There was no it. There was only the experience of connectedness. Then I was back in my body again. These moments, unsought and unarticulated, came to me from that time until my early twenties. And in a sense they saved me, first from loneliness and later from nihilism. When as a teen I read in Alan Watts's *This Is It* that underlying the great religious traditions of the world is "the sensation of basic inseparability from the total universe, of the identity of one's own self with the Great Spirit beneath all that exists," I applied it to what I had always considered my own singular experience. And to what I imagined people experienced under the tent. But of course as a five-year-old kid in Andalusia, Alabama, I was just trying to get from one part of my day to another. The clouds passed, insects crawled over my fingers, the sun burned a hole in my brain, the rain dripped, dripped, dripped, the bus groaned to a stop, Pam and Randall trudged up the hill, and time started again.

Pam took me to the side of the house, away from Randall, and opened her hand to show me little hard white balls wrapped in pieces of notebook paper. Atomic FireBalls. She had picked them up off the playground after other kids spat them out. She unwrapped each one, explaining that they were red when they were brand-new. We held them under the water hydrant and washed off the germs. I promised her I would never tell Randall ("He would want some"), or anyone else ("They wouldn't understand").

I daydreamed of living with Aunt Ruth, my mother's sister, or her brother, Uncle Dave. The last time I could remember seeing them was at Grandma's funeral. She had died after gallbladder surgery just as Brother Terrell had predicted. I thought my aunts, uncles, and my grandpa blamed Brother Terrell for her death, and that's why we never saw them. My mother told me later she avoided them because they were suspicious of her relationship with her employer.

One morning I woke up convinced that two of my youngest uncles were there. I had seen them roll a new red tricycle into the house for me during the night. It was the same tricycle one of them had backed his car over and mangled three years earlier. I climbed out of bed that morning eager to find the tricycle (never mind that I was too big to ride it now anyway) and eager to see my uncles. When I couldn't find either, I asked Pam and Randall where they had gone.

"Who?"

"Uncle Ron and Uncle James Earl."

Pam scraped the last of her grits away from the side of the bowl. She raised her head and paused before licking her spoon. "What are you talking about?"

"My uncles. They brought me a new tricycle last night, but I can't find it."

Randall smirked. "Keep looking. I bet 'chu find it before we get back from school."

Before Sister Waters put me out for the day, I peered in every corner of the house and looked under the bed and behind the sofa again and again. I pulled back the grimy little curtain that hung from the kitchen sink and watched as the cockroaches scattered. Outside, I searched under the bushes at the edge of the bare dirt yard and around the outhouse. Every few hours I sucked up my courage and knocked on the door to ask Sister Waters if she had found the tricycle yet. She looked out of her hard little eyes and issued a grunt that I took as a no. I threw myself down on the wooden front steps and tried to figure out why no one admitted seeing my uncles or the tricycle. I reviewed the places I had looked and realized there was still one place I had overlooked: underneath the house.

The pier-and-beam house sat high off the ground and I could see halfway back, but no farther. I crouched and took one step under the house, paused, then took another and another. Just as I reached the darkest part, a ball of daddy longlegs spiders fell on me and ran down my hair and over my face. I screamed and turned to run but smacked my forehead hard against one of the beams and fell onto the moist, mushy ground. Several spiders slipped under the collar and down the bodice of my dress. I yanked at the fabric with one hand and crawled back toward the daylight as fast as I could, yelling as I went. As I emerged from under the house, two plump hands grabbed me under my armpits and shook me in the air.

"What're you doing under there?"

"The spiders. My tricycle." I cried and flailed and whipped my head from side to side, trying to get the spiders off me.

Sister Waters put me under her arm and carried me into the living room. "I don't want to hear no more about no stinking tricycle. And I'll teach you to lie."

She threw me on the unmade couch and grabbed her switch from the corner. I danced a mad jig as the switch cut through the skin on my arms and legs. After a few minutes, she threw the switch aside and dragged me into the bathroom. The door slammed. She turned on the water at the sink, pushed my face under the faucet, and jammed a bar of soap into my mouth.

"This is what happens to kids who lie. Are you going to tell the truth from now on? Are you?"

I tried to answer, but my mouth and nose and eyes were full of water and soap and I was gagging. I tried to nod but it was hard because she was holding my face under the water faucet. Finally I went limp, stopped crying, and tried not to gag. *It'll be over soon. It'll be over soon.* My brother called my name from the other side of the door.

Sister Waters pulled my face from the sink and pulled the soap from my mouth. "Don't lie to me about nuthin' ever again. You hear me? Well, do you?"

I stared straight at her belly and nodded.

"Now tell me there wasn't no tricycle."

I started to cry again. "There wasn't no tricycle."

"Tell me you lied."

"But."

"You want some more?"

I shook my head no. "I lied. I'm sorry."

"Tell me you lied about your uncles."

"I lied about my uncles."

"Were they here?"

"No."

"What?"

"No, ma'am."

"No, ma'am what?"

"No, ma'am, my uncles never came."

"You made up that story about your uncles and that tricycle to get attention, admit it."

I admitted it, thinking all the while, *But it's true, it's true, it's true.*

"Good. Now go on ahead and git your bath before Pam and Randall get back from school. We're going over to Sister Currie's for the prayer meetin'. You understand?"

I nodded, but it was years before I understood. The red tricycle had been a dream. I had mistaken a dream for the real thing.

We stayed with Sister Waters for three months, six months, a year, less than a year. I couldn't really tell you. And then one day it was over. My mother drove up in her old black Ford, the same one we had driven away in when we first started traveling with the tent. We flung ourselves on her and jumped up and down and pulled her in every direction as she packed Gary's teddy bear and my one-armed doll and Etch A Sketch and all our clothes into a box. We were going to live with our mother in Houston. Pam and Randall would stay behind. They were in school when we left, so we didn't get to say good-bye. Mama said it was probably easier on everyone that way. She offered no explanation for our time with Sister Waters, and no explanation for why it had ended. I figured that was how life was. Things happened, and then they were over. No hard feelings.

When Gary and I saw Sister Waters at revivals in later years, we ran to her and she gathered us with those big soft arms and brought us to her breasts.

"My kids, my kids," she said.

We kissed her sweaty neck and told her we loved her, and it was true, in a way. I had not forgotten how she had treated us, but I had set aside those memories in favor of the kind, sweet woman who seemed so happy to see us. Then Pam reminded me one day of all that had happened during our time with The Waters, and I never loved the woman again.

Chapter Fourteen

MAMA EXITED THE FREEWAY AND GUIDED THE Ford into a labyrinth of suburban streets. Gary and I bounced up and down on the front car seat. "We're here. We're in Houston."

My mother was a self-described high-strung woman. Put her in a car with two attention-starved kids for five-hundred-plus miles and those strings were ratcheted about as tight as they could go. Each time she stopped the car in the middle of the street and consulted the directions she had scribbled on the corner of a page she had torn from a phone book, she breathed a little harder. She backed up and turned onto another street that led nowhere.

"Oh, sh-i-t."

Gary and I stopped bouncing and looked intently up and out the front window. He pointed at an airplane low in the sky without saying anything. I nodded. Mama said she had been here once before, last month, but she couldn't for the life of her remember how she got to the house; besides, all these streets looked the same. A few more stops and starts and she pulled into a driveway, turned off the engine, and let go a long sigh.

"Finally."

Our house—we claimed it as ours at once—was a slightly run-down replica of all the other houses in that unfinished but slightly run-down neighborhood of chain-link fences and dead-end streets. It was a rental with dark brown trim and, as my mother pointed out, "a real picture window" that looked out on the field across the street. I flung open the car door and Gary and I ran to the front door.

Mama stood on the stoop and fumbled through her keys, trying one, then another. "This one? No. Maybe this one. That looked like the one, no, must be the other one. I know it's one of these."

Gary and I twitched and shuffled until the key clicked and we stumbled through the front door. It was clean and modern with dark paneled walls, avocado-colored drapes, and a breakfast counter. We rushed to the gold sofa and honey-colored end tables, then down the hall to the two bedrooms, one with a double bed, the other with two singles. I stood in the hallway, stretched my legs and arms as far apart as they would go, and touched my fingers to the doorways of both bedrooms, ours and Mama's.

Gary ran back to the living room and looked out the big window. "It's got everything, even airplanes."

I threw myself on the couch. "Where did all this stuff come from? Is it ours?" I wanted it to be ours.

Mama stood in the middle of the living room and looked around. "Belongs to the landlord." Her voice trailed off the way it did when she had something else to say.

"Where's the table?" I pointed to the space under the hanging wagon-wheel light.

"We'll have to get one later. Right now, we have these." Mama walked over to the pantry in the corner of the kitchen and pulled out metal trays with stands. "TV trays."

"TV?" Gary looked around.

"She said TV *trays.*"

There was a peace about our early days in Houston that I found unnerving. I missed the chaos and the closeness of Pam and Randall. They had been a part of our lives for almost as long as I could remember, and there was too much room, literally and figuratively, without them. Mama assured me they were no longer living with Sister Waters; they were with their mother, she said. I hoped so, for their sakes. I never told her about life with Sister Waters, and she never asked. The quiet immobility of our new life made me jumpy. I missed the sound of car wheels moving on blacktop. When the sun went down in Houston, I begged my mother to take us for a drive on the freeway.

"Let's leave the windows down like we used to. It's warm enough."

My request brought long strange looks from Mama, as if she were trying to figure out what kind of kid would ask such a thing. But I think my mother understood my loneliness for our old life, because on some nights, she put us in the car and we drove all over Houston without saying much of anything.

From my bed at night I watched my mother's fish-belly-white legs lying inert on top of her blue-and-white bedspread, illuminated by the dim light cast from her bedside lamp. Her feet pointed straight up at the ceiling. I couldn't see the top half of her body, but I knew she was propped up on pillows, reading her Bible. When Gary or I woke in the night, she was by our beds before we could call out. She sat beside my brother on the tub while he soaked his flat feet in warm water and Epsom salt. She massaged away the growing pains in my legs. Every morning I padded into the living room, flopped on the couch, and watched dust mites slide down the shafts of light that streamed through the picture window. Mama made bacon and cinnamon toast while Gary charged in and out with a bath towel for a cape calling, "There's no need to fear. Underdog is here."

Gary had become enamored of Underdog while pretending to not watch the neighbor's TV. I threw him on the floor and tickled him until he begged for mercy.

Mama sounded a warning from the kitchen. "Kids, stop that. Go wash your hands. Breakfast is ready."

We ran to the bathroom, stuck our hands under the faucet, and flung water drops in the air as we passed the empty spot where the dinner table was supposed to go.

"Are we ever going to get a table?"

"One thing at a time." My mother set our plates down on the breakfast counter with a sigh.

I bit into my toast and studied her. "You tired?"

"Not exactly."

Her thin slippers slapped back and forth between the stove and the counter. More toast, more bacon, scrambled eggs, too, please. More, more, more. The beige plastic radio she kept on the counter broadcast one preacher after the next. Garner Ted Armstrong, Carl McIntire, A. A. Allen. The harvest was ripe and the workers were few and they made sure we didn't forget it.

"Can we turn off the radio? Please?"

We could not. The radio was my mother's lifeline. Brother Terrell was on twice a day now, and though the programs were exactly the same, Mama listened both times.

After breakfast, Gary and I met the neighbor kids in the field across the street to watch airplanes land and take off at nearby Hobby Airport. We lay in the tall weeds while the jets screamed over us like fierce metallic insects. My stomach dropped to my toes, and I breathed in the acrid odor of jet fuel. I could not believe how lucky we were to live so close to the airport.

As it turned out, it was design, not luck, that determined our location. Mama stopped us one morning on our way out the door to tell us she had a surprise for us; two surprises, really. Brother Terrell was coming to visit and we would go to the airport later that afternoon to pick him up.

We jumped up and down. "The airport! The airport!" It would be the first time my brother and I had been inside an airport.

I stopped and thought for a minute. "But where will they all sleep?"

"Who?" Mama brushed the hair from my eyes.

"Everybody. Pam. Randall. Brother Terrell. Betty Ann. The baby."

"We'll cross that bridge when we come to it."

My mother hummed and smiled all day. She swept, mopped, went to the grocery store, dusted, baked biscuits, and swept some more. She made us take baths and put on clean clothes while she curled her hair and sprayed perfume and picked out a dress that "put color in her cheeks."

At the airport that afternoon, Mama stood Gary in one of the airport's long windows to watch the planes, keeping one hand on his back to make sure he didn't fall. I rocked up on my toes to see over the ledge.

"There's one. Look!"

"Hey, there's another one."

Each time a plane landed, Mama murmured, "That's not it. That's not it." In between landings she glanced at the crowds rolling down the concourse until she glimpsed a familiar face.

"Wait. There he is. There's David."

She pulled Gary from the window and started to tell me to watch him. She was gone before she finished her sentence, moving like a homing device through the throng. I kept my eye on her back for as long as I could, then lost her in the ocean of elbows, chests, shoulders, and hundreds of unfamiliar faces. We stood apart from the crowd until it swelled and widened and engulfed us too. Gary tried to twist his hand free and I tightened my grip.

"Ouch. That hurts."

I backed us against the wall and we stayed put. Eventually the crowd thinned and there was enough space between the bodies that I could look for my mom.

"Do you see her?"

"Not yet."

And then I did. My mother and Brother Terrell stood at the top of the concourse, so close they almost touched. She looked up at him and they began to walk toward us. The closer they came, the more awkward I felt. To see them together like that, without Pam or Betty Ann or Randall or even the baby around, was odd, a bit like coming upon the tent in someone's living room. Out of context, out of place, wrong. Gary must have felt it, too, because by the time they reached us, neither of us could think of a thing to say. Mama asked us if we were going to say hello. We didn't answer.

"I brought y'all something." Brother Terrell reached into a bag and pulled out a pilot's cap with wings pinned to the front for Gary and a purse for me. I looked inside the purse and asked about Pam and Randall.

He stuck both hands in his pockets and shifted from side to side. "They couldn't come this time. Maybe next time."

"Okay. Just wondering." I slipped the purse over my shoulder and Gary slapped on his cap and we ran ahead of the grown-ups.

That night when my mother tucked us in, I asked the question that had nagged at me all through dinner: Where would Brother Terrell sleep?

"Right there on the couch. Why?"

I couldn't think of a single reason why I had asked the question or why I did not quite believe her answer.

I tiptoed into the living room the next morning before anyone was awake, determined to find out what was going on. There was Brother Terrell, curled up on the couch with the pillow over his head and the blanket pulled and twisted around him. He was there every night when I went to bed and every morning when I woke up. That arrangement began to shift as his visits became more regular. I often stumbled to the kitchen for a glass of water late at night to find only a blanket and a pillow on the couch. When I asked my mother where Brother Terrell went at night, she said he was probably walking around outside praying, like he did at the tent. I almost believed her until she introduced him to our neighbor Nila as her brother, her *real* brother. It wasn't a lie, she explained, because she had a brother named Dave, after all. And by the way, it would be better if we called Brother Terrell Uncle David in front of the neighbors.

"Why?"

"It just would. Don't back-talk."

It worked out okay, until Gary and I slipped and called him Brother Terrell in front of Nila from time to time. She cocked her head and looked at us funny. We kept playing and pretended not to notice. We also pretended not to notice when Brother Terrell/Uncle David eventually went missing from the couch altogether and reappeared from our mother's bedroom in the mornings.

Whenever Brother Terrell left, Mama moved through the house like a ghost. Her sighs were long and labored, and her face was vacant. She didn't talk unless we asked her a question, and sometimes even then she forgot to answer. It took a few days for her to find her way back to us. First Nila would come through the hedge that separated our houses to tell Mama she had a call from her brother. (We didn't have a phone.) It was always Brother Terrell, of course. These calls had a positive effect on my mother. Afterward, she stumbled into our room and told us we were going to Big Boy's for burgers and shakes. Everything was on its way back to our version of normal.

I don't know how long the three of us lived in Houston. My mother's memory is vague and my brother prefers to forget rather than to remember, so I am on my own when reconstructing this period of our past. My best estimate is three months. Despite my initial resistance to happiness, the end of it took me by surprise.

A plague of dead crickets littered the porches and sidewalks of our neighborhood and the sun flattened everything with its white light. Gary and

I had just taken our place at the picture window to watch the smallest and most unremarkable of planes make their way across a washed-out sky. We were just tuning up for the I'm-bored chorus when two black women glided up the cracked sidewalk to our house. They shimmered in the heat and humidity of the Houston summer, a mirage of leopard-skin pillbox hats and matching fur stoles. They pulled something big behind them, a console TV that sat high on a primitive wooden sled. There was something of the ancient caravan in their slow, rhythmic progress. They didn't stress or strain or stop to wipe a brow. Gary and I watched, arms and legs swimming against the glass. The women parked the TV at the bottom of our porch and climbed the steps.

"Mama, Mama, come quick."

Our mother opened the door before they could knock and there stood Rita, a long, inky black line, and Queenie, round as a butterscotch with skin the color to match.

"Mrs. Johnson? We talked to you on the phone t'other day, about your ad? These must be the children."

Cars slowed to a crawl as they passed our house that day and the long, white-stemmed necks in them turned like lazy Susans. It was 1963 and people of color did not live in, work in, or visit our blue-collar, all-white neighborhood. We should have seen those cars as a sign, a warning of what was to come, but Gary and I were too young to parse their meaning and our mother too naïve or too desperate to figure out what must have been common knowledge for most people.

We were not blind to Queenie's and Rita's skin color, but it surprised my brother and me far less than their leopard spots and television. I had sat with black women under the tent, hugged their necks, and draped white cotton cloths over their stout legs when they fell out in the spirit after a long shout. But those were holiness women, and they dressed like the white holiness women we knew. Plain, shapeless dresses. Dull, flat shoes chosen because they were on sale and good for navigating the uneven ground under the tent. Queenie and Rita were a different species. From their furs to their candy-colored lips (how did they get so red?) and the scent of Topaz and stale smoke that followed them into our house, they reeked glamour, youth, and sensuality. But even they could not compete with the lure of their television. Gary and I fidgeted our way through introductions, anxious to slip past the women and ponder the big box of sin left at the bottom of our steps.

Mama called TV "hellevision" and said she wouldn't have one in her house, which worked out well since we usually did not have a house. Brother Terrell had said television was a tool of the devil, another way the world would seduce us.

"First, you need Walter Cronkite to tell you what's going on in the world. Next thing you know you're missing church to watch *Bonanza* and Ed Sullivan. If God spoke to you, you couldn't hear him. You're too busy watching television."

He must have been right, because when Gary and I played in our neighbor Nila's living room, we could not take our eyes off her TV. Furtive glances lengthened into glazed stares, and when the other kids wandered outside to play, we stayed put, hypnotized by flickering images of the Lone Ranger, Tonto, and Hercules.

While Queenie and Rita sat inside drinking iced tea with our mother, we perched on the porch steps for what seemed an eternity, trying to figure out what it meant to have a TV right outside our door.

Please, God. We'll say our prayers and think of you all of the time—okay, most of the time. Please. Let the TV stay.

For once my prayer was answered. Mama came out and told me to cut through the hedge to Nila's house and ask her husband to help us get the TV up the steps and into the house.

I took off running.

The adults moved the TV inside, Nila's husband on one end, Mama and Rita on the other, and situated it catty-cornered to the picture window. Mama asked everyone to stay for dinner, but Nila had already cooked and Queenie and Rita said they needed to go. They had so much to do before they came back for good. My head snapped in their direction.

"What do you mean, for good?"

"Your mama will tell you, honey. Bye, you all."

The door closed and my mouth opened in a long, dry wail.

"Why are they coming back? Are you leaving?"

"Kids, I have something I've been meaning to tell you. Come sit on the couch with me."

Gary crawled on the couch. I kept my distance.

"I know this is hard. It's hard for me, too, but there are people who have never heard of Jesus. I'm going to travel with Brother Terrell and help him tell the world about Christ."

I put my hands over my ears. "I don't want to help anyone. I don't want to hear anything you say." I ran into my room and crawled under my bed.

Mama followed me and sat on the bed. Her voice rose and fell and rose and fell, saying all the things I already knew about Jesus and God and sacrifice. I couldn't bear to hear her talk. I wanted her to go, just go. My brother bawled like a baby calf in the living room. I would have felt better if I could have cried, but I couldn't squeeze out a single tear. The bed creaked and I watched the back of her heels shuffle away. I slid out from under the bed and headed for the front door. Out of the corner of my eye, I saw my brother and mother sitting on the couch. She held him in her lap and rocked him like a baby.

"Donna? Donna?"

The crack in her voice made me want to turn around, but I slammed through the door and headed to the brown, crunchy field across the street. Just a few weeks earlier, the tall green thicket of leafy weeds provided a jungle in which we played for hours. Now it was a bunch of tall sticks with a few gray leaves twirling in the hot wind. I picked up a long stick and began to walk and slash the dried stalks around me. With every step I repeated the same phrase: "I will never forget this."

Gary cried every night after our mother left and refused to eat much for weeks. He looked like a baby bird: big head, big eyes, bony little body. I busied myself practicing my letters and learning to read short, simple words. I wanted to be ready when I started first grade that fall. I took all my shots without crying. Then at the last minute, Queenie and Rita found out that because my birthday fell too late in the month of September, I would have to wait until the next year to start school.

I busied myself again, this time stealing candy from the store and change from Nila's counter. When Queenie and Rita asked me about the money, I told them I had found it in the yard. They believed me the first time, but the second time, they marched me through the hedge and made me give the money back. Nila said we were still friends, but I stopped going to her house to play.

With the other kids in school, Gary and I spent most of our days indoors watching Queenie and Rita's television. We stared at soap operas all day and Ed Sullivan and *Bonanza* on Sundays, just as Brother Terrell had predicted. We fell asleep in the living room almost every night watching newsreels and old movies and anything else that moved across the screen. Cigarette butts piled up in bowls. Lipsticks, bottles of nail polish, and plates of old food covered the end tables and the TV trays. I often woke early, poured myself a bowl of cereal, and turned the channel knob until I found a cartoon. On mornings when there was no milk, I took bills from Queenie's wallet and went to the nearby store. One morning as I handed a carton of milk and a fistful of money to my favorite cashier, a man I had nicknamed Mr. Whipple, he said something that shocked me.

"Honey, you need to go home and tell someone to put some clothes on you."

His voice was stern, but his eyes were traced with something that looked like sadness, only different. In that moment, I saw myself as he saw me: a skinny, dirty kid in baggy white cotton panties and nothing else. He said something else to me, but his words sounded thick and muffled. I stood there caught, not knowing what to do or say. Finally, a hand reached across the counter with my change. I took it and ran from the store. On my way home I played step-on-a-crack, break-your-mother's-back, and stepped on every crack I could.

Life flickered between triumph and tragedy that fall. News reports showed thousands of people, black and white, marching to Washington, DC, to hear about Doctor King's dream. When he spoke, the crowd went quiet and Queenie and Rita wept. Everyone locked arms and sang together and I was reminded of the revivals. I told Queenie and Rita about how blacks and whites sat together under the tent and how the Klan had beaten Brother Terrell. Less than a month later, four young black girls were killed in a Sunday-school bombing in Birmingham.

"*In church*, they killed them in church," Rita said. Two other people were killed in the riots that followed. The stations replayed scenes filmed just a few months earlier of Bull Connor turning fire hoses and dogs—*dogs*—on black kids. I worried about my mother and all the people who traveled with the tent, but the hatred and violence we saw on TV was much closer at hand.

Queenie and Rita lay stretched out on the couch, one head at either end, illuminated by the chalky light of the late-night TV test pattern. Gary and I were wrapped in a tangle of quilts and pillows on the floor. A scrape along the outside of the house caused Queenie's and Rita's heads to pop up like toast from the ends of the couch. Another scrape and a light tapping at the side window sent them screaming from the living room into the hall closet. I scrambled close behind and pushed my way into the closet with them. The door slammed with my brother on the other side. I kicked and yelled until they opened the door and pulled Gary in. The four of us stood there jammed in the closet until someone said they had to pee and absolutely could not hold it. Then we all herded into the bathroom, locked the door, and slept on the floor with folded towels for pillows.

Queenie and Rita laughed the next morning as we walked around the outside of the house and searched for the source of the noise.

"Probably a branch," they said, and laughed some more. They stopped laughing when they saw the broken bushes by the windows on the side of the house. Someone had climbed through that bush to look in the window. Little looks flitted between Queenie and Rita. Why someone would stand outside in the dark and tap on our window they would not say. The noises returned the next night, and every night after that. Sometimes we heard scraping, sometimes tapping. Sometimes voices moved in the dark outside our house. One morning we woke to find

NIGGER printed in big black letters on our sidewalk. I knew from the looks on Queenie's and Rita's faces; it was not a good word. We scrubbed and scrubbed, but the shadow of the letters remained. We hung sheets and blankets over our windows and began to sleep during the day. We sat up all night, watching the sign-off circles on the television and waiting for the noises. If we nodded off, Gary yelled and sent us stumbling through the dark into the closet. We stood there, flesh pressed against oily flesh, breathing in the musty scent of sweat tinged with fear.

"What happened?"

"Gary yelled."

"Why?"

"I don't know. Why, Gary?"

"I saw angels walking up and down a ladder in the living room."

Queenie and Rita sucked in their breath.

"A vision."

"Uh-huh."

"I will give my angels charge over them."

"That's right."

On November 22, 1963, our time in the Houston house came to an end. After a long night of interrupted sleep, we woke up late and had just turned on the TV to watch *As the World Turns*. Soap-opera tragedies never seemed far-fetched to me. Secret lives? Ditto. Preachers who turn into uncles. Okay. Two or three wives? So what. A few years later when TV was no longer a sin and my mother and I watched *The Secret Storm* together, she made a crack about how there was always a secret storm brewing on those shows.

"It's like real life."

"Whose life, Donna?"

If she didn't know, I wasn't about to tell her.

Queenie and Rita sipped their first cups of coffee that afternoon as Nancy and Grandpa sat down on-screen to have their coffee. Nancy told Grandpa her son Bob had invited Lisa to Thanksgiving dinner. Grandpa lifted his eyebrow and asked if she knew *why* Bob had invited Lisa. Before Nancy could answer, a slide clicked over the scene and a man's urgent monotone replaced make-believe family confidences.

"Here is a bulletin from CBS news. In Dallas, Texas, three shots were fired at President Kennedy's motorcade in downtown Dallas. The first reports say that President Kennedy has been seriously wounded by the shooting."

Rita stood up slowly and stared at the TV. She cupped her face with her hands.

"The president. They've shot the president."

Queenie groaned. Rita sank to the floor as if someone had let the air out of her. Queenie rolled off the couch, switched off the TV, and dropped to her knees. The television went dark and silent for the first time in months. Scattered like islands across our living room, we prayed without making a sound. Under the tent, people called on God as if he were hard of hearing. I had always thought of prayer as words, lots of words, until that day when a vast sorrow rolled across the country and a prayer of silence was the only possible response. I stayed hunched over until the sound of running water and clinking dishes signaled it was time to get up. Queenie brought two fresh cups of coffee into the living room and handed one to Rita. They took up their positions at either end of the couch and lit cigarettes. I switched on the TV. More reports followed. A would-be assassin in Dallas. In Dallas, *Texas*. Three bullet shots. The president slumped into the lap of Mrs. Kennedy.

"Oh no," she said, "oh no."

The helplessness of those words split me in two and my own grief came pouring out. Queenie opened her arms and waved me over.

"Come on over here, baby. Come on."

She wiped my tears and pulled me against her soft body. Walter Cronkite appeared on the screen to tell us the president was still alive, and Governor Connally too. Walter showed us a big room filled with people who had come to eat lunch with the president. They sat at long tables covered with white cloths and glasses that sparkled even on black-and-white television. They knew the president wouldn't be coming now, but still they sat there. A black waiter in a white coat leaned against one of the tables and covered his face with one of the big dinner napkins. When Queenie and Rita saw him, they let loose too. Then Walter appeared again in his white shirt with the news we already knew.

"President Kennedy died at one P.M. Central Standard Time, two o'clock Eastern Standard Time. Some thirty-eight minutes ago."

Walter pressed his lips together and took off his glasses. The world held its breath. Some of us never exhaled. We watched and listened to news reports into the evening. Queenie and Rita lit one cigarette from another. Walter told us Lee Harvey Oswald had been arrested. He showed us pictures taken of the president minutes before the rifle blew apart his skull. He looked like a man in charge. He looked like the president. In one picture Mrs. Kennedy held her hat on with a white-gloved hand. Such a small hand.

We forgot for a time the scrapes and taps and whispers we had lived with for weeks, forgot the fear that sent us running like rats for the small dark places that closed around us like tombs. We put aside our personal ongoing terror, but it came for us anyway. That night before the TV signed off, a thin voice called from outside our house.

"Here, nigger, nigger, nigger."

We didn't move. A horn blared, followed by the sound of breaking glass.

"Oh my God, they're coming in. Get out. Get out."

More horns and more glass. Images of the president's coffin handed gently, so gently from the airplane into a long station wagon flashed across the screen. Queenie and Rita threw open the windows that lined one side of the living room and we all jumped through them. We ran screaming through the hedge that separated Nila's yard from our own and pounded on her door. She cracked it open and pulled us inside. Her living room looked like ours, only neat and safe. Pools of light spilled across the ends of the couch. The long car with President Kennedy's coffin moved across the TV. Nila's kids had been in bed for hours and now they appeared in the doorway of the living room, rubbing their eyes. The police came with sirens and lights flashing. Nila sent her husband out to meet them and insisted Gary and I stay inside.

We pressed against the picture window to see what we could. Two cops and Nila's husband stood in a small circle, their heads pointed toward the center. Walkie-talkie voices crackled off and on, but the policemen ignored them and wrote stuff down while Nila's husband talked. They wagged their heads, then pulled out their flashlights and headed toward our empty house. After a few minutes they came through Nila's door, filling the space around them. Nila had wrapped Queenie and Rita in light blankets and sat them at her dining table with cups of coffee. The policemen sat down with them and asked questions. What were their first and last names? How long had they lived here? What were they doing here? Who were we? Where was our mama? Did they know the people who smashed our living-room windows? Were they sure?

Queenie's and Rita's voices shook. They kept their heads down and said, "Yes sir, no sir." Gary and I stood beside them until Nila took us by the hands and walked us out of the room. She took us into the bathroom, where she dabbed away at us with a warm, wet washcloth. The way she cupped my face with her hand made me miss my mother, but I did not cry. She pulled my dirty clothes up over my head without hurting my ears and replaced them with clean pajamas. Gary smiled and said he wanted to live with her. She said we could live there for the night. We woke the next morning to find Queenie and Rita on Nila's couch, one head at either end. We spent the day packing our clothes and toys into boxes. When the two taxis came that evening, we loaded the TV into the trunk of one and piled our boxes in the backseat. Then we slipped inside the other car and drove away.

We moved into a light-blue apartment complex. Our across-the-hall neighbor had a phone and told Queenie and Rita they could use it anytime. They called Nila and asked her to give the number to our mother when she called to check on us. With the exception of a light-skinned kid who said his daddy was Willie Mays, Gary and I were the only white faces. I never felt uncomfortable. When the neighbors heard what had happened, they gave us suckers and smiled as if we had just come home from the hospital. I wanted to tell them we were all right now, but I was afraid they would stop giving us suckers, so I kept my mouth shut.

We began to sleep through the night again after a few weeks. Queenie and Rita shared a bed in the only bedroom, and Gary and I slept on the couch. We watched Ed Sullivan on Sunday nights and mashed-potatoed and twisted up and down the living room. Queenie and Rita laughed and shook their heads at the way the white girls stretched out their arms and cried when the Beatles sang *oooh* and shook their funny hair. Sometimes Queenie and Rita put on their leopard-skin pillbox hats and fur stoles and met men in the courtyard. Gary and I hung on to them and begged them not to go. If someone could kill the president, no one was safe. They told us we could watch them through the window, and we did. I didn't understand how they could meet boyfriends and shop and pay bills as if everything were okay, as if the president were still alive, as if no one had chased us from our house. They said you couldn't dwell on evil, that you had to move on.

We had lived in the apartment a few months when I opened the door to a young man I had never seen before. He said our mother had sent him to pick us up. Gary and I hugged Queenie and Rita good-bye and cried all the way to the car. By the time we pulled onto the freeway, our eyes were dry. We were headed back to Mama and the tent. The world had resumed its natural order, or we thought it was about to. As the sun set that evening, the implications of not knowing exactly where it was we were going or who it was that was taking us there began to dawn. I was afraid if the man—a boy, really—was a kidnapper, and if I asked him where he was taking us, he might kill us. Better to say nothing and hope for the best.

Gary fell asleep in the backseat. My shoulders worked their way up to my ears. The longer we drove, the more the boy talked. About the revivals, the miracles he had seen since he began to travel with Brother Terrell. Goiters, cancers, blindness, cripples, you name it. He smacked his gum and went on about how the Lord and Brother Terrell had changed his life. A familiar monologue. The headlights from oncoming cars played across his long, broad fingers curled around the steering wheel. I liked the way he kept both hands on the wheel and the way he slowed the car around curves. My shoulders began to relax. My eyes closed. He wasn't going to kidnap us or kill us. We would see Mama again after all.

Chapter Fifteen

NO ONE KNOWS HOW WE CAME TO LIVE WITH the Smiths. When I ask my mother, I get her stock reply:

"Honey, there was so much going on at the time, I'm lucky to remember my own name."

I always want to say amen, but I never do.

I paw through odds and ends of memory, looking for some way to explain how we came to reside in that ramshackle Victorian house where everything strained and leaned and pulled away from everything else. I see my brother and me on our backs, staring up into the stars. The wooden bars of a folding chair push into my spine. We are lying down in chairs. A long face with ears the size of small boats floats above us. Skillet-size hands reach from white cuffs to pull us up. The scent of Noxzema signals my mother is nearby.

The scene stretches into a story, a story I had forgotten but remember hearing and telling while growing up. We were in yet another revival in Columbia, South Carolina. It had to be Columbia because that's where the Smiths lived. Pam and

Randall were there and we spent the evening running in and out of the tent until our mother grabbed Gary and me and planted us in two wooden folding chairs a few feet away from where she sat on the platform.

"I'll be watching, so don't you dare move, either of you."

And we didn't. Not even when the music took off and the spirit fell and a tall, gangly man in a white shirt and black slacks whipsawed toward us in double time, arms churning and flapping. Desperate to escape the human windmill headed our way, I waved at my mother. Her hands popped up high above the keyboard and her body bounced to the beat. Her gaze focused straight ahead on Brother Terrell. Just as he put his hand on his hip and began to move his feet in the shuffle step he was known for, the white shirt crashed into Gary and me. We flipped through the tent canvas onto the ground outside, where we lay for an instant, staring up into the heavens. The lower halves of our bodies remained under the tent, bottoms firmly planted in the chairs, legs sticking straight up like disjointed doll limbs. We were stunned but not afraid. The tall man in the white shirt stood over us now, but we didn't move until our mother gathered us close and pulled us back under the tent.

We blinked against the glare of the floodlights. Adults stumbled around us, drunk on the spirit, hands waving slowly, lips moving without uttering a word. Since Mama was with us, there was no music, but people continued to dance, some in marionettelike jerks, others in neat toe-tapping shuffle-slide steps.

The white-shirted man looked down at us. "You kids all right?"

Gary and I nodded. Mama said we were fine.

"When I start shoutin' I don't see nothing or nobody."

The next thing I knew, Mama was on her way to Barbados with the revival team and Gary and I were dodging Brother Smith's holy delirium on a regular basis. During the months we lived with the Smiths, two of the stained-glass windows in the church the family attended were boarded up, testaments to Brother Smith's spiritual abandon.

Put the head and face of Lyndon Johnson atop the body of Ichabod Crane and you've got the spitting image of Brother Smith. He was all knees, ears, elbows, and beaky nose, and he towered over most grown-ups, including Sister Smith. A small, wiry woman with brittle black hair and stooped shoulders, Sister Smith announced her entry into every room with an exhalation that spoke of her profound disapproval and bitter disappointment. The woman was a potent breather. While living with the Smiths, I officially developed a "weak stomach," a condition that was to a six-year-old what fainting was to a certain breed of Southern ladies in bygone eras. Anytime I found myself anxious or upset, I threw up. Our living conditions being what they were, I was sick on a regular basis. I didn't will it or fake it, but it did come in handy. Nausea excused me from countless long-winded sermons, and sometimes, if I threw up enough, I didn't have to go to church at all.

Wanda, the eldest of the three Smith teenagers, often accompanied me to the bathroom or the bushes or the side of the road, depending on where the urge struck, and smoothed my hair back from my face while I heaved. Afterward, she held my head in her lap, and if the situation allowed, placed a drippy washcloth on my forehead. She rocked and sang just under her breath a song about a girl dying in a car accident and how her boyfriend wanted to be good so he could see her in heaven. The lyrics made me tense, but I knew from the rapt, solemn expression on Wanda's long, pale face that the song was important to her, so I kept quiet.

"Don't tell anyone I sang this worldly song. Okay?"

I nodded.

Anything not related directly to God was a sin in the Smith household. Telling jokes. Smiling. Playing. Exhausted from doing too much of nothing, I tiptoed up the stairs once to the forbidden second story. Stacks of boxes lined the hallway. A splash of red and yellow peeked out of the corner of one box: a tic-tac-toe game, and below it books with drawings of kids and mice and rabbits in blue coats. I pulled out one of the books and ran my hand over it. I wondered whether Wanda or one of the twins would let me borrow the book or the game. Sister Smith's pinched, dour face came to mind. *Not in this life.* I pushed through the first door. More boxes; some neatly stacked and pushed against the wall, others scattered across the room and half-filled with old pictures, chipped whatnots, petticoats flung on top. A single bed, sheets and blanket smoothed and tucked into the sides, was shoved against the wall. A nightstand stood watch in the middle of the room, its crooked-neck lamp illuminating nothing. Faded wallpaper peeled away from the walls.

I wandered through an endless succession of rooms, all minimally furnished and filled with boxes. It was as if the Smiths had packed up their lives and were getting ready to move. But where? Maybe they were waiting for the rapture. Brother Terrell always said the time was short. I walked into the last room and noticed Betty's white sweater hanging from it. So this was her room. Betty was Wanda's younger sister and the twin of Eddy, the Smiths' only son. With their dark hair, big eyes, and petite frames, the fifteen-year-old twins exerted a powerful pull on my imagination. I gravitated toward them, but they did not gravitate back. I tripped on the corner of a box and a shoebox filled with letters tumbled off. Maybe love letters. I grabbed a handful of envelopes, stuffed them in the shoebox, and set it back. I had to get out of there before someone discovered me. But if the rapture came and I was left behind, I'd head to Betty's room and grab the shoebox. Never mind that I didn't know how to read. Miracles happened every day. When the rapture came, I would read those letters.

The Smiths were bona fide religious nuts, a distinction hard to achieve in our circles. The grown-ups who traveled with the tent fasted and prayed and used their hotline to heaven on a regular basis, but they also made jokes, enjoyed good meals, and listened to country music occasionally on the radio, if only to keep them awake during the long drives between revivals. Brother and Sister Smith honed piety to a sharper, more austere edge. Hunger was next to godliness and the family fasted several days a week. They also insisted my brother and I fast, though in deference to our ages they allowed us to eat one meal in the evening. The Smiths wanted to crucify the flesh, to rid their bodies and ours of earthly needs and cravings, so that we could all become more closely attuned to the world of the spirit. All that fasting must have worked because the Holy Ghost dropped in regularly. We might be washing dishes or sitting down for a rare family meal, when Brother or Sister Smith would begin praying aloud and speaking in tongues.

"Hallelujah. Praise God. Pass the sweet potatoes."

"Glory be to God, this meat loaf's good."

"Amen, Sister Smith. Shondalie. Condalie."

"Efna say ho li. Where's the gravy?"

We thought of the Holy Ghost as a direct experience of God. But it was a bit like the chicken pox, in that it was something you could "get," and people got it in almost every church service and revival. Everyone said the Holy Ghost changed everything, and that was certainly my experience. Despite the rift between Brother Terrell and the organized church world, the Smiths attended an Assemblies of God church located conveniently across the street from their house. Unless I was sick, I was in the pews every night. The services usually ended with an altar call. On this particular night, the preacher said he had a burden for young people and announced a special altar call for the youth.

"The Bible says God will pour out his spirit on all who seek him. And for many of you young people, tonight is the night. God wants to fill you with his spirit. Don't leave this church without saying yes to God."

Teenagers trickled up to the front. First came

the greasy-haired boys who slipped outside to smoke when the spirit overtook their parents. Next came the girls with tight blouses and too much powder, girls who often followed the boys into the darkened corners that lay just beyond the church doors. Then the altar call regulars, kids whose consciences pushed them forward with a litany of offenses real and imagined. I often fell into this third group, but that night I had something else on my mind: a pressing need to visit the ladies' room. I tried to tell Wanda, but a stern look from her shut me up. Up front, two to three adults gathered around each of the twenty or so kids kneeling at the altar and laid hands on them.

"Forgive her, Father. Wash away every sin. Let the power of your holy spirit flow through her, Lord. Now, Lord. Right now. Bless her, Jesus."

Prayers for forgiveness gave way to the earnest solicitation of the Holy Ghost. Adults held up the arms of penitents and new converts. Cries of "Bless her, Lord" and "Praise him" and "Fill him Lord, fill him" rang out over the moans of twenty souls. The prayers of a hundred people, some in English and some in those unknown tongues, echoed through the church.

Wanda jabbed me with her elbow.

"Go on. Get up there."

I made my way up the aisle and knelt below one of the stained-glass windows that had been raised to let in the soupy South Carolina air. I bowed my head to pray for the safe return of my mother and the Terrells. The smell of gasoline, motor oil, and exhaust fumes drifted up from the gas station next door and filled me with a strange longing for my dad: a man I had not seen since infancy and whose face I could not recall. I had often conjured the thought of my father when I needed to feel the spirit, but this was different. It was as if I had just lost him. I covered my face with my hands.

Brother Smith drawled in my ear, "Just pour your heart out to Jesus, honey. That's it. That's it. Do you know why you're crying?"

I said, "I feel the spirit for my daddy."

Brother Smith heard, "I feel the spirit, Daddy." This child he had taken in was feeling the movement of the Holy Ghost, and she had called him Daddy. He wrapped one of his long arms around my back. His big left hand cupped my shoulder. With his right hand he lifted one of my arms into the air.

"Just give yourself to the spirit, honey. Let him take over."

Someone raised my other arm and began to coach me in a stage whisper, "That's it. That's it. Now say, 'Shondi shondi shondi' over and over again."

I repeated the syllables.

"That's it. Now faster."

"Shondishondishnondi." My tongue tripped. "Shondiki . . ."

"That's it, baby. Let the Lord do the talking."

Brother Smith clapped me on the back. I stuttered again.

"Glory be to God, the Holy Ghost has got a holt of this child."

Shouts of "Hallelujah, thank you, Jesus" reverberated. A hand hit my forehead and I reeled back under the blow. I fluttered my eyelids and saw a clutch of adults gathered around me, determined to help me pray through to the Holy Ghost.

Getting the Holy Ghost Assemblies of God style could take hours. The petitioner pled with God to fill her with his spirit and practiced different combinations of consonants and vowel sounds to loosen the tongue. Believers mopped sweat off the brow and offered sips of water to keep the throat moist and the tongue moving. I've seen women and men turn pale after a few hours and look as though they were ready to faint. Just when the person reached exhaustion, the tongues came. If they didn't, the supplicant continued pleading and babbling.

I didn't have hours. What I had was an urgent need to pee. I opened my eyes.

"Don't fight him, honey. Let him take over."

I closed my eyes.

"That's right. Let God have his way with you.

Begin to thank him for giving you the Holy Ghost."

"Say, 'Thank you thank you thank you thank you thank you.'" Another hand hit my head and shook it.

"Thankyouthankyouthankyou . . ."

The syllables rattled round in my mouth, flowed together, and began to sound like something altogether different.

"Thanuthanuthathanunu."

The adults howled hallelujahs.

I ran my "thanu thanu"s up against the "shondi shondi"s. "Thanuthanushondishondithanu . . ."

The band of bodies around me broke as the adults began to shout and speak in tongues. The tall stained-glass windows beside me rattled as the breeze blew harder.

The preacher's voice shaped and narrated what was happening. "The Bible says the Holy Ghost blew upon them like a mighty wind. He's blowing through here tonight. Lift your hands, everybody."

I kept my tongue moving. "Thanu shondi condi thanu tha nu tha than u nu nu ah."

I opened my eyes and surveyed the situation. Everyone in the church was dancing. I closed my eyes and joined them. I longed to abandon myself to God, but something stopped me. Something always did. Usually it was my inability to escape my sense of self-consciousness, but on that night it was more basic. I had to go and soon. I crumpled to the ground as though slain in the spirit and lay there for a respectable length of time, then rose stumbling as I had seen grownups do and made my way down the aisle to the door marked LADIES. By the time I poked my head out of the lavatory, church was over. I walked out into the evening, where believers stood in small clutches discussing how the Holy Ghost had fallen on the young people and how different their lives would be from now on and how the Bible had foretold a great outpouring of the spirit in the last days and surely these were the last days.

Everywhere I turned, I faced the backs of people. I missed the spotlight that had so recently shone on me, so I closed my eyes and began to jerk and speak in tongues again. I felt a hand on each elbow. I fluttered my eyelids and saw a young man on one side and Betty on the other.

"Isn't it wonderful how God is blessing this child?"

"It is, and he's gonna bless her some more when we get home." *She knew.* I stopped jerking.

A permanent uneasiness took up residence in me that night. I couldn't decide if my initial experience with the Holy Ghost was real or faked. If it was real, why didn't I feel different? If it was faked, I had blasphemed and that was the point of no return that preachers had always warned against.

"There is one sin for which there is no forgiveness, and once you cross that line there is no way back. God will turn you over to a reprobate mind. Even if you want to find your way back to God, you won't be able to."

Did I have a reprobate mind? What exactly was a reprobate mind? Had God turned his back on me? These questions weighed on me for the rest of my childhood. Whenever I committed some wrong—watching *The Monkees* on TV, attending movies or high-school football games, making out with a boy, or God forbid, wearing slacks— they always resurfaced. I was never sure where God and I stood after that night, but I was pretty sure there was a vast amount of space between us.

One night after evening worship, the Smiths gathered around their small kitchen table with other church people. I walked in just as Brother Smith pounded the table to make his point. "The Assemblies of God is the only church today that stands by the truth. Everybody knows they only kicked David Terrell out because he had two wives."

His back was to the door that led from the living room to the kitchen, so he did not see me enter the room. Sister Smith shushed him, and he and the others turned to look at me. My face grew hot, and I felt as if the floor had given way, as if I was standing there with nothing to support me, nothing to save me. Brother Terrell's visits to our house in Houston, the gifts, the empty couch in my mother's living room all came together in that instant, and I knew that my mother was one of those two wives and that it was an awful, shameful thing and that her shame was my shame. I knew, and from that moment on there was no way to not know.

Gary and I passed our days swinging on the rickety wraparound front porch. We pumped our legs out as we arced up toward the peeling blue of the ceiling and snapped them at the knees as we swept back toward the edge of the porch. I looked over my shoulder as the swing rocked to and fro. Roses, ramshackle sheds, scuppernong vines, and patches of bare earth slick and shiny as Brother Smith's bald head jammed against the heavens and were gone. The world in all its misbegotten beauty rushed through me; glory, glory, glory. Wanda found me there weeping once, and asked what was wrong.

"Nothing's wrong. It's just so . . . you know, beautiful."

She held me at arm's length and looked me up and down. "Are you feeling sick again?"

The people who passed the porch on their way to work looked so different from the men and women I had known. I had never seen a man with a briefcase or a woman in a suit. The women in particular caught my attention. With their matching coats and skirts, purposeful strides, and straight-ahead stares, they constituted a third gender. I decided they were hermaphrodites, a word I had picked up from a recent sermon. Sometimes I imagined the porch breaking free with me and Gary aboard and gliding down the street past the suits, or sailing up past the clouds and the ghost of a moon on the rise. I wrapped my arm around a peeling column, curled my bare toes into the edge of the splintery boards, and peered into the sky. I had recently learned from one of the Smith kids that Earth was not fixed as it seemed, but was spinning in space and at the same time traveling in a vast circle around the sun. These facts I could not comprehend. I believed that if I looked long enough and hard enough and stood perfectly still, I might see some trace of the planet's turning, some vestige of its journey, but of course I never did.

Chapter Sixteen

AN ALARM SHOULD HAVE SOUNDED THE DAY Sister Coleman appeared at the Smiths' house: a siren's *whup whup whup;* the blast of a foghorn; an automated voice announcing, "Danger,

danger." No such luck. Gary and I watched from the front-porch swing as she turned in from the sidewalk and walked up the steps, moving at her own pace, neither fast nor slow. Church people were the only ones to call on the Smiths and they always came at night, after the service was over. I dragged my feet and slowed the swing. She stepped onto the porch and stood feet apart, hands on her hips. She stared at us as if deciding what she was going to do. Gary and I squirmed uncomfortably. My hand slipped nervously up and down one of the chains that tethered the swing to the porch ceiling.

"Are you here to take us to the orphanage?" I asked.

Her lips tightened into a thin line of a smile. "Are you expecting someone to take you to the orphanage?"

"Uh-uh." Gary and I shook our heads vigorously.

She walked over to the swing and eased herself down between us. "I'm Sister Coleman. I met your mama at the revival here a few months back. She asked me to keep an eye on you chillens while she's gone."

White people didn't use the word "chillens." She said it as though she were making fun of it somehow. I studied her a little harder. She wore her mostly gray hair pulled back into a bun like many of the women who came to the tent, but her knee-length wraparound skirt looked newer than the clothes they wore. Her attitude was different, too, more in charge, or maybe it was the rolled-up shirtsleeves.

"You sure you're not from the government or something?"

Again, the tight-lipped smile. This time the skin around her eyes crinkled.

"I'm sure. How can I convince you?" She pulled two chocolate bars out of her pocket and waved them through the air.

"I'm convinced." I grabbed the candy bars and handed one to Gary. We ripped them open. I wanted to eat mine slowly, square by square, but I couldn't, and it was gone too fast.

She cocked her head toward me and raised one eyebrow. "What do you say?"

On the other side of Sister Coleman, Gary held up his half-eaten chocolate bar. "Thanks."

How did he manage to make a candy bar last so long? Sister Coleman nodded her approval. Gary beamed a chocolate-covered smile her way. She laughed and hugged him. Everyone loved my brother.

I tugged at her sleeve. "Got any more?"

Sister Coleman joined us regularly on the porch after that day. She never went inside the house and the Smiths never came out on the porch when she was there. If we were still in our pajamas at the end of the day, she sucked in her breath and wagged her head. She asked what we had eaten and usually disapproved of our answers: beans, cornbread crumbled into powdered milk, or "Nothing yet, 'cause we're fasting."

"You chillens need to eat regular."

She told us about Bug, her adopted son. He was my age but he couldn't see, hear, walk, or talk. God was going to heal him soon. Sometimes she and her sinner husband took Bug to their lake house. She could tell he liked to feel the breeze from the water, because he closed his eyes and stopped making noises for a minute.

Gary jumped from the swing. "You have a lake?"

"We don't own the lake, but we have a house there."

My only experience with lakes was glimpsing them through a car window as we drove past. "You live there?"

"No. We live at our other house."

Two houses, and one of them on a lake. This woman was more interesting all the time.

Sister Coleman began to lobby my mother through letters and phone calls to let Gary and me move in with her family. She told Mama the Smiths neglected us, that we asked—begged, even—to come live with her. She promised she would give us a good home, and that my mom wouldn't have to pay her anything. Thus began our descent into the ninth circle of hell.

· · ·

The day we moved into Sister Coleman's house, she gathered us up next to her on the sofa and told us she had always wanted children, had in fact wanted *us,* and now the Lord had given us to her. Her remarks made me feel special, and uneasy. What did she mean, God had given us to her?

"You mean to take care of, while our mother is away."

"Excuse me?"

"God gave us to you to take care of until Mama comes back."

"Of course. What did you think I meant?"

I shrugged. "Plus, you already got Bug."

I pointed to the quilt on the floor where Bug lay on his side, legs in braces, eyes staring at nothing. He drooled and vocalized in the flat, toneless voice of a lost lamb or calf. Bug was big for a six-year-old, but Sister Coleman carried him everywhere. She would not put him in a wheelchair. I have no proof, but I believe it was Bug who first brought Sister Coleman to the tents. Each time a revival came to town, she lugged him to the front row and waited.

Gary and I were physically everything Bug was not, but emotionally we were a mess. My brother was a bed wetter with a nervous stutter and was prone to visions or nightmares, depending on your perspective. I was a thief who lied to cover my transgressions and committed the unpardonable childhood sin of sassing and talking back on a regular basis. Maybe Sister Coleman did not know this about us, or maybe she thought she could change us for the better. She made sure we went to bed and woke up at the same time, ate three meals a day, and visited the doctor when we were sick. She even took us on vacation once. When I turned seven, she enrolled me in first grade and bought me new clothes to wear to school. My blouses were tucked in, my socks matched, and headbands kept my hair out of my face. I looked respectable for the first time since Mama left us in Houston. Within weeks, Sister Coleman had given us more toys and clothes than we had ever owned: stacks of books and a big easel for me, trucks and a G.I. Joe for Gary.

The only material thing we lacked during the year and a half we lived with the Colemans was a room of our own. Their home was the newest and most comfortable house we had lived in, but it had only two bedrooms; Sister Coleman and Bug slept in one and the sinner husband had the other to himself. I camped in the living room on a daybed and Gary slept on a single bed pushed against a corner of the den. The Colemans seemed to like each other, or to have once liked each other. They laughed together when Gary or I told funny stories, and at those moments their eyes held and a wistful look passed between them, but they never touched. Brother Terrell's ministry may have been responsible for the rift between the Colemans. Women who followed the ministry often ended up alienated from their husbands. Sometimes men complained of the money their wives gave and sometimes they said the preacher had taken their place in their wives' affections. Brother Terrell explained his effect by paraphrasing Jesus: "I have not come to bring peace, but a sword, and a man's enemies will be of his own household."

Sometimes after school Sister Coleman picked me up and took me to her office, a three-room building surrounded by a dirt parking lot. On my first trip there, I was so distracted by the green metal vending machine in the hall (three kinds of snacks) that I didn't pay much attention to Sister Coleman's explanation of what kind of work she did. Until we walked into the main room. Teeth, sets of teeth, top and bottom, the whole pink and white inside of a mouth, many mouths, were scattered across counters, shelves, and the very table where Sister Coleman directed me to sit.

"I . . . I . . ." My hand flew across my mouth, as if to safeguard what was inside.

She nudged me toward the table. "Child, did you hear what I said?"

I shook my head no.

She took my hand away from my mouth. "What is it?"

I pointed around the room. "Whose are those?"

She laughed. "We make them at the lab, then bring them here for the employees and me to finish up."

I put my schoolbooks on the table and used them to nudge a set of dentures out of the way.

"They won't bite, you know."

I didn't know.

She walked back to the entry. "Come on out here. We'll get you a snack."

It took me a long time to choose between peanuts, orange crackers with cheese, and orange crackers with peanut butter. After changing my mind at least four times, I chose the peanut-butter crackers. I savored every bite, wiped the crumbs from my mouth, and crumpled the cellophane wrapper. "I could eat a dozen of those."

Life sometimes offers hints of what's to come, a foreshadowing that we can only decipher years later, if at all. People say, "I should've seen that comin'," but the signs are often subtle, saying one thing and meaning another. Once or twice a week we went with Sister Coleman to an abandoned movie theater where we met with about five other believers and "had church." These people, mostly women, were followers of Brother Terrell who had decided they could no longer tolerate the false doctrines of the institutionalized church. There was no minister and no music to accompany our strained renditions of old gospel choruses.

Someone, often Sister Coleman, opened the service with a prayer and asked if anyone had a testimony to share about how the Lord was moving in their lives. The Man Who Dreamed Hurricanes always had something to say. In his early twenties with tightly tucked shirts and a painful crew cut, the Man Who Dreamed Hurricanes regaled us with weather details from his latest vision. He said the Lord had given him the ability to see the storms before they hit so that he could warn us. Each week he set up his easel in front of the proscenium and, armed with a black Magic Marker and large flip tablet, became God's own weatherman.

"Last night the Lord showed me there's another tropical storm out there." He drew an ominous x somewhere in the vast blank space that represented the Caribbean. "It's gonna gather power until it turns into a storm as destructive as Hurricane Carla." He drew a scary swirled image with a black oval in the middle. "It will hit the Carolina coast and come right through Columbia." He drew a star to represent Columbia and little dashes to represent the path of the storm. South Carolina would be obliterated by hurricanes that year, thus saith the Lord.

Sister Coleman and her white-haired aunt Eunice sat in the wooden theater seats, nodding yes, yes. After service, women gathered around Weatherman and assured him he had a real gift, but no one stored up provisions, and no one made plans to leave the state. As it turned out, the hurricane season was one for the record books that year. In Florida.

As part of our bedtime routine, Sister Coleman read aloud to Gary and me from a book entitled *The Rapture*. The book weaves apocalyptic events into a story where characters wake to find that their Christian loved ones have been taken to heaven during the night, or raptured. Those left behind endure clouds of swarming insects. Rivers run in blood. Multiheaded beasts run through the streets. The sun burns the skin from their bones. And of course, the moon turns to blood too. The book turns the apocalypse into a story, and that story lived in my imagination in a way that sermons had not. Fear caused me to consider my sins in a more serious way; I did not want to be left behind when my mother and brother were raptured to heaven. Besides, Sister Coleman was so kind to me; she made me want to be good, really good, with no stains on my soul. One night as she closed the book, I looked into her eyes and told her about how Randall sometimes bribed me to touch him and how Pam and I took turns pretending to be the husband with each other.

"A girl with a girl? I've never heard of such a thing."

"Yes, ma'am. Does that mean I have a reprobate mind?"

She said she didn't know, but that I needed to kneel beside the bed and ask God for forgiveness. We prayed, and I cried so much I thought surely my sins had been washed away. Wrong. The next morning Sister Coleman announced Gary and I could no longer play together without adult supervision.

I was confused. "What do you mean? What do we do?"

She gave me a long, meaningful look. "Nothing. That's the point. You do nothing. You stay away from each other unless there is a grown-up in the room."

I thought she might relent, but she didn't. When Gary started kindergarten a few months later, she would not let us walk to school together. She made him leave first and let me go a few minutes later. She didn't know that Gary waited for me behind a bush just around the corner and that we finished the walk together.

The more Sister Coleman knew about me, the less she liked me. One day after meeting with my first-grade teacher after school, she strolled into the empty classroom where I waited, grabbed my arm, and squeezed it hard. Her voice was steady and even.

"Get to the car now."

I stumbled through the hallway and into the parking lot, with her hand heavy on my shoulder.

Once we were in the car, she turned the key in the ignition and pumped the gas pedal. The engine sputtered to life and she turned and glared at me.

"Why are you disappearing into the woods with boys during recess?"

"I'm not."

"They've seen you."

"It's boys and girls."

She gripped the wheel and gunned the engine. "You are a perverse child."

I didn't know the word "perverse," but I could tell it didn't mean anything good. I tried to explain.

"We go into the woods so they can repent and give their hearts to the Lord. I'm doing God's work."

It was true. I witnessed to my classmates during recess, then took them into the woods, where I had them kneel down and ask Jesus to be their personal savior. Tammy, the prettiest girl in my class, had almost gotten the Holy Ghost after only a few minutes of coaching.

"One boy said you kissed him."

"He said he wouldn't repent if I didn't."

She put the car in gear and we pulled out of the parking lot and away from the school.

"If you're so concerned about the Lord's work, why did you steal cookies from another little girl? And why did you lie when the teacher asked you about it? She *knows* you did it."

There it was, another sin. Two with the lie. Three if you counted the kiss, and I had to, considering how much I liked that boy.

I was not surprised when Sister Coleman began to favor Gary over me. As the chosen one, Gary dwelt in a land of perpetual smiles and kindnesses.

"Here, honey, let me help you with those buttons."

"Do you want another sucker?"

Or turning to her old aunt Eunice, "He's just the sweetest child I've ever seen."

She answered most of my questions with a terse yes or no and little eye contact. Questions that required further explanation were ignored. Her emotional coldness made me miserable, but I understood and accepted it as the penalty for my sins. I was always looking for ways to ingratiate myself with her. Once when we were on a long trip, I devised a game in which Gary counted gas stations and I counted churches. When Sister Coleman heard the rules, she sighed and responded exactly as I had anticipated.

"Honey, I'm afraid you'll always lose counting churches."

"That's okay. I don't mind."

The next time we stopped for gas, I got the sucker and the pat on the head, and Gary got nothing. I remained the favorite for a day or two, until I felt so guilty and so bad for my brother, I engineered my own fall from grace.

I pulled out a bag of books I kept under the daybed. In the bag was the oversize Bible storybook my mother had bought and for some reason Queenie and Rita had inscribed. The inscription read: "To David and Betty. May God bless and keep you always. Queenie and Rita." Everyone called my mother by her middle name, Carolyn, but Betty was her first name, and it was the name she had used in Houston when living incognito with Brother Terrell. I handed the book to Sister Coleman and asked if she would read us a story. She opened it and studied the inscription.

"Do you know what this says?"

I shrugged.

"Why do you think this is addressed to David and Betty? Isn't Betty your mother's first name?"

I nodded. "Yes, but everyone calls her Carolyn. They probably meant Betty Ann. David and Betty Ann. That book probably belonged to Pam and Randall."

She knew I had engineered her seeing the inscription and that I was lying about the ownership of the book, but she didn't know why. I didn't know either. What I knew but could not articulate was that sometimes I felt so awful, so sinful, that I wanted to pull everything down around me, wanted in fact for everything to fall on me like the dead weight of a felled tree and crush me into the ground. Maybe that "everything" was Sister Coleman. Tim-ber.

Sister Coleman opened the door to her lab and flicked on the light. My eyes lingered on the vending machine as we walked past and entered the main room. It was a Saturday and the employees were gone. Gary and Bug had stayed at the house with the sinner husband. I moved the teeth aside and placed my books on the table. The plan was for me to read and do homework while she caught up on work. She fished her white lab coat off the rack and pulled it on while I lost myself in a library book. A package of crackers fell onto my opened book. I looked up. She smiled and turned to study the dentures on the shelf. I opened the package, stuffed the crackers in my mouth, and went to the water fountain for a long drink.

I sat down at the table and picked up my book. Then I said what I always said. "I could eat a dozen of those."

Sister Coleman left the room without saying anything and went to the entryway. I followed. She put a nickel into the slot and pulled the knob. Then instead of handing me the package, she put in nickel after nickel and pulled the knob again and again. She handed the packages to me.

"Go sit down." Her voice had a flat, mechanical sound and there was an odd feeling in the room, a feeling of excitement and dread and something

I could not name. I walked to the main room and placed twelve packages of crackers on the table.

"I told you to sit down."

I pulled the chair out from the table a bit, cringing as its legs scraped against the floor, and wedged myself into it.

"Now, eat."

"But I can't eat all these."

"You said you could eat a dozen of them."

"I didn't mean it."

She wrapped her hand around the back of my neck. Her palm was cool and firm.

"You said you could eat a dozen, and you will."

Each package contained four cracker-cheese sandwiches made up of two crackers each. Eight crackers per package, ninety-six crackers in all. I made my way through package after package. Sister Coleman sat beside me, spine erect, knees and ankles together, hands relaxed and folded in her lap. A small, secretive smile settled on her lips. After a while, she stood up and began to check the teeth on the counter that ran along the longest wall of the room. She hummed under her breath. My mouth grew drier with each cracker until I began to gag. She glanced over her shoulder and pointed at the water fountain. I ran for a drink, careful not to let any of the mush in my mouth escape.

That night as Sister Coleman tucked me in, she planted a warm, dry kiss on my forehead, the first in a long time. "You know I love you chillens. I don't know what I'd do without you."

After dinner one evening, Sister Coleman called me and Gary to sit with her on the couch. She folded us into her arms just as she had when she first welcomed us to her home.

"There's something I need to tell you. It may be hard to understand at first, but it's better for everyone. Your mother has officially given you all to me. You're going to live here from now on."

Gary looked stunned. "You mean forever?"

She patted his arm and smiled. "Yes, honey. Forever."

I jumped off the couch and faced her, hands on my hips. "I don't believe you!"

She looked startled. "What do you mean?"

"Our mother wouldn't do that."

"Really? I have something to show you."

She stood and walked from the living room into her bedroom. I sat back down on the couch with Gary and whispered in his ear, "Don't worry. It's not true."

Sister Coleman walked back into the living room, holding a stack of papers. With her reading glasses on the tip of her nose and her sensible shoes, she looked like someone's favorite aunt. She flipped through the pages, licking her fingers in between to ensure she was turning only one page at a time.

"This is a legal document your mother signed, giving you both to me."

She pulled out a page and handed it to me. Our mother's signature was at the bottom.

Sister Coleman kept talking. She would adopt us. We would be a family. She wanted us to call her Mama. Wouldn't we like that? We nodded yes.

"Yes what?"

Gary spoke up. "Yes, Mama."

He gave her a quick hug. "Can I go now?"

"Go ahead, sugar. I'll call you for dinner."

The worst had happened. We had lost our mother. There was nothing left to say. Nothing left to do. I curled up on the daybed and fell asleep.

Gary and I found it almost impossible to eat after Sister Coleman's announcement. Food stuck in our throats, and breakfast especially proved difficult. Every morning Sister Coleman placed giant bowls of oatmeal in front of us and told us to eat. The cereal refused to stay down. We started each day hanging over the toilet and throwing up. I was late for school almost every day.

One morning when I began to gag, Sister Coleman would not let me run to the restroom. I was going to eat my breakfast, she said, no matter what. Again that cool, firm palm on the back of my neck. I swallowed, took a bite, and the oatmeal came back up. My cheeks bulged. I flailed and scrambled to get up, but she held me in the chair. I threw up in the bowl and all over the table. When I finished she held my face and wiped it gently with a napkin. Something sour streamed from my nose. I was sorry, really sorry. She smiled and handed me the spoon.

"That's okay, hon. Just clean your bowl."

"But . . ."

"Go ahead. Eat it." She held my head over the bowl.

I cried and pleaded and ate what was in my bowl.

After a while, she replaced the oatmeal with mackerel. It was salty and fishy and the vomiting lasted all morning.

We never told Sister Coleman's husband what was happening in his suburban home, and we never told her aunt Eunice. White-haired Aunt Eunice sometimes sat with us while the Colemans worked. Her body was soft and comforting as a favorite pillow and she had enough patience to teach a seven-year-old to embroider. She shuffled her thick legs behind a walker and talked about the day the Lord would heal her.

"I just want to walk without pain one more time before I die."

The three of us, Sister Coleman, Aunt Eunice, and I, were desperate for God's attention: Sister Coleman for Bug, and Aunt Eunice for her legs. As for me, I prayed all the time for forgiveness. I was sure I had done something to make God hate me. How else to explain my mother's abandonment. How else to explain Sister Coleman, a woman who couldn't decide whether she loved or hated us. How else to explain why no matter how hard I prayed or what I promised, no deliverance came.

Sister Coleman strapped Bug into his special seat in the back of the car and Gary and I climbed in beside him. Aunt Eunice lowered herself into the front seat, her walker stowed in the trunk. Sister Coleman slid behind the wheel. Her aunt grabbed her hand. "I believe Bug is going to walk out of the tent tonight, Lib. And I may leave my walker at the altar and walk out with him."

The tent was smaller than Brother Terrell's but everything else about it looked and smelled like home. The dust from the cars driving across the field, the moldy canvas, the sawdust, the way people greeted one another.

"Sister Mayfair, how are you? Come on over here so I can hug your neck."

The familiarity filled me with despair. Sister Coleman marched us to the front row of the middle section, so that we could sit in front of the prayer ramp. She had me spread a pallet for Bug on the ground. Once he was settled, she bowed her head. Aunt Eunice positioned her walker to the side of her chair and eased herself into the seat.

She looked around, bright and expectant. She had told me once that she never left disappointed.

"Even if you didn't get healed?"

"That just means the healing is still out there waiting for me."

I covered my eyes with my hand and pretended to pray. The organ music started, and it sounded so familiar that for a moment I thought it might be my mother sitting at the Hammond. I opened my eyes and raised my head. I recognized the woman. Evelyn. She had approached Mama at one of Brother Terrell's revivals and said she wanted to play just like her one day.

I recognized the preacher too: Ronnie Coyne, the man who could see through a glass eye. A picture of Brother Coyne would eventually end up on the cover of the *Weekly World News*, a tabloid cousin of the *National Enquirer*, under the headline, IT'S A MIRACLE AND A MYSTERY, SAY DOCTORS. That night he yelled into the microphone for a long time, then he taped up his good eye and had someone write a few words on paper and hold it in front of him. He read the words aloud and everyone went crazy. Once he had quieted the crowd, he invited them to form a prayer line. Sister Coleman knelt on the quilt beside Bug and gently rolled him into a crumpled sitting position. She threw his arms around her neck and struggled to her feet, one arm under his bottom, one cradling his back. She carried him through the line and the preacher laid hands on him. The tent workers helped them down the ramp, Bug's head lolling on his mother's shoulder, legs dangling, useless, outlined in the heavy metal braces. Sister Coleman put Bug back on his pallet and sat down. Up on the prayer ramp, Aunt Eunice planted the walker in front of her and pulled one leg and then the other until she was even with the preacher. Her lips moved constantly as Brother Coyne laid hands on her, then it was back down the ramp. When she reached the ground, she took one hand off the walker and raised it into the air, and then she raised the other one. Maybe this would be the night. She lowered her hands to the walker and pulled herself back to her seat. She sat down and leaned over to her niece.

"The Lord's presence was so sweet tonight, Lib. Thank you for bringing me."

Then it was over and we were packing up. Sister Coleman gathered up Bug. "Donna, get the pallet and bring it to the car."

I folded the quilt, tucked it under my arm, and turned to follow her out of the tent. But before I could think twice about it, before Sister Coleman could stop me, I grabbed Gary's hand and ran toward the back of the platform. I had not known I was going to take off, had not thought about it beforehand. Sister Coleman called after us.

"Come back here. Where are you going?"

"To visit people," I called over my shoulder.

I pushed the canvas curtain aside and pulled Gary around the tent man who asked us what we were doing back there. I had to find Evelyn before the tent man told us to leave, before Sister Coleman came to get us. I spotted her standing in a small group with her back to us. She was tall and slim like my mother, with brown hair that fell almost to her waist. Like my mother, she wore a long skirt that dragged the ground. I ran up to her and grabbed her arm.

"Evelyn. Do you remember me, I mean, us?"

She turned and studied us, her brows coming together. My chest heaved. After a moment she knelt down and brought her face close to mine.

"Of course I do." She reached out and hugged me. "You look just like your mama."

I broke into sobs.

"What is it? Is your mom here?" She peered over our heads.

"No. I mean no, ma'am."

"Where is she?"

"I don't know. We live with Sister Coleman now."

"Who is Sister Coleman?"

I felt a hand on my back and looked up. Sister Coleman stood over us, her mouth pulled into that thin line that was something between a smile and a grimace. "I hope these kiddos aren't bothering you."

Evelyn stood up. "No, not at all. I know their

mother. She still traveling with Brother Terrell?"

"They were on a mission trip to Central America and Mexico last I heard. I expect they are back in the states by now. I've got to get these chillens to bed. School tomorrow."

Without saying anything more to Evelyn, we turned and walked away.

She called after us, "Y'all visit again before the revival is over."

As we stepped through the curtain, Sister Coleman warned me. "Don't ever run away like that again. Do you hear?"

I nodded.

"And pick up that quilt, you're dragging it through the sawdust."

We went back to the revival every night so that Sister Coleman and Aunt Eunice could offer their burdens to the Lord. Every night Evelyn waved to us from the platform and we waved back. I wanted to talk with her again, but I did not know how to bring about a meeting without risking the wrath of Sister Coleman. The night before the revival ended, Evelyn's mother came and sat with us before service began. She carried two large brown grocery sacks and without asking Sister Coleman for permission, she handed one to Gary and the other to me.

"Evelyn wanted to give y'all something before we left."

We held the sacks in our laps until Sister Coleman nodded her permission. Gary pulled a canister of Tinkertoys from his bag and I lifted a doll, about twenty-four inches tall, from mine. She had two tiny teeth, reddish-blond braids, and pink cheeks. She looked old-fashioned, like a picture of a child in a storybook.

"I've never in my whole life seen a doll like this."

Evelyn's mother laughed. "Probably because they don't make them anymore. It was Evelyn's first doll. She wanted you to have her. Let me show you something."

She took the doll and stood her on the ground. "Look, if you hold her hand, she walks."

I walked the doll through the sawdust while Evelyn's mom talked with Sister Coleman. "Evelyn has the doll clothes in her purse. She wants to give them to Donna after church, and to say good-bye to the kids before we leave."

I waited for Sister Coleman to say no, but she said yes, and the two women hugged each other's necks.

"Good, then. See you kids a little later."

After service that night Gary and I headed behind the platform. I stood by the ladder that led to and from the platform. I needed to make sure I caught Evelyn as soon as she came down. She would play until everyone had left the platform and most of the congregation had gone home. I knew this would take a few minutes, but my eyes would not leave the little half gate at the back of the platform. I strained to hear the last note. *Any minute now, any minute.* Silence. There it was. The gate opened, and I saw Evelyn backlit on the top step, her face in shadow.

As soon as she was within reach, I grabbed her hand. "I need to talk to you. Please. Right now. Hurry."

She stepped to the side and I told her everything, about the vomit and the crackers and how Sister Coleman said our mama had given us to her. She dropped into a nearby chair.

"What do you mean, gave you to her?"

"She said she was our new mama." Gary and I both were crying.

Evelyn sat down and pulled Gary into her lap. "Wait a minute. You threw up and she made you eat it? You're not making this up?"

She had to believe me. I talked faster and louder. "She feeds us this salty fish for breakfast, Evelyn. She does it to make us sick. She likes us to throw up, we can tell."

Gary nodded as I talked. People around us were staring. Evelyn's mother joined us. "What's going on here?"

"I'll tell you later, Mom."

Evelyn's arm encircled me. "I am going to find your mama. It will be okay. I promise. Don't say a word to Sister Coleman. Can you do that?"

We nodded. Gary climbed out of her lap, and we turned to go.

"Wait." Evelyn opened her purse and handed the doll clothes to me. "Remember, not a word, even if she asks. I'll handle this. Don't worry."

I worried all the way home that evening, through a long night of tossing and turning, and during school the next day. Life could get harder, much harder, if Sister Coleman found out I had confided in Evelyn. And what if Evelyn could not find our mother? Or what if she did, and our mother did not want us back? What else could I have done?

I walked home from school, noticing how the homes were so well cared for, no peeling paint, no dirt yards, gardens dark and empty, at least until next spring. I came to Sister Coleman's house and looked up the driveway. Empty. She was still at work, so she must not know. When I started second grade, Sister Coleman had given me a key to wear around my neck and told me I was old enough to stay by myself after school some days until she could make it home. I pulled the key over my head and fitted it into the front-door lock. Inside, everything looked exactly as it did every other afternoon. I didn't know what to do with myself, so I followed my routine. I made up the daybed and wandered through the kitchen into the wood-paneled den. A large white tablet stood on my easel, waiting for pictures and stories that had never come. Just beyond the easel, sliding glass doors framed a backyard made up of green on green. We should have been happy here, but things had gone wrong. I had helped them go wrong. Why had I told Sister Coleman things I knew would make her hate me?

A car pulled into the driveway. Car doors opened and closed. The front door creaked. *Might as well get it over with.* I trudged into the living room. Sister Coleman stood with her back to me, facing the door. Bug's head rolled on her shoulder. "Come on, Gary. We don't have all day." She bent down and placed Bug on the daybed, then turned to face me.

"We've got a lot to do here tonight. Some people made sure of that." She walked toward me. "I guess you're happy with yourself, Miss Smarty-Pants. I hear you told Evelyn how *mean* I was to you all."

She turned to my brother. "You think I'm mean, Gary?"

He shook his head no.

She bent down and pulled my face to hers. I stared at the crease between her thin, pale eyebrows. "You think your mama wants you? If she takes you back, it will be for a minute; then she'll send you to the next person who feels sorry for you. I wanted to give you kids a stable home, something you could count on, but you stabbed me in the back with your lies."

She raised her hand to slap me. My eyes met hers and she started to cry. Gary moved over to us and we put our arms around her.

"I'm sorry, Mama. Please don't cry. I'm sorry." I was sorry. For so many things.

Sister Coleman fed Bug and put him to bed. She asked us if we wanted dinner, and for the first time in months, we did. We ate grilled-cheese sandwiches and reminisced: about the time her husband took us fishing at the lake, the swinging bridge in the Smoky Mountains, the first time I saw her lab.

"You had the funniest look on your face. I really believe you thought we were robbing people of their teeth."

We all laughed, and I was sorry again.

After dinner, we packed our clothes, books, and toys into a small suitcase and a few paper bags, and sat down to wait for Evelyn and her mother. Sister Coleman's husband came home and told us he would really miss us. He pulled us to him and I felt tears on his scratchy face. Aunt Eunice came by to wait with us. She gave me embroidery hoops and told me not to give up on embroidery or faith. Evelyn and her mom drove up late that evening to find all of us sobbing and hugging.

Sister Coleman handed our suitcase and sacks of books and toys to Evelyn and her mother. "These kids have been crying all evening."

Evelyn loaded us into the car and backed out of

the driveway. Once we were in the street, she turned to look at Gary and me sniffling in the backseat. "I don't understand. Don't you want to leave here?"

We nodded yes and continued sobbing.

"Why on earth are you crying? After everything she's done?"

We shook our heads and cried on.

After a few miles, Evelyn spoke up again. "I have some news from your mother." We stopped sobbing.

"Your mama didn't give you to Sister Coleman."

I sat up and moved my head close to the back of Evelyn's shoulder. "But I saw her handwriting on that paper."

"She gave her something called power of attorney. That way if there was an emergency, she could take you to the doctor."

"Really?"

"Really. She's in Baton Rouge, Louisiana. We'll be there in the morning."

I woke the next day as I always did, with the image of my mother's face fixed in my mind, only this time it didn't recede. She looked at me through the car window, then the door opened and we tumbled into her. I buried my face in her neck and wept into her hair.

"You're here. You're really here."

Gary climbed all over her. "Mama, Mama, Mama," he called again and again.

"Yes, yes, I'm really here. It's okay. It's okay now."

That morning in Baton Rouge Mama promised she would never leave again. By the time the revival ended, she had changed her mind.

"It's just for two or three months, kids. There's no one to play for the revivals right now, and until we find someone, I have to do it."

She said it broke her heart to leave us, and I believe it did. She cried and cried as she climbed into the backseat of someone's old black Chevy. My brother, a quiet, easygoing kid, fell apart as the car drove away. He climbed the chain-link fence and when someone pulled him down, he kicked and flailed and cut his legs on the pointed metal pieces at the top. Blood ran in small streams down his legs as he raced the length of the fence howling, "No," his mouth stretched into a wide, red *o,* like the entrance to a fun house. My mom's face, framed in the car's rear window, wore a look of surprise. Her arm waved from side to side, good-bye, good-bye. I watched the car grow smaller and smaller until it disappeared into that thin space where heaven and earth meet.

The End-Time

1966–2001

SUPPOSE YOU BREAK THIS WORLD TO BITS,
ANOTHER MAY ARISE.

Johann Wolfgang von Goethe,
Faust

Chapter Seventeen

GOD WORKS IN SEVENS. THE RAINS CAME seven days after Noah shut the door of the ark. Egypt had seven fat years and seven lean years. The book of Revelation refers to seven churches, seven spirits, seven golden candlesticks, seven stars, seven lamps, seven seals, seven horns, seven eyes, seven angels, seven trumpets, seven thunders, seven thousand slain, seven heads, seven crowns, seven last plagues, seven golden vials, seven mountains, and seven kings. The only thing missing is seven swans a-swimming and the tune to "The Twelve Days of Christmas."

Gary and I wandered through seven households in three years, and then Mama reappeared. Her return was as unfathomable as her departures. One day we looked up and there she stood. The kind and seemingly mute old couple we had lived with in Baton Rouge was gone. Baton Rouge was gone. We blinked and found ourselves back in Houston, living with Mama in a series of run-down apartments, each with its own built-in tragedy.

The yellow cinder-block ghetto that housed our first apartment backed up to what I remember as a highway. Mama told us not to go near the road, but the store on the other side exerted a powerful pull, and one day we could no longer resist. We stood by the side of the road with a group of kids, waiting for a break in the traffic, one leg in front of the other, rocking forward and back. An older boy was supposed to shout, "Go!" But before he could say anything, Gary wrenched his hand from mine. A horn blared. Tires screeched. Cars slipped all over the road and came to rest at odd angles. A woman opened her car door and began to wail. I ran toward her. My brother lay on his back, surrounded by chrome bumpers and grills. Blood covered his forehead. He tried to sit up, but the woman pushed him down. He told her he was okay, that Jesus had protected him, and pulled a Sunday-school picture of Jesus from his back pocket to show her. Someone called an ambulance. Someone else ran to our apartment where Mama was visiting with Brother Terrell. She arrived, hair, tears, and snot flying, and crawled into the ambulance with Gary. They returned from the hospital a few hours later. Gary had a Band-Aid on his forehead and the picture of Jesus crumpled in his hand. For months he told every person he knew, every person he met, the story of how Jesus had saved his life. I felt more wretched each time he recounted the story. If I had watched over my brother the way I was supposed to, if I had resisted the neighbor kids when they said, "Aw, come on," my brother would not have been in harm's way and Jesus could have gone about his business elsewhere.

After Gary's accident, we moved to an apartment located far from the highway but in the heart of sin city. Strippers and sad-eyed drunks in need of encouragement populated the new complex. When my mother wasn't writing articles for Brother Terrell's magazine, she was "trying to help" the neighbors. She listened to long, troubled sagas over coffee in our kitchen or theirs and told them about how God could straighten out their lives. Late one night, the husband of one of those neighbors muscled his way through our front door and grabbed Mama by the throat. He pushed her through the living room, where Gary and I slept, to her bedroom. Just as he began to tear off her clothes, Brother Terrell called. Mama grabbed the phone and the man, thinking that Brother Terrell was in town and on his way over, ran out of the apartment. According to Mama, God and Brother Terrell saved her from being raped. While she fended off the would-be rapist, Brother Terrell was busy discussing a business proposition with another preacher after a late-night tent service. My mother says the Lord caused Brother Terrell to become so distracted and so uncomfortable that he was compelled to break off conversation with the man midsentence and call her. Gary and I slept through the incident and woke to policemen swarming our apartment and our mother's shaky voice recounting what had happened. The police advised her not to press charges, telling her the man's lawyer would try to make her look like a whore. What seems likely, though hardly fair, is that Brother Terrell's visits to our apartment may have figured into their assessment. A single woman with two kids who allowed a married man to come and go from her apartment would not have been in much of a position to file attempted-rape charges in 1964.

I was in third grade when we landed in the *Leave It to Beaver* house, a white two-bedroom frame job with green shutters, shaded by big trees and surrounded by grass instead of dirt. I began to do well in school, and my teacher moved me to the top reading group. She gave me permission to check out books designated for fourth- and fifth-graders and I did so at every opportunity, even though I had to skip words, paragraphs, and sometimes most of what was on the page. I dreamed of becoming an artist and drew pictures of three-legged horses: one leg at either end and a third, foreshortened, coming out of the rear of the belly. Inexplicably, the girls who lived on our street began to like me. I had been friends with boys, but other than Pam Terrell, I had never had a girl for a friend. They taught me to play Barbies and we gathered in their living rooms to watch

The Monkees or sat on the grass and sang Supremes songs as loud as we could.

I began to feel a part of instead apart from the world. My mother let it happen, and in some ways she encouraged it. She gave me a hot-pink transistor radio through which poured the satanic sound of rock and roll. The Lovin' Spoonful. The Monkees. The Beatles. Sam Cooke. I plugged in my earpiece when Mama was around, to keep from aggravating her. It seems odd that my mother would allow me to listen to rock and roll. She wanted Gary and me to fit in, to belong in the communities in which we lived. Or more accurately, she wanted us to avoid the pain of not fitting in. Her childhood stories had always revolved around the theme of being chosen, called by God. As I matured, the flip side of her theme surfaced: She was the kid who never fit in, the girl whose dedication to God was not always by choice. The missed field trips (too worldly and no money). The unrequited longing to play high-school basketball (Holy Rollers didn't wear shorts). The fantasy of strutting down the field as a majorette (something Mama's preacher father wouldn't have let happen even if God hit him over the head with a baton). Mama was caught in a tug-of-war between what she wanted for us and what she thought the Lord required.

Brother Terrell dropped in about every three weeks, on his way to and from revivals. He arrived in the middle of the night, and when Gary and I woke up the next morning, we found the briefcase he now carried sitting by the living-room door and his pile of change on the kitchen counter. A carefulness settled over the house during his visits, but we didn't talk about it. I don't remember what we talked about. Family life was deep space. No road maps. No signs. Just light-years of uncharted territory. Brother Terrell and Mama once again held themselves out as brother and sister in the neighborhood. At the tent revivals and the independent Holy Roller church we attended, Uncle David morphed back into Brother Terrell. And in the privacy of our home, he was someone else entirely: the man who slept in my mother's bed. I never knew what to call that person. The laws of behavior were determined by which role Brother Terrell played: Uncle, Man of God, or Mama's Whatever. The basic rules were: (1) Run to meet the uncle's car and introduce him to neighbors as Mama's favorite brother without looking shifty; (2) Act shy around the Man of God under the tent and wait for him to invite a hug; (3) Try not to gasp when the Whatever smooches Mama long and hard on the lips. The situation made me tense, but I did not find it especially confusing. I understood our life with Brother Terrell occupied a parallel universe, and that my job was to tap-dance between worlds without stepping in anything.

My mother stumbled about for days after Brother Terrell left, muttering about how she was going to write a book about "this whole sorry mess," but she never did. Her favorite antidote for loneliness was to drive us down the road to the doughnut shop across from the drive-in theater. She ordered six glazed and three tiny cartons of milk at the drive-thru window, pulled around the building with the winking fluorescent lights, and parked the old Ford with its nose toward the drive-in. The three of us sat in the front seat and gorged on doughnuts and every image that flickered across the giant screen. We strained to catch any bit of dialogue from *Cat Ballou*, *Born Free*, *The Dirty Dozen*, and my favorite, *Bonnie and Clyde*. I argued with Mama on occasion that it couldn't be more of a sin to actually drive in to the theater and listen to the movie than it was to watch in silence across the street.

"Fine. We'll stay home, then."

Gary rolled his eyes and asked me why I couldn't for once just let well enough alone. We joined forces and pleaded and when the sun went down, we headed back to the doughnut shop to watch Bonnie bounce like an unstrung puppet to the *tat tat tat* of the machine guns, the only sound that drifted across the street with absolute clarity.

Brother Terrell was putting up the tent in Dallas, and though Houston was four to five hours from

Dallas, Mama said we were going. Our tent-revival attendance had become spotty. There was school and there was also the matter of keeping our secret life with Brother Terrell a secret. When we did go, I didn't always get to see Pam. Like my mother, Betty Ann had retired from the tent circuit and settled down so that Pam and her other daughters could go to school. Randall traveled with his daddy and was omnipresent at the tent, though I am unclear about where he went when Brother Terrell came to see us.

I was excited. Gary and I had not traveled with the tent in five years, but somehow I still considered it our real life, our real home. Plus, Mama told me that since it was summer, Pam would be there. In the days leading up to our trip, she knelt in front of me several times, rested her hands on my shoulders, and reminded me not to tell everyone everything I knew. Especially about Brother Terrell.

"You'll have to keep your mouth shut. Pam may try to pry information out of you, but you can't tell her anything, not even where we live. It's important."

"But why is it a secret?"

"It just is. And it's important for you to keep it. Do you hear me?"

"Yes, ma'am."

The gravity of these talks made me feel important. At ten, all I knew was my mother trusted me with her secrets, and that I had to be very careful not to say or do anything to betray her trust.

The world's largest tent took me by surprise, as it always did. When I remembered the tent, I thought of the smaller one with a crowd capacity of about three thousand, not this monster that could accommodate more than five thousand people. My mother ushered us down one of the central aisles. People stopped her to ask her where she had been and to tell her how good it was to see her. She said she had taken time off to raise her kids, that we needed her. The words sounded less convincing each time she said them.

"How long's it been since you traveled with Brother Terrell?"

"A year and half? Maybe two?"

"My word. Don't you miss it?"

"Every day."

Everyone said the music wasn't the same without Mama. It was good, but it didn't have the same anointing. Mama waved her hand as if to brush away the compliment, but I could tell she was glad to hear it.

We finally made it to our seats, middle section, second row. Brother Terrell liked to be able to see my mother. Before he started to preach, he would have her stand and introduce her as an old friend of the ministry. Everyone applauded. As my mother and Gary settled into their seats, I told Mama I wanted to go find Pam. I was anxious to show her my go-go boots and fishnet stockings. She said okay, and gave me a meaningful look. I walked until my boots pinched my toes and still I had not made it around the tent or seen anyone I recognized. The faces had changed since the time we traveled with the tent, or maybe the people I knew were just lost in the crowd. I was about to head back to my mother when a young woman walked by and touched my arm.

"Aren't chu gonna say hello?"

"Pam?" I recognized the voice and that was about all. Her hair was piled on top of her head in a mass of curls. She wore a simple white blouse, a dark knee-length straight skirt, and heels. She had breasts and hips. At twelve, she didn't look a day under seventeen. I felt the full weightlessness of my ten years, and the silliness of my paisley skirt and go-go boots. She gave me a quick hug, the kind where shoulders almost touch but not really.

I took her hand. "Hey, can I sit with you?"

"I guess so."

We took about four steps and she pulled her hand away.

"Donna, we're not kids anymore."

"What do you mean? I'm still a kid."

"Well, I'm not, and if we walk around holding

hands, people will think we're, you know, like those weird women."

"You mean hermaphrodites?"

"Sorta."

Half a football field away, someone waved. Pam waved back.

"You know Mary Sue?"

I shook my head no.

"She's Dockery's daughter. She's sixteen. We've been best friends for a while now."

The gates to the Garden of Eden clanged shut, and I was on the wrong side. I followed Pam to where the older girl waited for her. Mary Sue moved her purse off the one seat she had saved and Pam slid into it, pulling her skirt down, crossing her legs at the knee. I stood there in the tight space between the rows of chairs, trying not to look pitiful but unsure of what to do. A group of women who sat next to the girls took pity and moved down. I took a much-coveted seat next to Pam just as Brother Terrell took the platform.

He said he wouldn't preach that night, that he felt a spirit of discernment. This spirit enabled him to see what was wrong with people. He roamed the audience, calling people out and telling them all the details of their mostly invisible maladies. A young man hindered by a lack of confidence in his call to preach would from that day forward possess a new boldness for Christ. A woman suffered from female problems

297

for years. From the top of her head to the soles of her feet, she was now whole. Another woman had lost her family in a car accident and couldn't stop grieving. God mended her broken heart on the spot.

After two or three hours, Brother Terrell made his way back to the front, the music came up, and several men fanned out in front of the platform holding the big white offering buckets I remembered. Only there were more of them. Brother Terrell walked to the back of the platform and turned his back on the audience. When he turned around he was wearing a chef-style apron with pockets, lots of pockets. He nodded to the organist and the music became a low purr. The apron, he told the audience, was for love offerings, personal donations that went to support him and his family. Everything that went into the buckets was spent on the ministry and nothing else. Forty-five minutes later the offering was over and bills spilled out of the buckets and apron pockets. Brother Terrell took off the apron and spoke into the microphone.

"The Lord is showing me right now that there are a hundred people here tonight that need to prove God with a hundred dollars. You know who you are. If you stand with this ministry, that loved one who needs healing or deliverance will be taken care of."

About fifty people, mostly women, approached

the front and arranged themselves in a semicircle around Brother Terrell, heads bowed. He took the money from each of their hands and prayed with them individually. They stood straight and still, absorbing whatever it was Brother Terrell and God promised. As they walked away, Brother Terrell once again issued his call.

"There are fifty more of you out there. God is dealing with you right now. Come on up here and help us take the message of Jesus to hundreds of thousands in India who have never heard his name. We need your support."

Another twenty made their way down the ramp. "I'm not asking for me. I'm asking for God. You better think twice about denying God."

Thirty minutes of coaxing and mild threats yielded a total of about eighty believers willing to part with a hundred dollars. In the end Brother Terrell handed out twenty pledge envelopes addressed to his office in Dallas. The Lord would have to rely on a lick and a promise to get the rest of his ten thousand dollars.

As the service wound down, Pam leaned over and asked if I wanted to come back to the motel and spend the night with her. She put her arm around me. "Don't look so shocked. Don't you know I love you, Donna?"

My mother gave me permission to go with Pam. Mary Sue drove us to Mama's room, where we picked up my pajamas and toothbrush, and then we went back to their motel. We turned past the blinking NO VACANCY sign (believers had filled the place) into the parking lot of a moldering cinder-block motor court, the same kind of place we had stayed in on the road from time to time as kids. Brother Terrell had since graduated to the Holiday Inn, as had my mother. I couldn't believe how grown-up we were when Pam put her key in the door. We were practically on our own. Mary Sue said good night and closed the door between the adjoining rooms. I brushed my teeth while Pam smeared something like Pond's Cold Cream over her face. She said she was traveling with her daddy all summer, on her own—well, except for Mary Sue. Her daddy paid the older girl to keep an eye on her.

"Mostly 'cause she needs the money. She's more of a friend than a babysitter." She tissued the white goop off her neck. "What do you wash your face with?"

"Soap. Sometimes."

I padded toward the bed. An off-white trench coat, hanging in the recessed area of the room that passed for a closet, caught my eye. I stopped and fondled the sleeve.

Pam eyed me in the mirror. "What is it?"

"Nothing. Whose coat?"

"Mary Sue's. Why?"

"Mama has one just like it."

"Well, Mary Sue's isn't some cheap raincoat.

It's a London Fog." She met my eyes and said in a very deliberate tone, "Daddy bought it for her."

There was something about the way she said "cheap" that sounded like a slur against my mother, and something about her daddy buying the coat for Mary Sue that felt like a threat to Mama. I let the sleeve fall from my hand and said in my most casual voice, "He bought one for Mama too." I turned my back and in an instant Pam had backed away from the sink and hurled herself on me and knocked me to the mildewed carpet.

She straddled my back and grabbed my hair, drawing my head back. With her other hand she twisted my arm behind my back. I yelled for her to get off me and she yelled for me to keep my mouth shut about her daddy. Mary Sue burst through the door and demanded to know what was going on.

"She tried to insinuate something about Daddy and her mama."

Mary Sue knelt beside us. "Let her up, Pam, come on." Her voice was low and soothing.

"I'll let her up when she takes it back."

"Get off me, you, you . . . you mean thing." I tried to flip over but couldn't.

"What do you want her to take back?"

"She said Daddy bought her mama a raincoat just like he bought you." She was crying. "Why would he buy her a coat, Mary Sue? Why would he?"

She let go of my hair. Mary Sue pulled her off me, and then turned to help me up. Pam buried her face in the older girl's chest. Mary Sue put her arms around her and rubbed her hands up and down her back, like an older sister, like a mother. Pam cried long, heaving sobs. I felt miserable and useless. I had used a seemingly casual remark as a weapon against a girl I loved like a sister, and worse, I had aimed it at what I knew was a tender spot. Mary Sue walked her to the bed and sat down beside her.

"Look, Pam, that coat don't mean nothing. Your daddy bought one a few months back for all the women who work for him. He bought one for Martha Joyce and Sister Sonnie and Brother Starrs's wife."

Pam snuffled. "Really?"

"Yes, really. Now you and Donna make up so we can all go to bed."

"Sorry" seemed a flimsy word, but it was all I had to offer. Pam and I hugged each other's necks and fell into bed, exhausted by everything we had said and all the tension created by what we had left unsaid. The next morning, when Mary Sue went to the tent service, Pam and I walked to the store. She pulled out twenty dollars—from her daddy, she said—and bought bags of notebooks, paper, files, pens, stamps, envelopes, and other office supplies. We went back to the room and played secretary. I filled out forms and Pam signed them. We wrote about twenty-five letters to people who didn't exist, sealed them in envelopes with fake addresses and real stamps, and dropped them in the out-box of the motel office. We ran back to the room and fell on the bed laughing. With our pretend work finished, we fixed each other's hair, put on Pam's best dresses, and pretended to be secretaries, then singers, then actresses. Ann-Margret and Sandra Dee, out on the town. We held out our pinkies and drank Coke from the stubby motel glasses. We giggled and vamped as the light outside deepened and shadow spread across the room. Pam was right; we were not kids anymore. At least we never would be again, not together. Mama picked me up early that evening before church started, and without a word of protest, I climbed in the car. It was time. I waved briefly through the dusty car window and turned to face the front, sad and relieved to be on my way.

Chapter Eighteen

LIFE CHANGED THE DAY I SLAMMED BILL Dodge's arm down for the third time on our front porch in Houston.

"Ta-da! I'm the arm-wrestling champ."

His face flushed and the red rushed all the way up and through his blond crew cut. He pulled himself up and stood by my front door, the same door he had walked out of so many times carrying a stack of Mama's homemade oatmeal cookies. His cheeks puffed a couple of times, and then he blew.

"That man is not your uncle, and everybody knows it!" He yelled loud enough for everyone on the block to hear, and hopped on his bike.

I ran after him. "You better pedal fast, weeny arms."

The veil of normalcy under which my family and I thought we were hidden had been ripped away. None of my friends had questioned the identity of the man I called Uncle David, not to my face. I put my dog, Prissy, in the basket of my bicycle and rode up and down the streets for hours, soothed by the motion.

That night at dinner Mama asked me what Bill had yelled. I told her it was nothing, that he hated losing to a girl, but I could tell by the way she looked at me that she knew better. A month or so later, she announced we were moving to the country. I blamed Bill Dodge, but larger forces orchestrated the move. I wept when I told my teacher. She tried to ease my misery by pulling down the state map in our classroom and tapping her long pointer at the exact center of the map.

"What do you see?"

I sniffled. "A red heart."

"That's where you're moving, to the heart of Texas."

I looked closer. Printed next to the heart was the word "Waco," the future scene of the Branch Davidian siege.

Waco was the cover story. It was the place I was told to say we were headed. This was part of Mama's and Brother Terrell's strategy to throw off the Communists or the Antichrist or perhaps Betty Ann (though no one said that), should they come looking for us. We actually landed six miles outside of Marlin, a tiny community thirty miles east of Waco. Still, it made me feel better to think of us living *close* to a city that looked like a valentine on the map. Any romantic imaginings vanished when I laid eyes on our new home, a secondhand trailer squatting a few feet off Highway 6 on a hard patch of ground that would have been completely barren except for two spindly trees that produced bushels of inedible pears and no shade. An old white house with peeling paint and rotting wood leaned to the left of the trailer. Long stretches of mud-clotted land with outcrops of mesquite trees, ramshackle barns, and outbuildings separated us from the patchwork houses of our neighbors. Barbed wire delineated property lines. Everyone lived far away from everyone else.

Mama tried to soften the blow. "You'll have your own bedroom! This is ours. We own it." When Gary and I remained unconvinced she added, "Look on the bright side, you can have more dogs."

My mother made good on her promise of more dogs, but they began dying soon after we moved in. First to go was Prissy, kicked to death by cows. Then we found Suzy, Prissy's replacement, dead on the highway. A giant, sweet-tempered German shepherd named Kelly met his fate there, as did Brutus, a black adolescent Great Dane whose first and last attempt to mount the long-legged and more experienced Guinevere had ended in a broken and bandaged penis. I spotted him one morning as I stepped out of the trailer. He lay stretched out on the far side of the two-lane road, his taped and splinted member glowing white against his dark fur. The neighbors shrugged and said too bad 'bout those dogs.

Gary and I had been raised by country people, but we were not country kids. Until we moved to Marlin, we had never cleaned a horse stall, rounded up cows (just wave your arms when they stampede toward you), ridden a horse, or raised an animal destined for the slaughterhouse. The kids who lived around us had plenty of experience at these things and had developed a mental and physical toughness we lacked. They sniffed out weakness and pretension like bloodhounds.

The first Monday Gary and I stepped up onto the school bus, it went silent. Twenty pairs of eyes took our measure. Why, oh why had I worn the go-go boots? Blood thrummed in my ears. I focused on the unshaven face of the bus driver. His cheeks hung down to his chin. His eyes drooped. His lips drooped. Someone had let the air out of this man a long time ago. Mama had taught me it was my Christian duty to lift up the downtrodden. I read the nameplate on the dash and said in my most grown-up, citified voice, "Good morning, Mr. Nix."

A dark, juicy wad issued from his mouth and landed with a splat in the big coffee can he kept beside his seat. He threw the bus in gear and we lurched forward.

That night at dinner, I told my mother about saying hello to poor old Mr. Nix. She looked at me with admiration.

"I hope you always have the gumption to do what's right."

"But how do you know what's right?"

"You feel it. Like you did on the bus this morning."

The next morning I stepped into the bus, took a deep breath, and said, "Good morning, Mr. Nix." Before I could sit down, a chorus of kids echoed in my own prissy falsetto, "Good morning, Mr. Nix." On Wednesday, a barrage of spitballs followed the chorus of mimics. On Thursday night, I prayed Mr. Nix would die in his sleep.

Gary and I stood in the middle of our caliche drive Friday morning, dreading that smear of yellow on the horizon, hoping as we would for the next two years that we had somehow managed to miss the bus. He picked up a smooth, round stone and with a flick of his wrist, sent it skipping one, two, three over the blacktop. We grinned at each other. He stepped back from the highway and stood beside me. We turned our heads and eyed the bus lumbering toward us. Gary ran his sneaker over the loose rocks, clearing a small path through them. "You don't have to do it. I don't think it makes him feel better about being disgusting and all." The bus huffed to a stop and the door opened. My brother looked over his shoulder before he stepped inside. "I won't tell."

I took my seat at the front of the bus that morning without saying a word. Dead silence. Followed by a hailstorm of spitballs and laughter.

My mother introduced herself to neighbors as Mrs. Ter-*rell,* with the emphasis on the last instead of the first syllable, a mispronunciation intended to throw off anyone who might connect Mr. Ter-*rell,* with Brother Terrell. They decided a certain amount of disguise was necessary, and Brother Terrell began to go incognito in lime-green leisure suits and straw fedoras. This in a community where Wranglers and cowboy hats were standard male dress. Then there were the big black Jackie O sunglasses he and my mother insisted on wearing indoors. A waitress who worked the dark cavern of Marlin's "nicest" restaurant once suggested they take off their sunglasses if they wanted to actually see the menu.

"Or you could stand under the Schlitz sign over there by the counter."

They raised their sunglasses slightly to peruse the menu and lowered them again when she returned to take our orders.

Brother Terrell fueled rumors with his habit of paying in cash for everything from the most expensive saddles in Barnett's Feed and Seed to land. A neighbor told us the townspeople speculated he was a professional gambler, mobster, drug dealer. He squinted at my mother in her dark glasses and waited for her to fill him in. She tried to dance around the question.

"Oh, he does a little of this and that." The neighbor pressed her and finally she said her husband was a traveling salesman. What did he sell? "Oh, cars, heavy equipment, land, things like that."

The neighbor said, "Uh-huh, I see."

Whatever people suspected, the great silver heist probably confirmed. The Lord revealed to Brother Terrell that as the Mark of the Beast approached, U.S. paper currency would lose its value and silver and gold coins would be the only money worth anything. Around the same time, he heard the government was withdrawing silver dimes, quarters, half-dollars, and silver dollars from circulation and replacing them with coins that had either less silver or no silver at all. He began to bring home sacks of change from the offerings.

Mama held a large cloth bag over my bed and the coins rushed from it like water through a broken dam. She emptied another and another. A metallic smell filled my closet-size bedroom. The smell was so strong I could taste it on my tongue. Mama shook another bag and hundreds of dimes fell onto the inverted cone-shaped mountain of coins. I thrust my hands into the pile, buried up to my wrists in money.

"Careful, now. You don't want to scatter everything." Mama stood over me, folding the bags in half one by one, running her fingers over the crease in each one, like she did the sheets when we folded laundry. She stacked the bags on my dresser and sat on the edge of my bed. She picked up a dime and held it between her thumb and pointer finger, turning it so the edge was toward me.

"You want to look for edges that are silver like this. We'll keep those." She threw the dime into a bucket on the floor, sifted through the pile of money again, and pulled out a second dime. "The ones that have this coppery edge? We'll give those back to Brother Terrell."

The mindlessness of sorting the coins appealed

to me. Mama brought peanut-butter sandwiches and milk and set them beside my bed, and we ate and sorted together. Over time we filled six to eight large trash cans with silver. We stored the trash cans in the old house that stood beside our trailer, next to the room where we stored hay and feed for the livestock. We padlocked the front and back doors of the house. The arrangement worked fine until my mother hired someone to feed the cows and horses. Maybe the guy was looking for feed and stumbled upon the coins or maybe he just took a peek one day. Either way, the next time Mama checked the trash cans, they were only three-quarters full. She balked at calling the sheriff. She said she felt bad for the man who worked for us, that he was poor and black and had a bunch of kids. She did not say that she was reluctant to explain to the sheriff why she kept so much money squirreled away in trash cans. Eventually she did press charges and the man went to jail for three months. We drove to his house each week while he was in jail and gave his wife a check for the same amount of money he had made working for us. It was the least we could do after putting temptation right in front of the man, Mama said. She bought a new lock for the doors, but she didn't move the money.

Not long after our move, my mother called Gary and me into the living room and made a somewhat breathless announcement. "I've got something to tell you both. Y'all sit there on the couch." She smoothed the full skirt of her shirtwaisted dress, sat between us, and took our hands. It was Mama's version of a June Cleaver moment. All I could think was, *Uh-oh, here we go*. She looked at Gary, then at me, and ran her tongue over her lips. "I know this move has been hard on you, leaving your friends and all. But something good has come from it. From now on, you can call Brother Terrell 'Daddy.'"

Gary broke into cheers. "We'll have a real daddy."

My brother called every man he spent more than ten minutes with "Daddy," so Brother Terrell's latest incarnation suited him. I had spent every year of my life since I was one living apart from my dad, but I had never thought he was gone for good until that moment.

Mama put her hand on my shoulder. "Donna, you've got that lip so far out, you could ride it to town."

I didn't say anything.

"I thought you loved Brother Terrell. What is it?"

I didn't know where to begin. There were so many "it's" piled one on top of the other in a big sticky mess. My real daddy. Pam's and Randall's real daddy. My mother's coming and going. Sister Coleman. Moving from one crappy place to the next. Always talking about the Truth, but living a lie. I did not know how to choose my words or pull apart the grievances. In the end it didn't matter. The words chose me.

"He is not our daddy! You are not his wife! This is all a big, fat lie!"

My mother's eyes met mine and in one awful instant I knew. This was the big "it." Her hand popped across my face. The slap registered, but the euphoria of saying what only seconds before had been unsayable and the righteousness of knowing I was *right,* numbed the sting. I could not stop myself. "The Bible says thou shalt not commit adultery, but you do it all the time."

"Do you just want to hurt me?"

I did want to hurt her and in the next second I didn't. "I'm sorry, Mama. I'm so sorry."

She wiped her tears with the back of her hand. "Well, for your information, men in the Bible usually had more than one wife. They took a woman into their tent and they were married. They didn't go through all the rigmarole we do today. In the eyes of God, we are married."

In the eyes of most people, Brother Terrell was still married to Betty Ann, but I decided to let that one go.

My mother waved her left hand through the air and said in the breathy voice of a new bride, "Aren't they beautiful?" Brother Terrell had given Mama a set of diamond-encrusted wedding rings he had pulled from the offering. When believers had no money to give or when they wanted to "prove God" for a miracle, they made an offering of their most treasured possessions. The thought was that the goods would be sold and the money transferred to the ministry, and that God would honor the sacrifice and answer the prayer of the giver. Jewelry, they dropped directly into the offering buckets. In the early years, Brother Terrell announced from the platform that we didn't have the time to sell the items, but people continued to give them anyway. He stopped making that announcement after a while. After the evening services, someone separated the trinkets from the money and put them into a different bucket. It wasn't unusual to see members of the evangelistic team at the back of the platform going through the jewelry and taking what they wanted. Sometimes they paid for it and sometimes they didn't. Mama contended that Brother Terrell always paid for what he took. He brought home several sets of china that we never used, silver, stereos, antique furniture, hand-woven Indian bedding. I was the only girl in fifth grade with a diamond watch. Mules kicked the china to bits. Someone tore holes in the Indian blankets. I lost the diamond watch. We didn't possess the capacity to value such things. They meant almost nothing to us.

The one exception was the rings. My mother

loved those rings. Every time we went to a revival and Brother Terrell asked people to prove God by digging deep and giving something they could not afford to give (he meant money), Mama slipped the rings from her purse and dropped them into the offering buckets surreptitiously. She took seriously the concept of proving God. She believed if she gave God everything she had, he would work things out so that she and Brother Terrell could be married properly and she could wear the wedding rings he gave her under the tent as well as out in the world. Brother Terrell fished the rings out of the offerings many times and gave them back to her. One night, someone got to the rings before Brother Terrell. He had to find another set and the cycle began again.

My mother believed she and Brother Terrell were soul mates ordained by God to be together to build a great ministry. He received the visitations, and she translated them into their own brand of theology and wrote articles under his name explaining the revelations. She encouraged his ambitions to take his ministry worldwide and helped him develop a strategy to do so. She believed he would "do right" by her. All she had to do was pray and keep the faith. I know all of this because when we were not arguing about her relationship with Brother Terrell, she confided in me. She had no one else. She kept her affair with Brother Terrell a secret from her family and the longtime friends she had made while traveling with the tent. Neither her family nor her friends knew where we lived. The neighbors she befriended thought she and her "husband" were flashy dressers and secretive, but they chalked it up to their citified ways. They had no idea how secret their lives really were. To talk with anyone other than me about what was going on would have been to betray what was most important to her: Brother Terrell and the ministry.

I was desperate for my mother to save herself, to save us. Especially after she told me she was pregnant. She said we would manage by keeping the baby a secret from everyone in the ministry, and from her family. When we traveled to the tent revivals, we would leave the baby with a sitter. Simple. I cast and recast the reasons she should leave Brother Terrell, out loud and to myself. He couldn't leave Betty Ann. The baby would grow up and someone someday would have to know the identity of the father. I told my mother that if Brother Terrell loved her, truly loved her, he wouldn't want her to be so sad. I thought clear, compelling arguments would make the difference. Instead they made me my mother's adversary. She couldn't stand to hear me say what she was thinking and our "talks" inevitably ended in argument.

People have called Brother Terrell a sociopath, but I don't think that's true. He had a conscience.

I woke to him crying in the middle of the night more than once, calling out again and again, "My kids, oh, my kids. What am I going to do about my kids? Oh God. My children."

The first time I heard him, I slipped out of my bed and felt along its edge until I found the door and pulled it back an inch or two. He was on his knees in the living room, holding his head in his hands. Mama held him and the two of them rocked to and fro in silhouette. A crescent moon grinned in the window behind them. *What the hell are you grinning at?* I eased the door shut, climbed back into the bed, and fell asleep with my fingers in my ears.

The road between sin and hell was turning out to be long and circuitous instead of short and direct. I could deal with that. On days my mother dropped Gary and me off in town to spend the afternoon wandering in and out of stores, I rolled up my knee-length skirts to hit midthigh and flirted with older boys. We set up meetings in alleyways and in nearby houses where I let them kiss me, keeping their tongues out of my mouth and their hands away from restricted zones. On occasion I smoked and said "damn." My brother charged me a percentage of my allowance not to tell. It's strange to think that our moral code was such that this delinquent behavior did not make me feel half as guilty as saving up to buy my first pair of jeans. When I pulled on those pants, I was bucking one of the strongest and most visible tenets of holiness. Mama told me to take them off, but I wouldn't. She stalked me through the fake-wood-paneled trailer, paraphrasing scripture in Deuteronomy: "It is an abomination for a woman to wear that which pertaineth to a man." Not just a sin, but an abomination, she stressed. That meant it was something God hated. I reminded her that a few verses down it warns against plowing with an ox and an ass together and allowing men with crushed testicles to enter the assembly of the Lord.

She put her face so close to mine I could count the pores on her nose. "And we don't do those things, do we?"

I backed out of slapping range. "How would we know? I don't see anyone asking the preachers to drop their pants before they step on the platform."

All those long talks about Brother Terrell and their future had begun to shift the balance of power between my mother and me. She relented finally, saying I could wear my filthy old pants to ride horses, but that was it. I walked outside wearing my abomination and climbed on Red Rose, the bag of bones I had spent the last year trying to ride. I thought she might throw and trample me for my sins, but she settled for her usual routine of scrubbing me against the barbed-wire fence until she was bored, then plodding back to her stall and standing there while I unsaddled her. It was business as usual, but this time my legs weren't bleeding. Thank you, Levi Strauss. Once I had those jeans on, I didn't want to take them off. It was so much easier to run, jump, and play baseball. Plus, my skinny legs looked better covered up. Mama threatened to burn them, so I hid whichever pair I wasn't wearing under my mattress.

I sat in the backseat of Brother Terrell's Thunderbird and smoothed the flounces on my fanciest dress. I always wore a dress when he was around, out of respect, and maybe a bit of fear, too, though he had not come after me with a belt in years. Gary sat beside me and flexed his bicep muscleman-style. "Feel it, just feel it."

I ignored him and looked out the window. The car rocked toward the local diner, with Brother Terrell driving in his signature style: one foot on the gas, the other on the brake, accelerating and slowing down, accelerating and slowing down. Mama sat beside him, almost glamorous in her big sunglasses. Life looked so much better from the white leather interior of the T-Bird. I contemplated ordering something sophisticated for dinner, maybe a club sandwich and a TaB. We were almost to the city-limits sign when Mama turned to Brother Terrell, adjusted her sunglasses, and made one of her announcements.

"David, Donna has been taken over by a lesbian spirit."

Gary lowered his arm and we stared at each other. Brother Terrell turned toward Mama, and then back toward the road so fast he jostled his fedora. A lesbian spirit was as bad as it got in our circle. I didn't know whether to speak up or wait until she said something more, something I could defend myself against.

Brother Terrell straightened his hat and shook his head. "What are you talkin' about?"

Mama sniffed and lifted her chin in the air. "She never wants to wear anything anymore but pants."

I envisioned myself rolling in the sawdust with Brother Terrell trying to pin me down and cast the devil out of me. I was relieved to hear him tell my mother, "Look, we need to, uh, you know, I think, well, let's pray about this, okay?"

Before she could answer, he punched in his new eight-track tape and turned up the volume. I was not a Johnny Cash fan, but "Folsom Prison Blues" sure sounded good that night. Brother Terrell had decided that while rock and roll was blasphemous and rebellious, and he didn't mean that in a good way, God actually liked country music.

I was eleven, going on twelve, nearing the Age of Accountability, that time when a kid becomes an adult and God begins to record every sinful thought, word, and deed on a permanent spiritual record. Mama confirmed that holiness people considered twelve the cutoff point between childhood and adulthood. It depended on the individual. She raised her eyebrows and quoted from the New Testament: "For everyone to whom much is given, from him much will be required."

I knew what she meant. All those years of hearing Brother Terrell preach the Word meant God had higher expectations of me. That did not seem fair. But neither did having the world end before I grew up. The end had been in sight for as long as I could remember. I took for granted that God, the devil, and the Communists had signed some sort of foreordained annihilation pact that was already unfolding. What I found more disturbing was that the more I learned of the outside world, the more it seemed to corroborate the apocalyptic visions on which I had been raised. At school they had us crouch under our desks, put our hands over our heads, and wait for the end. I read about the assassinations of Martin Luther King and Robert Kennedy in the issues of *Time* and *Newsweek* my mother brought home, and even between the ads in *Seventeen* magazine. I saw photos of boys who looked like high-school students fighting in Vietnam, pictures of other kids fighting in the streets with the police, pictures of blissed-out teenagers, half-naked, listening to rock and roll. Proof we lived in the last days. And yet, I wanted to be in those pictures.

It was a Saturday afternoon. I was walking along Highway 6, beating at the long grasses with a stick I had picked up. My destination: the cemetery located about a mile from our trailer, the only place close enough to reach by foot. I couldn't ride my bike because there was no shoulder on the road and the burrs would flatten my tires. Horses were too moody a mode of transportation. The day had gone cold and gray. A pickup passed. An old car. An eighteen-wheeler. All going somewhere. Everyone talked about heaven as a place where time stood still, but other than saying it had streets of gold, no one said much else about it. I imagined an embalmed sort of place. No color. No feeling. No gravity. People and angels flying off at random. I passed a neighbor's house, tiny and cramped with a warren of rooms, each added on as time and money permitted. On the other side of the highway, a field of turned earth rolled on forever, or at least as far as I could see. Somewhere on the other side of all this, the world waited. The world with its music and books and cities and violence and terrible beauty. I paused and poked through the ice that skimmed the surface of the ditchwater. My next thought came to me with a certainty so clear and strong it frightened me: I did not want to go to heaven. *I didn't mean it. I'm sorry. I'm sorry.* But

I wasn't sorry. Surely God knew that. I turned into the drive of the roadside cemetery. The tombstones on either side looked as though they had been stuck in the ground on a whim: one here, another there, two more on the diagonal. Why not in straight orderly rows? I walked to the end of the drive and turned around, then wandered among the graves. So many young children, babies really, with lambs and roses and cherubs etched into the stones. I sat down and leaned against the back of one of the stones. I had a soul, and God and the devil had everything else. I closed my eyes. No pictures crossed the screen of my mind and no thoughts either. I could feel my heart beat all over my body. I took a deep breath.

"Look, Devil, I'll trade you my soul for the world. I'm not talking about a little bit of the world, I mean the whole wide world."

I looked up from the weedy graves of the people who had lived and died right next to the heart of Texas. The sky was still there, the ground too. I dusted off the back of my jeans and walked home. I rarely thought about my deal with the devil after that day. Nothing changed much. I invoked the blood of Jesus to protect me from demons when I went to the bathroom at night. I prayed when I remembered, but there was less guilt, less remorse. I had made my choice. I would live in the world. In truth, it wasn't that easy, but it was a beginning.

Chapter Nineteen

SAYONARA, HELLHOLE, WE WERE MOVING. Brother Terrell had bought property about thirty miles away, outside a town with the improbable name of Groesbeck. An enigmatic smile perched on my mother's lips each time I asked her about our new house. "Just wait till you see it," she said. "Just wait."

Mama switched on the blinker in her dark green Thunderbird and turned off the highway onto a long circular drive. We glided past crepe myrtle trees in hot-pink bloom and an acre of the greenest front lawn I had ever seen. She stopped the car in front of a yellow two-story house shaded by giant oaks and turned off the engine. This was the kind of house that girls with long shiny hair and braces disappeared into every afternoon, girls with "Homecoming Queen" stamped on their future. I hung over the back of the front seat and shook a rattle in the general direction of my new sister. Mama insisted on putting baby Carol's carrier in the front passenger seat, "in case of emergency." That way, if she had to put on the brakes, she could throw her right arm out and save her.

I craned my neck to see around the house to the garage apartment or trailer in back. "Where is it?"

My mother glanced over her shoulder. "Where's what?"

"Our house."

She opened the door and paused before getting out of the car. "This is our house." She walked around to the passenger's side and lifted Carol out of the carrier saying, "Hi there, hi there," in that sticky voice people use with babies. Gary and I were right behind her. He looked up at the trees, then turned to face the house, spreading his arms out as if to encompass the view. "We're going to live *here?*"

"This is it, and your room is at the very top. It's a converted attic."

He ran up the steps to the long porch and threw himself into one of the three white rockers that seemed to be waiting for us. Mama shifted the baby to one shoulder and asked me to grab the diaper bag.

"And Donna, close your mouth. You'll catch flies."

We unlocked the front door and stepped into something called a foyer with a hanging light and a wall-mounted gold mirror with a table underneath. We huddled in the doorway looking into a white-carpeted living room with nine-foot ceilings and furniture that was decidedly not early American. A dark blue low-slung couch stretched along a wall punctuated by three tall windows. Cream-colored floor-length drapes framed the windows and were pulled back by wide black ribbons at either end. The black fabric shades were a revelation; who knew they came in anything other than white plastic? Outside each window, just below the midway point where the shades stopped, hung a yellow-and-black garden spider. A little jewel of color located at the central point of each of the three large webs. *Even the spiders are color-coordinated.* Islands of glass-topped tables floated through the room. Gary and I took off our shoes and slid our feet through the white shag carpeting. We ran our fingers over everything, including the empty built-in bookshelves. We passed without speaking through the wide arched opening into the dining room. My mother flipped a wall switch and a chandelier spilled light over a long dark table with eight tall chairs.

"Oh." The word came out as a soft sigh from all three of us. Off to the side, an empty china cabinet awaited its new charges. It would have to make do with the Harvest Gold dinnerware Mama had bought with green stamps. We pushed through a door into the kitchen with its floor-to-ceiling cabinets, a second table, and a pantry almost as large as Gary's old bedroom. So much space. Half our trailer would have fit in the kitchen.

We rounded the corner and traipsed up the stairs, through the bedrooms fully furnished with beds, dressers, tables, lamps, and a picture or two. Where had all this stuff come from? I peeked in the closets, relieved to find them empty. The dressing room attached to my mother's bedroom was the only unfurnished room in the house. Mama nodded toward the longest wall. Her voice broke the spell. "The crib will go there."

"Mama, all this furniture, whose is it?"

She laughed and handed me the baby. "Ours now. We bought it all from the people who lived here. Just like that." She snapped her fingers.

"All those years of sacrifice, and now the Lord is blessing the ministry. Brother Terrell is going to get that divorce from Betty Ann. Things are going to be different." Her voice sounded like a kid who couldn't believe her luck.

Things were different, and seemingly overnight. Right after we moved in, Brother Terrell had Longbotham Furniture deliver a huge TV to our door. Mama made a weak protest, but she couldn't say no to Brother Terrell, and the hellevision became a permanent fixture in our living room. Brother Terrell spent every evening after dinner stretched out on the big couch, watching that screen. It wasn't so much that he liked TV, Mama said. He just needed a break from the pressures of the ministry.

In the early to midseventies, the Lord's work officially took in about a million dollars annually, though since all transactions were made in cash, the accounting was vague at best. Edited versions of Brother Terrell sermons were broadcast on about thirty-five stations across the United States, and his magazine, *The Endtime Messenger*, went out monthly to over one hundred thousand subscribers. Radio and publishing costs came with an annual price tag of close to a half million dollars. Brother Terrell had purchased a second version of the world's largest tent, this one in red, white, and blue. His annual missionary trips to India drew hundreds of thousands. He was on the verge of being discovered by a broader audience. The rise of the Charismatic movement brought middle-class tongue-talking Methodists, Baptists, Presbyterians, Lutherans, Episcopalians, and Catholics to the tent. Someone approached Brother Terrell about a television show. Someone else wanted to write a book about him. A religious film producer wanted to make a movie about his overseas revivals. Brother Terrell bragged that country-music star George Jones had approached him after service one night and requested prayer. Another night, bluegrass legend Lester Flatt, a personal hero of his, came to the tent and asked for prayer. Brother Terrell prayed for Flatt several times over the years, usually by phone, but the musician kept getting sick. After hearing Flatt was back in the hospital, sicker than ever, he called my mother in tears. God healed people all the time in his services, he said, so why wouldn't God heal Lester Flatt? And more important, why hadn't God healed Randall?

I stood by the table in the breakfast nook and listened as my mother consoled him over the phone. Of course God heard his prayers. Of course he hadn't done anything wrong. The devil was using Lester's and especially Randall's sickness to make him doubt himself. Randall continued to vacillate between health and illness. One minute he was shouting the victory and the next he was getting yet another blood transfusion. The scripture about God visiting the sins of the fathers on the children came to mind. I wondered if Mama or Brother Terrell ever thought of it.

Mama ended her pep talks to Brother Terrell with a reminder that he was God's chosen vessel. It was a vocation for which he was increasingly well paid. Our garage held two new Mercedes and a Lincoln Continental. The driveway at the back of our house was filled with his-and-hers Thunderbirds, a new pickup, and a station wagon. My mother wouldn't drive the fancier cars, so once a week, we went from car to car, turning them on and letting them idle in place to keep the batteries from running down. These were our personal automobiles. There was also a fleet of corporate vehicles that included more Mercedes, a few Cadillacs, a couple of run-of-the-mill Ford LTDs, a luxury bus, a prop plane, and a six-passenger jet. Brother Terrell drove up to the house one day towing a horse trailer with a movie-star horse inside. He had admired the horse on *The Virginian*, his favorite TV Western, and when it came up for sale, well, didn't the Bible say God grants the desires of our hearts? A movie-star horse couldn't live on an ordinary farm, so Brother Terrell bought a fancy horse farm in Tennessee. He bought other properties as well, including a ranch close to Brownwood, Texas; a house with acreage in Palestine, Texas; and a two-hundred-and-sixty-acre farm outside Lampasas, Texas.

I asked my mother on occasion where all the money came from, and she replied in a haughty, you-shouldn't-ask-that-kind-of-thing voice that everything we had was paid for with love offerings, money people gave Brother Terrell for his personal use. Besides, Brother Terrell traveled so much, he needed reliable, comfortable transportation. And he had grown up poor as dirt and had given up so much for the gospel; he deserved a few nice things. And no one thought a thing when the people of the world, movie stars and entertainers, bought fancy things.

She gave Brother Terrell an entirely different perspective, reminding him that people sacrificed, some giving everything they owned, so the gospel could be preached, not so we could pile up riches on earth. Her refrain became: "How many cars can you drive? How many houses can you live in? How many suits can you wear?" He darted away without answering and said he had to go to town to make a few business calls. He couldn't make calls from our house phone, he said. Someone might trace them. The persecution complex was turning into paranoia, nursed along by tussles with law enforcement, the Klan, and no doubt by his secret relationship with my mother. Mama rationalized it as a natural response to all the horrible things the Lord had shown him in visions. The Old Testament prophets were not happy-go-lucky guys, she said. Probably not, but I hoped Brother Terrell would not pull a Jeremiah and take to the streets of our new hometown, crying judgment and eating dung. Anything was possible.

The people in Groesbeck were the friendliest I had encountered outside the tent—a congeniality purchased, at least in part, with our newfound affluence. Bankers, lawyers, and shopkeepers went out of their way to say hello on the street. Kids at school assumed I was worth knowing. A seventh-grade cheerleader wanted to be my best friend. Girls invited me to slumber parties. I threw parties, and kids actually came. I nagged my mother into letting me see a movie endorsed by Billy Graham that was playing at the local theater. Afterward, I was able to see every movie that came to town, no matter the rating. Football games, bowling, and skating outings followed. Groesbeck gave me a chance to fit in, to be normal, but I couldn't quite pull it off. After hours of making and hanging posters encouraging the junior-high football team to "Fight, Goats, Fight!" I was jonesing for excitement. Normal was not in my repertoire, nor was it in Mama's. She didn't have a clue that I was the only girl in seventh grade who dated high-school seniors. By eighth grade I was dating college guys, with Mama's blessing, and smoking pot (no blessing involved). The only caveat: My boyfriends and I had to attend the Bible study she led on Friday nights before we headed down one of the country roads to make out or get stoned. She never questioned why I showed up late for curfew (ran out of gas, again) with glassy red eyes (oh, those dusty roads). She didn't want to be suspicious like her daddy, she said. She didn't want to make me feel guilty every time I looked at a boy.

In reality (whatever that was), my mother didn't have much time to wonder about my activities. She cared for my sister and brother, wrote the magazine, duplicated tapes for the radio broadcast, kept up the house and its surrounding thirty acres, and fed and saw to the care of the menagerie of birds, monkeys, dogs, horses, and livestock Brother Terrell brought home. Then there were the preparations for the end-time:

planting and harvesting two vegetable gardens large enough to feed a small community and canning and freezing the produce from those gardens. Plus, she was pregnant again, with twins. She broke the news with a dazed look on her face as Gary and I slurped cereal one morning. My brother laughed—twins, ha, how funny—and went out to play in his tree house. I was stunned.

"Mama, y'all aren't married. He's not even divorced."

She stared past me. "He's working everything out."

"But what will you tell the kids when they grow up?"

"Jesus will come before then. David said so."

I studied my cereal bowl in utter defeat.

For the first two or three years of my sisters' lives, we dropped them off for long weekends with a neighbor once or twice a year while we attended one of Brother Terrell's tent revivals. We climbed into the car as the middle-class Ter-*rell* family from Groesbeck and emerged a few hours later in Dallas, Houston, San Antonio, or wherever the revival happened to be, transformed into Sister Johnson, Brother Terrell's longtime associate and ghostwriter (the one secret everyone seemed to know), and her two obedient kids. Gary replaced his sleeveless T-shirts with a long-sleeved button-down, and I traded my jeans for a dress. We looked the part. People under the tent congratulated Mama on bringing us up with God-fearing ways.

"It's like the Bible says, you train your children up the way they should go and they shall not depart from it."

Under the tent I became the person believers thought I was: a good and virtuous Holy Ghost girl. When I wriggled into my jeans and played with my sisters at home, I was my other self, and still another when I smoked a joint and went skinny-dipping, and yet another when I read Yeats and scribbled bad poetry, and someone else altogether when I pinned on my homecoming mum with its long red and white ribbons and plastic dangling footballs. I was all of these people. Maybe that's why Brother Terrell's latest incarnation did not shock me.

He walked onto the platform dressed all in black, carrying a seven-foot staff with a crook on the end, a far cry from the dandy who zipped in and out of Groesbeck in a powder-blue Mercedes. He walked down the prayer ramp, stood level with the audience, and stretched out the staff. He was Moses parting the water. Ezekiel calling up the dry bones. Elijah calling down the fire.

"The Lord God Almighty has called for a famine on this land. Hordes of locusts, clouds of grasshoppers darkening the sky. Crops are destroyed. They're eating everything: corn, beans, tomatoes, wheat. I see hungry people everywhere. Hungry children. I see people throwing their money in the streets. Their money is no good. Banks are failing. Babies are hungry, asking their mamas for food, but they don't have none to give."

He shook the staff in the air and began to weep. "Woe! Woe! Woe! Woe to the cities. Woe to the merchants. Woe to those who call good evil and evil good." He threw down the staff, pulled his shirttail from his pants, and ripped one side and then the other. He stalked the aisles with his torn shirt flapping.

"Judgment, judgment, judgment. Judgment on America! Judgment on America! The only people who survive will be those who have made themselves ready, those who heed the word of this man"—meaning himself—"those who move to the country and become self-sufficient. The Great Depression won't be nothing compared to what's fixing to hit this country."

The prophecy rambled on for hours, ending with predictions of earthquakes, floods, and airplane crashes—all disasters God would allow so that we would know Brother Terrell was a true prophet. With the last "thus saith the Lord," he walked back up the ramp to the platform. A woman minister who sat behind him on the platform brought him a box of handkerchiefs. He pulled them out of the box and rubbed them over some part of his face or neck, talking into the microphone the entire time.

"The Bible says the prophet will sustain you. The Lord told me that these handkerchiefs will work miracles. Tie them on your cars and your door handles. The anointing of God is in them. Get me some more handkerchiefs. I want everyone to have one. Y'all line up around the tent and come on up here."

Some say it was my mother who first placed the prophet mantle on Brother Terrell's shoulders. If that's so, she sealed her fate. As a prophet Brother Terrell came to believe that everything he said, everything he did, and everything he *thought* was sanctioned by God. He said this from the platform, and he said God would not tolerate those who questioned his anointing. The emergence of the prophet changed the dynamic between my mother and Brother Terrell—she had no right to question him about money or anything else. It also changed the dynamic of the ministry. Employees who once feared Brother Terrell's temper now feared the word of the prophet. That fear overshadowed the love that had always been present. People who questioned the prophet died. It was biblical. Brother Cotton and several other longtime colleagues had left or been replaced by employees who bowed and scraped when they approached him.

"Ah, Brother Terrell, sir, if you don't mind, I

was wondering if I could talk with you for a minute, please, only if you can spare the time. Yes, sir, yes, sir. Thank you, sir, thank you."

They disapproved when his children or Gary and I treated him with familiarity. Young ministers and even the tent hands who traveled with him began to adopt his mannerisms and dress. I stepped behind the platform one night and witnessed six iterations of Brother Terrell pacing about, hands jammed in pockets, change jingling. Their impression of him was pitch-perfect, down to the lean, haunted expression on their faces and the incessant movement of their lips in prayer. I laughed out loud and their necks popped up from their collars. I knew our reality was not sane, but that knowledge didn't stop me from tying "blessed" handkerchiefs around the doorknobs in my room when I got home. When friends asked me what they were for, I shrugged.

"I dunno. Something my brother did."

My mother called me and my date into the living room at the end of her Friday night Bible study. The date was a twenty-two-year-old law student I had gone out with for a year, and despite his professed agnosticism, my mother liked him. The neighbor family who attended the study had already gone, and the room was quiet and mostly dark. A small lamp squatted on a tabletop at either end of the couch and cast the only circles of light in the room. My mother waved us over to the couch. We anchored one end and she took the other.

"I don't know what y'all are going to do about this, but I thought I should tell you that we are going to be moving in a few months."

For several months, my mother and siblings had met Brother Terrell for prolonged visits at some "ranch" out in the middle of nowhere. He was worried that our house in Groesbeck was not remote enough, that "the enemy" would find him. I refused to go with them for these visits, and when my mother tried to tell me about the ranch, I left the room with my hands over my ears. And now here it was, the big announcement. I told my mother I couldn't bear to move, that I would not move. The boyfriend spoke up.

"Look, we'll go to Oklahoma and get married. I think the age of consent is fifteen there. I know for sure it's a lot younger than it is here."

Mama didn't say anything for a moment. When she spoke, her voice was smooth and fat with satisfaction. "Well, now, y'all don't have to do that. We can have a wedding, a real wedding, before the move."

I had planned to break up with the law-school boyfriend. He was kind and smart and talked to me about Nietzsche and existentialism, but I also felt overwhelmed and voiceless around him. And there was a boy in high school. A boy with whom

I felt, for the first time in a long time, like a kid. I didn't want to get married. I wanted to continue waking up in the yellow house every day, and going to school and coming home until it was time, really time, to do something else. All of this had seemed possible, but it wasn't and probably never had been. My choices were to marry or to move to the middle of nowhere and wait for the end of the world.

I married a month before I turned sixteen. Mama sold the house, and my family hightailed it out of town. I quit school. It's one thing to leave home and another to have home leave you. I missed my family. Everything that had been familiar began to look and feel like a foreign object, including me. I stopped eating and was hospitalized for pneumonia. I began to talk to God. *Please help me. I am so lost.*

One day a friend from the nearby town of Mexia (a Spanish word mangled as "Ma-hair" by local farmer-rancher types) dropped by, and for lack of anything better to do we took a stroll around the courthouse. I pointed to the statue of the World War II soldier and told him about the time a visiting movie star, a hometown boy made good, got drunk and hung a dead skunk from the bayonet of the statue's rifle, just in time for the homecoming parade. My friend said something about being surprised he hadn't read *that* on the front page, and pulled a folded copy of the *Mexia*

News from his jacket. There on the front page was an AP wire story on evangelist David Terrell, along with a photograph. I stammered through an explanation of why we kept my stepdad's profession a secret, and heard my mother's voice.

"It's so he can get some rest. People would bother him day and night if they knew where he lived."

My friend shrugged. "I kinda knew. Rumors have been going around for years."

I scanned the story. Brother Terrell's followers, dubbed Terrellites by the press, were descending en masse on backwaters in Texas, Georgia, Alabama, Tennessee, Arkansas, Oklahoma, and South Carolina. People were selling everything they owned and moving to makeshift camps in these "Blessed Areas" to survive the coming apocalypse prophesied by Brother Terrell. A six-year-old girl had died in the camp in Bangs, Texas, from a minor kidney ailment that could have been treated had her parents taken her to a doctor. They had opted for prayer instead. With winter approaching, the local authorities worried about more deaths. The reporter wrote that some of the Terrellites lived in tar-paper shacks and gave everything they had to the prophet, who traveled between revivals in a Mercedes-Benz. That, at least, sounded familiar. The prophet owned property all over the United States and was under investigation by the IRS. The IRS? No wonder my mother had been in such a hurry to get out of town. I pulled my sunglasses out of my purse and put them on.

My friend laughed. "Pretty weird, huh?"

Since Groesbeck and Mexia were only a few miles apart, everyone in town knew about the newspaper story, but no one asked about it. I wanted to call my mother and ask her what was going on, but I couldn't. She had decided it was best if I didn't have her new phone number or her address. That way, when the Communists or the Antichrist came looking for them, Mama said, I wouldn't have anything to tell them. She didn't mention the IRS. One day as I scanned the radio dial in my car, I happened upon Brother Terrell's broadcast. He was scheduled to preach at an auditorium in San Antonio. Maybe it was a sign.

My husband and I arrived early for the morning service. I leaned against the half wall outside the auditorium and watched people stroll in while my husband sat in the car and studied. A woman with a boy of about eight walked over and stood beside me. The boy picked up a stick the size of a pencil, turned his back to me, and pretended to write on the wall. I asked him what he was writing. He didn't look up or indicate in any way that he might have heard me.

"He doesn't mean to be rude. He can't hear."

I turned to look at the woman. She was Mexican American, in her thirties, and she wore a regular knee-length dress, not the ground-dragging garb that was more and more the uniform of the women who came to hear Brother Terrell preach.

I didn't know what to say, so I told the woman I was sorry, as if I had something to do with the boy's deafness.

"He's never been able to hear. I saw the ad in the paper for this preacher. He heals people?"

I nodded. God and Brother Terrell healed people, at least sometimes. What that meant about either of them or if it meant anything at all, I didn't know.

"How does it work?"

"I'm not sure . . . but it seems to work."

"No, I mean how do I get him to pray for my son?"

I told her about the prayer lines and how sometimes Brother Terrell called people out of the audience to pray for them. "But he may not do either and if he doesn't, try to grab one of his associates and tell them about your son."

My husband walked up from the parking lot. I said good-bye to the woman and turned to enter the building. She grabbed my hand. "You have seen people healed by this man?"

I nodded. She looked so eager to believe. "Please pray he will heal my son."

Brother Terrell spent the service prophesying about famine and the end-time. I despaired for the woman, the boy, and for myself. After the offering, Brother Terrell began to prowl the audience. He called out an older man and a younger man and prayed that God would heal them of alcoholism and nerves. *Please. Please. That little boy. Please.* Brother Terrell walked back toward the platform. I prayed harder. He stopped and turned around.

"There's somebody else here. Someone who feels like this is their last chance." He walked down one of the two aisles. "You there. The lady with the little boy. Stand up, ma'am. Your son too. The Lord is showing me he's deaf."

The woman began to cry and Brother Terrell put his arm around her. "I know what it's like to see your son suffer, to weep and cry for his healing. The Lord of Hosts has heard your prayer today."

He knelt before the boy and cupped his hands over the child's ears. "In the name of Je-sus. Stretch out your hands and pray with me, people. In the name of Je-sus. Be gone, you foul spirit of deafness. Release this child."

Brother Terrell moved behind the boy and clapped his hands. The boy whirled around and the crowd rose in unison. They moved toward Brother Terrell and the boy from all directions, pressing against them. *Yes Lord. Yes Lord. Yes.* Brother Terrell asked the boy to repeat what he heard and the mother translated his request in sign language. Again he moved to stand behind the boy.

Brother Terrell said the word "baby." The boy said, "Bah-bah." *Hallelujah.*

Brother Terrell said, "Mama." The boy said, "Maaaaaaah." *Amen. Praise God.*

Brother Terrell said, "Dad-dy." The boy's response was lost in a din of praise. *Thank you. Thank you. Thank you.* A haze of light seemed to fall on the upturned faces and hands. My husband, an introverted cynic, stood with his hands raised at shoulder level, a tentative posture compared with the outstretched arms of those around us. His eyes were closed and he wore a beatific smile. Tears dripped off his chin. I raised my hands, too, letting go of the questions and the arguments and all the resentments, reaching for a place where everything belonged, even me.

That afternoon as my husband and I drove through the parking lot, I saw the woman and her son sitting on a bench beside the road. The boy's head moved from the right to the left and back again, over and over in a rhythmic pattern. I asked my husband to stop the car so that I could talk to the woman. She smiled as I approached.

"That man. He healed him. My son can hear."

I looked at the boy, sitting on the edge of the bench, his head turning from side to side. "What is he doing?"

"He's listening to traffic. He's never heard it before."

Chapter Twenty

NONE OF THE HEALINGS I WITNESSED GROWING up had ever felt so immediate, so personal. Maybe it was having contact with the boy and his mother before and after Brother Terrell prayed for them. Maybe it was because I didn't know how to live without Brother Terrell and his ministry at the center of everything. Or maybe it was because I was sixteen and longed to go home. With the miracle of the deaf boy, God seemed to beckon me. "You belong *here*," he seemed to say. "Here" was among the Terrellites.

My husband agreed. He continued going to law school but swore off atheist philosophers. I swore off pot, scoured the scriptures for obscure references to the end-time, tried to like Richard Nixon (an honest man chosen to lead the country, according to Brother Terrell), and switched the radio station in my car from rock and roll to country and western. We bought and stored extra food in our pantry to prepare for the famine. I burned my jeans and wore long, hippie-looking dresses. When my mother called, I told her of my conversion experience and she gave me her phone number. We both agreed it was best that the whereabouts of her ranch remain a secret, if only to thwart the devil. I tied a blessed handkerchief around the steering column of the car and we began making the three-hundred-and-sixty-mile round-trip between Groesbeck and Bangs on most weekends.

Located at the western edge of Brown County, ten miles outside the county seat of Brownwood, Bangs is situated in a sort of borderland along which the rolling gentility of the central Texas landscape gives way to the windswept desolation that eventually becomes west Texas. Until the big tent came to town in 1972, a truck stop and a convenience store were the most visible landmarks along Highway 84 West. The wind blew all winter long, and in the summer, the sun beat the land into submission. Wind, dust, and truck-stop grease. Still, one person's hell is another's Promised Land, or at the very least, Blessed Area.

The Terrellites descended on Bangs like a biblical plague. They came in their broken-down trucks and leaky campers and station wagons that rattled when they rolled. A few drove new cars, all that remained of the middle-class life they had abandoned. The women, in their high-necked, ankle-length dresses and bird's-nest hair, resembled refugees from the Grand Ole Opry. The men, perpetually pale and skinny from months of fasting, had taken to shaving their heads, a look locals associated with Charlie Manson or Hare Krishna devotees, neither of whom were popular in and around Brown County. Some believers applied Old Testament admonishments to modern life and went about their daily business dressed in sackcloth and ashes. One early arrival told a reporter, "You think we look bad? Wait'll you see the ones coming from behind."

They came from California, the Dakotas, New York, Colorado, Maryland, Pennsylvania, Kansas, Florida, and from all across the South. The influx began in 1972. Within a year, Bangs's population of twelve hundred had almost doubled, and the Terrellites were spreading to surrounding communities. Other Blessed Areas scattered across the South experienced similar growth. The population of rural areas around Fort Payne, Alabama, increased by twenty-eight percent. No one in Bangs could figure out why these people were coming or how long they would stay. Finally they read the explanation in the paper: The Terrellites were there to wait out the apocalypse. They would be there until the end of the world. Meanwhile, they would build a tabernacle. The tent would remain up until the church was finished. This put no one's mind at ease.

Locals blamed Brother Terrell for bringing the first homosexuals, hippies, and blacks to the community. The town of Coleman in nearby Hamilton County saw its black student population increase from sixty to one hundred and twenty within months. Just a few years earlier a sign posted inside the city limits of the Hamilton County seat had read: IF YOU'RE BLACK, DON'T LET THE SUN SET ON YOU IN HAMILTON. Believers were blamed for everything from vandalism to cattle mutilations, but nothing stuck until the death of that little girl I'd read about in the Mexia paper. The sheriff, judge, and district attorney had called for an investigation. Reporters from Dallas, Fort Worth, Abilene, and the wire services swarmed. An AP story quoted the stepfather of the girl as saying he didn't just *let* his stepdaughter die.

"I believe it was the will of God, and if he wanted her to die, it didn't make no difference if I took her to fifty doctors."

Brother Terrell and his followers said the child died because the parents did not have enough faith. Even in my new nonrebellious mode, this explanation was hard to swallow. The girl's parents had prayed and they had asked Brother Terrell and several of the ministers close to him to pray, and now everyone said the parents didn't have enough faith. I argued the issue with a friend in the ministry. Jesus had said that faith equal in size to a mustard seed could move mountains. Surely these people had at least that much faith, or they wouldn't have been living in a tent in Bangs.

The friend shrugged off my argument. "You better make sure you know exactly how much faith you have when you decide not to take your kid to the doctor."

I filed the deaths under "unknowable," but that didn't feel right either. If the child had received medical care, she would have lived. That much we knew. My prayer became, "Lord, I believe. Help my unbelief."

Brother Terrell's notoriety turned to full-blown infamy. Newspapers ran photos of him arriving and leaving the tent in Bangs in his Mercedes or Lincoln. They showed him stuffing his pockets with love offerings and ran the photos alongside the squalid living conditions of some of his followers. They emphasized that no one really knew where or under what conditions he lived, something my mother gave thanks for daily. After the article was published, Brother Terrell said from the platform that the reporters were out to get him, and we all nodded and said amen, including those of us who knew that the newspaper articles were a fairy tale compared to what was really going on.

He railed against the press. "These bunch of lying reporters better watch out. The Bible says, 'Touch not my anointing.' They come against God, and they'll wish't they hadn't."

But the reporters kept on coming. A follower knocked one out of her chair during a tent service when he raced up behind her, grabbed her camera, and ran out of the tent with it. She ran after him and into a line of men with folded arms. Yes, they had a seen a man with a camera. No, they wouldn't tell her which way he had gone.

Brother Terrell responded to the media coverage with increasingly grandiose claims. "In the Bible Paul said, 'Follow me as I follow Christ.' All this fasting and praying has purified my body, my mind, and spirit."

He leaned toward the audience as he spoke and trembled. He danced in place, and then hopped on one leg across the platform. "I'm pure like Paul. I'm without sin like Jesus. You can follow me all the way to glory, hallelujah, hallelujah, hallelujah!"

The preachers and supporters who sat on the platform stood and shook their fists in the air, yelling amen. Mama stood with them, clapping her hands, shouting, "Preach it, preach it." My mind rebelled. *How can he say he is without sin?* Rowed up at the back of the tent, so that they could be the first ones out and escape unwanted attention, sat three little girls. My sisters lived with my mother, but none of the tent crowd in Bangs knew about their existence. When Mama attended the services in Bangs, she handed them off to a woman she had taken into her confidence in Groesbeck. When my mother moved, the woman and her family moved also. They lived on one of Brother Terrell's properties close to my mother's farm, though of course they didn't know the exact location of the farm. The story, should anyone in Bangs ask, was that these girls were the woman's grandchildren.

"God has sanctified me. My body is a living sacrifice for the gospel. I've been washed in the blood. Purified by his word. I'm a Jesus man! Everything I do is holy!"

Everyone around me stood and applauded, including my husband, who knew everything I knew. To ponder whether the content of Brother Terrell's sermon matched the reality of his life was the equivalent of grabbing a spiritual fire extinguisher. My brain said, *Wait a minute,* and my instincts compelled me to step into the flame of belief and burn, burn, burn.

Doubt is a lot like faith; a mustard seed's worth changes everything. Away from the tent, the questions kept coming. *How can Brother Terrell claim to be without sin? Why doesn't it matter that he is committing adultery and lying?* Mama tried to explain.

"Perfection in God's eyes is not the same as our idea of being perfect."

"King David had a man murdered, and the Bible says he was a man after God's own heart!"

No matter what Brother Terrell did, God loved him. We loved him. I, on the other hand, failed the holiness dress code, and that was something neither the Lord nor his people could forgive. Two new converts, hippie girls turned Holy Rollers, informed me my sleeves were too short and my neckline too low. They were kind in that churchy, bless-your-heart kind of way. I bit my tongue and borrowed a sweater. In the summer months, when the tent turned into a canvas steam bath, I tried to steal a little comfort by going braless under loose blouses and covering the evidence with a shawl. Things jiggled when I raised my hands to pray, and people were scandalized. I couldn't please God or the Terrellites, and I couldn't stop the questions. Why was it more important to look holy than to live holy? Why did Brother Terrell and my family have so much stuff, when Jesus said to sell everything and give it to the poor? Why had an omnipotent God let that child die? I broached these issues with other believers as much as I could without betraying my family, and was urged to pray harder and not give in to the devil. My old misgivings about the ministry returned, and my resentment against God, the all-or-nothing ego at the center of the universe, grew. It was all his fault: my mother's abandonment of my brother and me, the sadness at the center of her life. Then there was the secret of my sisters' existence. The way they met their daddy in a roadside park after a tent service, so they could hug him through the car window. And there was the loss of that high-school boyfriend, a small grief that grew larger as I tallied the offenses.

I tried to discuss my doubts and resentments with my mother, but I couldn't get past her defense of Brother Terrell. Jesus had said that the poor would always be with us. It wasn't his fault that he had to keep his family (her and my sisters) a secret. It was the fault of his enemies, who would use the information to destroy the ministry. Couldn't I see that? When she wasn't defending Brother Terrell, she was calling to tell me how depressed she was.

"Sometimes, I just wish the Lord would take me." It seemed to me that my mother saw death as the only way out.

After nine months of trying to be a good Terrellite, I quit. I lacked whatever it took to live right, which in my mind was to abide by Terrellite doctrine. I also lacked the ability to stay married. My husband and I divorced, and I spent the next three years careening between sex, drugs, and rock and roll, and the increasingly paranoid reality of the Terrellites. With their big egos, infidelities, and cash transactions, these worlds were surprisingly alike. All I had to do was change clothes and I felt at home.

Despite Mama and Brother Terrell's attempts to keep the whereabouts of her ranch a secret, IRS agents showed up in the small town close to where she and my sisters lived. This scared Brother Terrell. He stopped visiting my mother's house and bought another ranch about an hour and a half away. No one, including my mother, knew where it was located. There was just one problem: getting my mother and sisters to the ranch without revealing its whereabouts. I wasn't along for these outings, but my sisters recount the experience from time to time at family gatherings: Brother Terrell is behind the wheel of his dark green Mercedes with Mama beside him in the passenger seat. My sisters are in back. They rock along some gravel farm-to-market road with Brother Terrell hitting the brake and the gas pedal, the brake and the gas pedal. They pass some rancher poking along in the opposite direction, raising his hand at every vehicle that passes, howdy-howdy (pronounced "hidy" in Texas). The sun in his eye makes him question what he saw. *What's a Mer-say-dees doin' out here? And that woman on the passenger's side, what was that white thing over her eyes? Somethin' over the kids' eyes too.*

Brother Terrell wrapped blessed handkerchiefs the size of bandanas around the eyes of my mother and sisters, trying without success to avoid tangling strands of his daughters' fine blond hair in the double knots he tied at the backs of their heads. Just another happy family out for a Sunday drive, mother and kids blindfolded. The trips to the ranch were plagued by bouts of motion sickness, forcing Brother Terrell to pull over and let one or all of the girls heave, blindfolds lifted just enough to let them see, and miss, their feet. When the car finally stopped, my sisters found themselves in the middle of a seven-hundred-plus-acre ranch with a guitar-shaped swimming pool. The pool was modeled on the one Elvis had put in at his Memphis house. My sisters thought of the ranch as a mysterious place. They parked their bikes in one place when they left and found them in another when they returned. Their toys, too, seemed to have a life of their own and were always someplace other than where they had left them. When the girls asked their dad what was up with the toys, he said they had most likely forgotten where they had left them or that the cleaning people had probably put a few items back in the wrong place. The truth was more surreal. Brother Terrell had another secret family he brought to the ranch between my mom's and sisters' visits. He had become involved with a woman preacher who traveled with him, and they had a daughter together who was the same age as the twins. They kept the girl's parentage a secret by telling her and everyone in the ministry that she was adopted. To complicate matters, Brother Terrell had adopted a young boy from Mexico around the same time, and he and the girl grew up as adopted siblings.

Years later, the girl and the boy would tell my sisters that they had often wondered why there were three ponies, three beds, three bikes, three of everything, when there were only two of them.

I became suspicious of Brother Terrell's relationship with the woman when I noticed on my visits to Bangs that they were almost always together. Instead of referencing Mama from the platform as he had once done, he talked about the preacher woman, calling her a great woman of God. She had replaced Brother Starrs, who had replaced Brother Cotton a few years back, and was now the one who introduced Brother Terrell. She had become his de facto second-in-command. I often glimpsed them getting out of the Mercedes together at the back of the tent. Then one day I saw her with Pam and Brother Terrell's other daughters. There was something about their body language, the ease and familiarity with which the Terrell girls interacted with her, as if she were a family member. I asked my mother about the relationship one afternoon as she drove me, blindfolded, from Bangs to her farm for a visit. She admitted that Brother Terrell was involved with the woman. She didn't mention the daughter.

"He said it was a mistake. He got himself into a mess with that woman, and now he says he's working everything out. I believe him. He's always done right by me and the girls."

I adjusted the blessed handkerchief that covered my eyes, careful not to let it slip.

The walls that divided Brother Terrell's lives began to crumble. My mother confronted the preacher woman and told her about my sisters. The woman didn't believe her. Someone broke into the prophet's ranch house. The next week, the *Fort Worth Star-Telegram* printed a long piece describing the ranch and the house in detail. The guitar-shaped swimming pool received special attention. Brother Terrell told my mother IRS agents had broken into the house with the reporter. Around the same time, Randall spotted my sisters during a tent service in Bangs, noticed the resemblance they bore to his own sisters, and confronted my mother.

"Carolyn, I know those girls are Daddy's. They look just like him."

My mother admitted the truth. Randall confronted his daddy, who admitted nothing. Randall made it his personal cause to force his father to publicly recognize my sisters. When Brother Terrell and the preacher woman arrived at the tent before the service started, they saw Randall walking around with my sisters in the area at the back of the platform where all the insiders would be sure to see them. Brother Terrell gave Randall a quick nod on his way past. My sisters looked the other way.

• • •

During the mid-to-late seventies, Brother Terrell fasted more than he ate. My mother told me he weighed one hundred and twenty pounds, not much for a man six feet tall. She was afraid he was dying. I made my way to Bangs to see him preach for what my mother said might be the last time, though I could not imagine the world without the force that was David Terrell.

His shaved head gleamed under the lights; his all-black attire hung off his ruined body. He paced around in that aimless way I remembered from earlier fasts. "Y'all know I been prophesying the destruction of America for years; well, God told me the time has come. I asked the Lord the other night if there was anything I could do to hold off what's coming."

He pulled his shirttail from his pants and began to unbutton it. "God told me there was only one way."

The people around me began to rock and moan. I don't know if they knew what was coming next. I didn't. Brother Terrell slipped out of his shirt, revealing a short-sleeved white T-shirt underneath. He unbuckled his belt, pulled it through his pants, doubled it, and held it at both ends. Clutching the waistband of his trousers with one hand and the belt with the other, he walked over and stood in front of one of the young men seated on the platform. He looked

358

down at the man and extended the belt to him.

"Brother Walker, God told me he needed someone to stand in the gap. I need you to stand up and take the belt." The man did as he was told.

"The prophet always has to bear the signs in his own body." Brother Terrell walked over to an empty folding chair and Brother Walker followed, the belt dangling from his right hand. Brother Terrell knelt in front of the chair and took off his shirt.

"God told me someone has to take the whipping for America."

Brother Walker dropped the belt and backed away, shaking his head. Brother Terrell looked over his shoulder. "Pick it up, Brother Walker. I know you don't want to do this, but you have to. I have to."

The younger man picked up the belt and beat the prophet. When Brother Walker collapsed in tears, Brother Terrell called one of the other ministers to take his place. After the second whipping, the welts began to bleed. Everyone in the tent wailed and cried, and I was right there with them. *Oh God. Oh God. Oh Lord.* He called preacher after preacher. If they did not hit him hard enough, he looked up and told them that if they didn't want to see children running through the streets of America with their skin melting from their bones, they better hit him harder. We screamed and moaned with every lash. The blood ran down his back. After about an hour, he pulled his T-shirt over his head and a couple of men ran to help him up. Blood seeped through the cotton of his shirt as he stumbled offstage between the men. The preacher woman spoke over the microphone as the men led Brother Terrell offstage.

"We've just seen an innocent man take a whipping for the sins of this country. I want everyone to gather in the altar and pray. Pray for Brother Terrell. Pray for America."

I skipped the altar and headed for my car. I passed my sisters, crying in the back row, fists stuffed into their mouths. Their fake grandma was on her knees. I wanted to comfort them, but that would have frightened them more. I stepped out into the night feeling purged of every transgression and wondered if Brother Terrell felt the same. The whippings continued off and on for several years and most of the men associated with the ministry, including Randall, had to take a turn with the belt. Brother Terrell never handed the belt to my mother or the preacher woman, who sat on opposite ends of the platform.

Not long after I witnessed the whipping, Brother Terrell sent word through my mother that if I didn't get right with God, I wouldn't live past twenty-five. Right on cue, I came down with an illness that doctors could neither diagnose nor cure. Sores erupted on my body. I was beset with fever and chills. My bones ached and my energy dwindled. No matter how much I ate, I lost weight. After several months, I made my way to the tent in Bangs. Brother Terrell began calling people out of the audience almost at once that night. He made his way to our section. I tried to catch his eye but he looked over my head and asked a man in the back to stand up. He prayed for him and moved on to the young mother across the row. Finally, he pointed at my most recent live-in boyfriend and told him to step into the aisle. He clapped his hand on the man's forehead and told him he had been bound by the powers of Satan and from that moment forward, he was free. The boyfriend hit the ground so hard he had a lump on the back of his head for a couple of weeks. He later told me he lost consciousness as soon as the prophet laid hands on him. He estimated he was out for ten minutes, maybe longer.

Brother Terrell placed his hands on my head next, and it was as if a curtain fell over my senses. Sight, sound, smell, and touch were gone. The I that was me, separate and distinct, released its hold, and I experienced myself as a vast and bliss-filled darkness. I did not shout or speak in tongues. I did not fall to the ground as my boyfriend had. I was there, but I was not there. I don't know how long I drifted like this before slowly becoming aware of sound and of being back in my body. When I opened my eyes, I knew

Brother Terrell had prayed for me, but I didn't know the content of the prayer. It didn't matter because the sores, fevers, and lethargy that had plagued me for months disappeared that night. The healing increased the dissonance between what I believed and what I thought. I believed Brother Terrell was a prophet and a healer. I knew he was a liar and an adulterer. I did not know how to reconcile the two. I also believed the Terrellites were right about what God required—complete withdrawal from the world and sacrifice in every aspect of life—and I knew I was not capable of that. I was seventeen when I left Brother Terrell's ministry for what would be the last time. There were no epiphanies, only a sense of regret and failure. I pushed these feelings away when they surfaced, and over time they turned to anger and then, to my relief, something that felt like indifference, only heavier.

It was well after midnight. The bars had closed and my friends and I had taken the party to someone's house in the country. Bodies packed every room. We were smoking and drinking and hovering over the pile of cocaine on the coffee table. Musicians ran up and down guitar scales, and somewhere in the back of the house, someone pounded out the drum solo from "Wipe Out." We talked and talked about terribly important things. Out of that din, a clear, mellifluous voice sang:

Though God slay me
I will trust him
I shall then come forth as gold.

Everything fell away but the song. It was "Job's God Is True," a song Brother Terrell often sang under the tent.

For I know that he is living
I can feel him in my soul.

I followed the sound to the front porch. A young blond woman who fronted a local band and who minutes earlier had bent over the cocaine with me sat on the porch swing, strumming her guitar and singing. I asked where she had learned the song and she told me she had attended Pentecostal churches, even tent revivals, as a kid.

"There's power there. Can't deny that." She looked up and smiled.

I nodded and walked back inside.

Over the next five years Brother Terrell and my mother drifted further apart, but she didn't seem to realize it. After a while, only the preacher woman and her family accompanied him to the ranch, but Mama maintained he was working everything out. Eventually a grand jury convened to examine the IRS evidence against him. It came out in the hearing that my mother had made a down payment on a property with thirty thousand dollars in cash. The attorney who handled the transaction remembered it ten years later as one of the strangest moments of his career.

"This woman hands me all this money in a bag. A brown paper bag! I kept waiting for the wise guys with machine guns."

My mother told the grand jury she had borrowed the money from an individual, but she wasn't at liberty to tell them who had loaned it to her. She had promised the person she wouldn't. The jury sent her home to reconsider, but her answer remained the same. She spent several weeks in the Wichita County jail for contempt. Eventually the person she had "borrowed" the money from (she told me it was not Brother Terrell) released her from her promise and she answered the jury's question. Mama told me later that while she was in jail, the preacher woman and Brother Terrell had been in Hawaii ready to leave the country "if things went wrong." It was the closest my mother ever came to saying a bad word against Brother Terrell. She wouldn't elaborate on which things could have gone wrong. I assumed she meant answering the grand-jury question in a way that would have incriminated Brother Terrell. I remembered that during the weeks my mother was in jail, he had called me almost every day.

"I'm really concerned about your mama," he

said in that hoarse, overworked preacher voice.

I asked my mother what she thought about a man who would have left the country when she was facing legal repercussions for protecting him. Instead of answering my question, she voiced a fear around which she had detoured for almost twenty years.

"I guess he didn't really care what happened to me." She looked tired and defeated.

If anyone had asked me at the time of this conversation if I still believed in David Terrell, I would have said no, and I would have been wrong. Belief, like love, can go underground. It can become a part of our operating system, without our knowledge or approval. As my mother spoke of Brother Terrell's betrayal, another layer of faith fell away even as I recognized its existence. What a surprise to feel its absence. Within hours, the illness from which I had been healed returned. I had been symptom-free for nine years. One doctor said the symptoms I experienced can occur and then disappear and remain dormant for years. I nodded, thinking all the time, *You have no idea.* I sometimes think that the timing of my healing and my relapse were weird coincidences. What I believe, or what I think I believe, is far less rational. I had faith once in a man's connection to what I thought of as God. Strange as it seems, that faith, misplaced and undeserved, made me well, and when the last remnant of it deserted me, I fell ill again. The symptoms remained for two years until we found a drug to control them. These days I am mostly well.

After an investigation that lasted almost a decade, Brother Terrell's case went to trial. I'm not sure how much of a role, if any, my mother's answer to the grand jury played. We learned during the trial that Brother Terrell had fathered a child with Sarah, the woman he had taken home after a tent service more than twenty years earlier. Pam murmured during the trial something about hoping there were no more children hidden under a bush somewhere. Her dad was found guilty of criminal income-tax evasion and sentenced to three ten-year sentences, to run concurrently. It wasn't until my mother tried to see Brother Terrell in prison that she realized he had finally worked everything out. He had put my sisters on the visitors list as his daughters. The preacher woman was listed as his wife. My mother's name was not on the list.

There is a small tree—I picture it as a skinny, overgrown bush—in the yard of the prison where Brother Terrell served his time. He told my sisters that when he finished his work as a prison janitor, he went to the tree to read his Bible and pray. Since praying and pacing were synonymous for

Brother Terrell, he walked around the tree and called out to his God, sometimes in silence and at other times aloud. Did he beg forgiveness and ask for a second chance? Did he call down the wrath of Jehovah upon his enemies? Knowing Brother Terrell, I would bet he did both.

My sister Carol met a man who served as chaplain of the prison after her daddy left.

He told her that her father had become something of a legend. Five years after his release, the longtime prisoners still talked about the tent preacher, and when they were troubled, many of them visited what had become known as the Prayin' Tree.

Chapter Twenty-one

AFTER SEVERAL FALSE STARTS AND STOPS, I found a path that led away from the tent and the Terrellites. I went to college and studied philosophy, literature, and journalism. For a long time I felt like a cardboard cutout of a person, flat and one-dimensional, propped up with a plastic stand, nothing behind me. I watched the students, teachers, employers, friends, and colleagues around me and picked up cues on how to be in the world: Look them in the eye, firm up the handshake, file down the emotion, read good books, wear good shoes, dark colors, the best haircut you can afford. Fake it till you make it. Gradually, the years between me and the tent stacked up until they formed a wall of experience that separated me from my former self. Upon meeting my relatives who remained in the ministry, my husband and friends commented, "I don't know what to think. They're so different from you." The eleven-and-a-half-year-old girl who sold her soul to the devil in exchange for the world—the very thing everyone under the tent warned against—had gotten exactly that: the world, in all its messy glory.

When casual acquaintances asked where I grew up, or where I came from, as we say in Texas, there was a long and uncomfortable pause. After a moment I might say, "Oh, we moved around," or "We lived all over," which led to questions about whether my "stepfather" was in the military. If I felt brave, I laughed and said, "Oh, something like that," and made a fast getaway. Most times I stammered and shifted my eyes until the conversation limped off in another direction. The question of where I came from struck me as a paradox. I had not lived anywhere long enough for a place to stamp itself upon my psyche in the cozy shape of a Monopoly house. Brother Terrell's ministry was the only home I had known, and that did not constitute an answer anyone could understand. I experienced myself as an exile, an orphan, a ghost girl, all of the above.

There was the time I had passed through and the time I now inhabited. I had no way to connect the two. Until my sister's telephone call and Randall's funeral.

Randall knocked on death's door off and on for forty years. Maybe that's why when the door finally opened and he slipped through, it came as a shock. With the help of his daddy's prayers, he had spent most of his life proving doctors wrong, and I guess some of us thought he always would. One of his sisters sobbed, "I thought he was going to get a miracle." All the hemorrhages and death sentences he had survived didn't count.

On the night prior to the funeral, family members gathered in the funeral home in Brownwood, the largest town close to Bangs, and greeted one another with exclamations of surprise at how long it had been since we last saw one another. The old animosities no longer held. Betty Ann gave me a long hug and said, "How's your mama? Tell her I love her." Only my mother and brother were missing; they had begged off, saying neither of them felt up to it. Betty Ann drew my sisters to her and they clung to her like a long-lost aunt. The preacher woman's daughter was there, laughing and talking with my sisters. I marveled at the banality of the scene. After all the lies and secrets, we were, finally, like any other family. Voices, soft and layered one upon the other—how you been, have you seen so and so, that's her over there, her husband died ten years back, oh no, it's been so long—all spoken in half whispers, as though we feared to wake the dead.

At the edges of the crowd, the conversation was of an entirely different nature: *Should* Brother Terrell raise Randall from the dead? Maybe he should leave him in peace. He was so sick when he died. Well, God had promised Randall a miracle. But he had already been *embalmed*. Wasn't that a problem? If only Randall hadn't been sick so long. If only Brother Terrell had gotten to him before the mortician. No one said, "Look, this isn't going to happen." Several of us had left the ministry decades earlier to pursue nursing, software development, accounting, and other careers built on reason and rationality, but that evening we had once again taken our places in a universe where the impossible could happen, whether you really wanted it to or not.

The next morning, my husband steered the car down Highway 84 toward the funeral in Bangs. I gazed out the window, puzzled at the unreality of finding myself en route to a place I had left so far behind, a place I turned away from at every juncture. When friends said things like, "Nothing happens in God's world without a reason," and "There are no coincidences," I rolled my eyes and shuddered. They had no idea where that kind of thinking could lead. Everything within me had shifted, from belief to atheism to agnosticism to a sort of "cultural Christianity," yet the stretch between Brownwood and Bangs remained unchanged. I thought I recognized every dusty outcropping of rock, every stand of cedar and pad of prickly pear. The person who looked out the window, the woman who had changed the way she thought, spoke, dressed, prayed, or didn't pray, the woman who had sold her birthright, she was the one I didn't know.

I pointed out a gravel road. "Slow down. Turn right."

My husband swerved, and all at once we were there. Dusty cars of every make and model were scattered across the scrubby field. Small groups of people streamed toward a large utilitarian building, the Terrellite church, positioned in what appeared to be the same spot the tent had occupied during the run-up to the end-time. My husband parked the car and we stepped out into the sunlight of a mild November day. A light breeze played at the edges of my suit jacket. No west Texas gusts pulled or pushed at me. No need to pull my coat tighter about me. No need for a coat at all. We picked our way across the dry, rocky terrain, moving ever closer to the church. I remembered the times I had backed away, literally and figuratively, from anything that had evoked this place, these people. The pop singer who crooned "Job's God Is True" at the after-hours party, the sad little gospel tent in Boston Common, the voice of a street preacher wafting through a hotel window ten stories above San Francisco, the French Holy Rollers who tried to convert me in Nice. Trickster spirits that winked at me from unexpected corners of my life, reminders that all was not as it seemed, that I was not as I seemed.

Family members clustered outside the church doors, arranging themselves in two long wobbly lines. My sisters stood near the front of the line, an ordinary and astonishing sight. A remnant of scripture came to mind: ". . . and the last shall be first." Unsure of whether to join the family or take a seat inside, I positioned myself to the side of the line. Was I family? Friend? Foe? Pam walked over, took my arm, and settled the question. I filed into church that morning with all of the women and children who had lived separate and sometimes secret lives with Brother Terrell. Legitimate and illegitimate, adopted and semiadopted, steps, halves, and blood relatives, mistresses and wives paraded down the aisle, two by two. The existence of my sisters and other children born outside the sanctity of marriage had become known fifteen years earlier, but the funeral marked our first and only appearance as a family. We numbered around seventy as we filed into the center section of the church. My husband and I took seats behind my three sisters. The secrets Brother Terrell had gone to such lengths to conceal had names and faces and sat shoulder to shoulder in his church, and yet it was a day like any other. The Earth didn't shift on its axis. The sun didn't fall from the sky. One less person drew breath, one less person sat among us, but the world creaked on and on.

Most of Brother Terrell's longtime followers and supporters had left him by the time Randall died. After his release from prison in 1987 he put up tents that seated twenty-five hundred, small tents by his old standards, and was lucky to draw two hundred people. Some believers had drifted away years earlier when news of his relationships with my mother and the preacher woman became known. Others left when he divorced the preacher woman and married a woman young enough to be his daughter. On the day of the funeral, many found their way back. The Bangs church, built to seat about twenty-five hundred, was full. Old friends flew toward one another, often meeting in front of the casket, laughing and talking in subdued voices while Randall slept on, hands folded on his chest. The family sat quiet and subdued.

A minister who was a friend to Randall and a colleague of Brother Terrell's opened the service with a prayer. He spoke of Randall as a man of faith, a preacher. This image of Randall did not fit with my memory of the boy who could not sit through a tent service, the boy who was always angling for a chance to play husbands and wives. The minister looked down at the casket.

"Brother Randall fasted, prayed, and believed the Word, just like his daddy. He taught me so much about faith. I know many of y'all came to hear him preach over the years and heard the story of how time and time again God raised him up from his deathbed."

The family shifted from side to side. We studied our fingernails. I noticed a long scuff across the toe of my right boot.

"I know there are others out there who have stories of how Brother Randall's testimony blessed and changed your lives. I invite you to come on up."

Pam's husband walked up the prayer ramp and took the microphone. "Randall taught me a lot, and some of it was about what not to do. I remember the time he convinced me we could make extra money by charging people who came to the tent twenty-five cents to park. The money was nothing compared to the whipping Brother Terrell gave us. Randall also taught me the rules of fasting; if you can get it through a straw, it ain't cheatin'."

Only the family laughed. We were not here to testify for Brother Randall. We were here to say good-bye, or hello, depending on how things went, to the boy Randall. My sisters approached the front of the church next. There were those who thought it wrong that these girls, women now, never publicly acknowledged by Brother Terrell, should speak in his church, but this was not their day. Without rehashing or explaining anything, my sister Carol said Randall was the first to welcome them into the family and had treated them as sisters from the beginning. Lisa spoke of how Randall loved to fish and how he had taken them fishing with his daughter. Laura recounted the time Randall took them to their first circus.

When the family remembrances were finished, someone introduced Brother Terrell. The door at the back of the platform opened, and a small, silver-haired man with hunched shoulders stepped forward. He looked like an old man, not the fiery prophet I remembered. He wandered aimlessly about, crying into the microphone. He walked down the prayer ramp and peered into the casket. Family members cast worried looks at one another. He pulled a handkerchief from the pocket of his suit jacket and wiped at his eyes. He tried to speak and sobbed instead. At another funeral someone would have led the grieving father away. But this was Brother Terrell, and no one was going to lead him anywhere. After a few minutes, he pulled himself together and began to speak. His speech was slow and halting as he recalled the many times death had tried to take

Randall from him. He said no matter where he was in the world, he had always sensed when his son was sick. He talked about the times he had called Randall and urged him to fight the most recent death sentence the doctors had given him. He talked about calling his son from Haiti, India, and Africa and praying for him, and how Randall always got better. He paused in front of the open casket where his son lay.

The crowd called out encouragement. "Help him, Jesus. Strengthen him, Lord."

He drew strength from their responses and was gradually transformed from grieving father to who he really was, who he had always been. He was the healer and prophet plucked by the hand of God from the Alabama countryside and given a worldwide ministry of faith and deliverance. He was a son of God, a voice crying out in the wilderness. Oh, hallelujah, he knew who he was, and the devil couldn't take that away from him. His shoulders straightened and his voice grew stronger. The eulogy turned into preaching and the preaching wandered across a broad expanse of subjects. The 9/11 attack had come to him in a vision where he saw the towers fall. When he prophesied, you better believe it came to pass. The intermittent response of the crowd lengthened into a steady buzz of "amen, uh-huh, hallelujah, that's right" running underneath and alongside every sound that issued from his mouth until his words and theirs formed one single affirmation.

He began to pace and then to dance up and down the platform. His words came faster until he was shouting into the microphone. "There's comin' a revival, a dead-raising revival!"

Family members, tense and silent, shifted in their seats.

"It's a revival that will restore everything the devil has stolen, a revival that will return everything that's been lost . . . everything that's been corrupted, everything you've lived without."

They jumped to their feet, waved their hands, and danced and danced. They understood that life takes it all, your last dime, your last hope, your last breath. They understood, and they laughed and shouted and careened about the church, drunk on faith. My husband, one of the most reserved and cerebral men I have known, had his hands in the air. My sister's husband shouted "amen" until his face turned red. The funeral had turned into a revival meeting for everyone except Brother Terrell's children, who sat red-eyed and rigid in the middle of the church facing the coffin.

With the congregation in his thrall, Brother Terrell abruptly stopped preaching and handed the microphone to one of his associates. As the amens and hallelujahs softened, the associate minister waved forward a group of preachers.

One of them carried a bottle of olive oil. They walked down the ramp to the casket. The church went silent. My sisters glanced over their shoulders, eyes wide. One of Pam's younger sisters buried her face in her hands. The minister who had been Randall's friend took the bottle of oil and tilted it onto a white handkerchief. He put the cloth on Randall's forehead and spoke while the others laid hands on the corpse.

"Brother Randall, in the name of Jesus, if you want to come back, then go ahead and come on. In the name of Jesus. We'd be glad to have you."

After what must have been one of the shortest prayers in Holy Roller history, the preachers stepped away from the body. Shoulders relaxed in the family section. Randall would remain dead and his body would stay in the coffin. The organ music swelled and Brother Terrell moved to the side of the coffin. The audience lined up to shake his hand as they had years earlier. As they filed by, they gripped his arm, pulled him close, and offered their condolences.

"So sorry for your loss."

"We're praying for you every day."

"Don't give up. God's gonna see you through."

After everything they knew about Brother Terrell, after all the affairs and lies and moneygrubbing, these people had only soft words for him. I brought my hand to my face. It was wet. Only then did I realize I had cried silently and steadily throughout the funeral. Not over Randall or the loss, so much loss; not the visions of family or redemption laid to waste. It was something else, something alien and familiar as my prodigal heart. I watched an elderly couple make their way through the line. I saw the concern in their faces as they approached Brother Terrell and grabbed his hands, eager to convey all they carried in their hearts for him. He inclined his head as he listened and nodded.

"Okay. Okay. We 'preciate that. Bless you, now." A flash of a smile that moved from shy to showtime in an instant, his eyes sliding off to the next in line. The couple walked past me, hands clasped, each leaning on the other, faces shining. They looked . . . blessed. Yes, that was the word. By a con man? A prophet? A performer?

I had spent a lifetime deciding, and each time I thought I knew, the answer proved too small to encompass my experience. Or was it the question? Maybe it wasn't about Brother Terrell, but two worlds: one under the tent and the other outside. Each time I turned toward one, I turned away from some part of myself. I watched the people move through the line. Women with their arms folded across their chests, hugging their elbows. The men with their straight-ahead stares. Kids tugging at their parents. I recognized no one and yet, I knew them. I had always known them. There was no separation, no division, no choice to be made. They had been with me all along, and without knowing it, I had been with them. After all this time. It wasn't belief or unbelief. It was love. It could not have been otherwise.

I walked to the front of the church and took my place in line. When it was my turn, I took his hand and told him I loved him. His expression, practiced and perfect, showed no recognition. "Thank you. 'Preciate that."

I looked into his face. "Brother Terrell, it's me, Donna."

He stammered and I fell toward him. He pulled me close. After a few seconds we pushed away from each other, shy and embarrassed. He patted my arm. There was nothing to do but move on. As I made my way back to my seat, I saw the old man and woman framed in the doorway of the church; beyond them stretched the beginning of the West Texas sky, and the world, the big, wide world. I'd be there again soon enough.

Acknowledgments

I am grateful to the Mayborn Literary Nonfiction Conference for its recognition of an early chapter and the impetus to finish this book; the Ragdale Foundation for the gift of time, space, and amazing food that sustained spirit and body (thank you, Linda); the Writers' League of Texas, especially Cyndi Hughes and Jan Baumer for ongoing support; and to the Austin Bat Cave and S. Kirk Walsh for workshops that inspired and encouraged me to believe in my story.

Many thanks to Theresa May, editor in chief at the University of Texas Press, for her cheerleading and "safety net," and to writers P. J. Pierce, Mary Day Long, Elena Eidelberg, and Christine Wicker for reading the pages and listening. Special thanks to the women of the Secret Sports Club (you know who you are) for beating back the demons. My sister Carol Terrell Lamb and my mother, Carolyn Richardson, provided background materials that breathed life into the past and for which I am truly grateful.

The persistence and patience of agent extraordinaire Dan Conaway turned a prologue into a book and my editor, Lauren Marino, at Gotham kept the faith through missed deadlines.

A number of texts provided context and inspiration for this book: First and foremost, *Can*

Somebody Shout Amen! Inside the Tents and Tabernacles of American Revivalists, by Patsy Sims; *Salvation on Sand Mountain*, by Dennis Covington; *The Gospel Singer: A Novel*, by Harry Crews; *All Things Are Possible: The Healing and Charismatic Revivals in Modern America*, by David Edwin Harrell Jr.; *Border Radio* (page 318), by Gene Fowler and Bill Crawford; *Journey to Dharavi: The Life and Ministry of David Terrell*, by Earl W. Green; and *Beyond the Valley of the Shadow of Death*, by David Randall Terrell.

Thanks to William Martin, senior fellow for Religion and Public Policy, Baker Institute at Rice University, for sharing his notes and observations of David Terrell and other revivalists.

Finally, I owe everything to Kirk Wilson, my husband and partner, for his tireless support and unshakable faith.

Center Point Publishing

600 Brooks Road ● PO Box 1
Thorndike ME 04986-0001 USA

(207) 568-3717

US & Canada:
1 800 929-9108
www.centerpointlargeprint.com